Bodymakers

LESLIE HEYWOOD

Body

Rutgers University Pres

A   Cultural

Anatomy

of Women's

Body

Building

makers

ew Brunswick, New Jersey, and London

Library of Congress Cataloging-in-Publication Data

Heywood, Leslie
   Bodymakers : a cultural anatomy of women's body building / Leslie Heywood
     p. cm.
   Includes bibliographical references and index.
   ISBN 0–8135–2479–2 (cloth : alk. paper). — ISBN 0–8135–2480–6 (pbk. : alk. paper)
   1. Bodybuilding for women—Social aspects.   2. Women—Social conditions.   3. Body,
Human—Social aspects.   4. Women in popular culture.   5. Feminist theory.   I. Title.
GV546.6.W64H49 1998
646.7′7′082—dc21 TOC 97–27016
                                                           CIP

British Cataloging-in-Publication data for this book is available from the British Library

Photo opposite page 1 by Bill Lowenburg
Photo opposite page 192 by David Tuttle

Manufactured in the United States of America

For the strong women who continue to inspire me:

Jennifer, Susan, Susan, Sandy, Heidi, Melissa, Martha, Beth

Contents

Contents

Bodymakers

1

Introduction

Monsters, Feminists, Babes

Behind the image there is emptiness, so deep it is almost its own source of light. We put on the image when we go into the world and in it we can live, mark or mock the appearance of life. But we return, retreat home to the place where the image splits, evaporates in the darkness without mirrors. No mirrors without others; we don't exist if we can't be seen. Postmodern Persephones we've lived with the images in palpable form ever since we were born, drawn to our own form of coldness and hell that marks the space without image, the space where the light disappears, where we are nothing and create ourselves over and over again. What am I if not that Reebok ad? The Calvin Klein? The Polo Ralph Lauren? The bodies there, that body, me. Mirror, image, source of light, there is nothing that I can feel or see I've lived so long with specters, source of life. My body left over, burden, daily life, unshaped. I'll go out in the world again to live. The gym.

■

Welcome to the world of bodybuilding, where the absurd and the spectacular meet each other head on. Where bodies parade around dressed in bright tights, flexing their forearms, shaking their willowy legs, circling each other like so many peacocks unfurling themselves for display. Where an extra five pounds lifted is a cause for joy; where the magazine racks are full of paper curled up by the sweat of the thousand hands that turned over their pages while making the Stair Master or treadmill churn through its lonely mechanical course. Where every afternoon bodies turn up in these twelve thousand-foot spaces all over the city: Fed Ex delivery persons, bankers, fake ID makers, schoolteachers, country singers, lawyers, electricians, and students of every color, stripe who gather to strip to their undies or what looks like them, bare their chest hairs and lumpy torsos, spend their spare time repping out iron from the same stretched racks week after week, perpetually communing with chest press, triceps, abdominal machines, checking the progress of each others' pecs and buns.

We enter the gym like family members who maintain no particularly close personal ties, a wary wolf pack happy to greet each other, in this, the only space we share, but not particularly eager to develop relationships that go on outside. Yet we provide each other with a sense of stability and order in tumultuous lives. When a regular disappears this occurrence may not be spoken by those who remain, may not be registered consciously, but he or she will be missed. An anonymous fabric that provides us with one of the strongest senses of community we have, gods and heroes, goddesses, heroines, us.

We enter ordinary people, a thousand details weighing down our lives, the weight of gravity and years dragging us thickly, flesh spreading a bit around the middle, tangerine-skin bulges wrinkling the buttocks that once stood out clean. Blood churns sluggishly through our bodies, barely warming up the skin, and we are the employee reprimanded by the boss, the teacher harassed by her students, the waitress with one too many moody tables, the lawyer with sick kids and three cases and research to do all while she feeds them. Our partners have fought with us, told us we're not their truest loves, our electric bills have gone up, the car has developed a stutter. We are overworked, hassled, tired, harassed. We are small, the stoop of our shoulders weighed down by our shoes.

But then, we are here and by magic we are casting our ordinary uglinesses free. We aren't middle-aged women who think we're losing our looks, or students worrying about job prospects or bad grades, or parents with funds running out and two birthdays to cover next week. We aren't men who can't seem to get girlfriends or girls who just can't seem to find the right job, aren't single mothers without nearly enough energy to do what we've got on us, or fathers deserted by former friends. No. The gym is the world of gods and heroes, goddesses larger than life, a place of incantations where our bodies inflate and we shuffle off our out-of-gym bodies like discarded skins and walk about transformed. We have expanded past our bosses' words of diminishment that sent us seething into smallness behind our desks, beyond parking attendants that forget our change or that paper we just can't seem to write. Here, ten minutes into a workout our muscles fill up with blood. Here, in this space, we begin to grow, to change. The transformation has begun, and our flawed humanity is falling off fast. We are picking up our shoulders, elevating our chins, shaking ugliness from our torsos with a series of strokes, the glistening dumbbells, listening to our blood's rush. Our pasty misshapen bodies are developing clean lines. Our day's tribute of trials and heartaches is fading, for here, in this gym space, we become kings and queens. Larger, invincible, gods in ourselves.

Our breathing is quick, our skin flushed, our hearts are pounding thickly. Each day we come out a little stronger, each day we feel more anchored to the earth, more certain we are tangibly here. Through an endorphin haze our minds become expansive, bringing us pictures, ideas we've never seen. Taking the risk, going up the next ten pounds and getting the lift convinces us we are someone who can do things, someone who is competent, proud. Declarations of independence, female strength where before none existed. The kind that lets you pile your own firewood or pry the lids off your own jars. And that other, less tangible kind that lets you stand straight like you've got your own spine. The right to stride through space.

B O D Y A M E R I C A

Women who bodybuild are a recent cultural phenomenon, so recent that, while it generates a good deal of interest—positive or negative—we don't yet understand this phenomenon and can't assess its importance, if any, to our daily lives. As women's bodybuilding photographer Bill Dobbins puts it, "The association of women and muscles developed to [the] degree [that

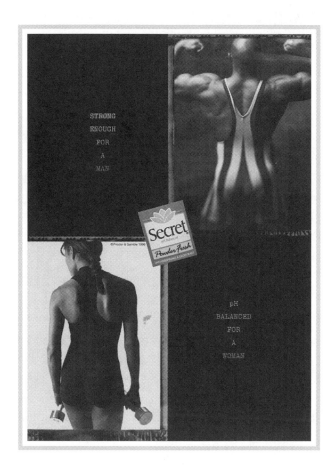

Gender traditions, nineties style: Pumped masculinity, toned femininity. (Ad in *Seventeen*, March 1997)

female bodybuilders have developed them] is unprecedented in history. . . . Muscular women are a contradiction to, even an attack on, our sense of reality."[1] This newness, along with the ways in which muscular women challenge traditional ideas that associate women in general with physical weakness and incompetence, femininity with diminution and childishness, and the female body with softness, has led to the widely held belief, within bodybuilding circles as well as outside them, that the cultural impact of female bodybuilding is limited to a very small subculture.

Indeed, when explaining why he excludes an examination of women from his recent book devoted to an exploration of the muscular body, Kenneth R. Dutton asserts that "women's bodybuilding remains very much a minority activity even amongst athletically-minded women . . . [and is] often seen as a kind of erotically-tinged curiosity. . . . The body as presented and interpreted in terms of its muscular development . . . is restricted almost exclusively to the male body."[2] The public imagination has few images of and associations with the muscular female body, but the one that most stereotypically comes to mind is: steroids. They're all on steroids. Women can't really get big; their muscles can only be purchased by technological means. General discussions of steroids in bodybuilding often talk about the health risks for men, but for women the main fear seems to be that steroids ruin their femininity and have permanent side effects like enlarged clitorises and deep voices. The knee-jerk reference to steroids and the assumption that all female bodybuilders use them are easy ways to marginalize and dismiss the sport, even though steroid abuse is a problem in most sports, and even though many female bodybuilders, especially those who don't compete, have never used them.[3] Since the discussion of steroids is often a red herring used to dismiss and marginalize female bodybuilders, whether specific women take steroids to enhance their musculature will not be the focus of my arguments here. In my arguments about female bodybuilding, I refer to a wide range of women—competitive and noncompetitive—who work out regularly with weights and for whom this activity is an important part of their lives, and I discuss cultural representations of muscular women within the wider context of popular culture. I try to show ways of thinking about female bodybuilding in a much broader sense than it is usually discussed.

Although Arnold Schwarzenegger allies female bodybuilding with more general cultural changes when he writes that "women have all the same muscles that men do and should be free to develop them as they wish. . . . Women are becoming involved in all manner of activities and professions that were once denied to them. . . . Bodybuilding for women is just one more example of this cultural transformation," even the small amount of work that has been done on female bodybuilding continues to consign the sport to a ghetto by means of the form that work takes.[4] A cultural study of female bodybuilding that devotes an entire book to the subject—why would we need that? Discussion is usually limited to chapters or sections of chapters in books whose subjects range from male bodybuilding (such as Alan M. Klein's *Little Big Men*) to the culturally constructed body more generally (such as Mascia-Lees and Sharpe's *Tattoo, Torture, Mutilation, and Adornment*), and to film (such as Yvonne Tasker's study of gender and genre in the action cinema, *Spectacular Bodies*).[5] My work here is indebted to these studies, and especially to the work of Anne Bolin, Laurie Schulze, and Marcia Ian, all of whom, bodybuilders and theorists themselves, have formulated some of women's bodybuilding's most contradictory complicities with and revisions of dominant cultural paradigms of gender.[6]

While most people seem to have an opinion *about* and considerable positive or negative interest *in* muscular women, most also would insist that female bodybuilding is a marginal rather than central concern. Although it may be true that, as Marcia Ian has written, "there is [no] significant audience for female bodybuilding . . . a minority within a minority," what drives bodybuilding, the most basic desires and motivations of those who practice it, shares a great deal with the larger culture.[7] In fact it may be seen, as Ian has argued, as a practice that blurs the line between the bodily preoccupations and practices of the dominant culture and the subculture specific to competitive bodybuilding: "Bodybuilding . . . makes it possible to disavow, for at least a couple of hours a day, any rigid demarcation between the 'hegemonic' and the 'alternative.'"[8] One of my arguments is that although seemingly marginal and actually marginal in some ways, women's bodybuilding can be seen as a microcosm of many characteristic elements of dominant culture—an example, in miniature, of much larger social conflicts and issues. Rather than an extreme oddity that exists on the fringes of cultural life, women's bodybuilding is an apotheosis of the American fascination with individual empowerment and sovereignty and the way the second-wave women's movement extended opportunities to act on that fascination to some women.

As the work of such recent photographers as Bill Lowenburg has shown,[9] bodybuilding reflects us in all of our ugliness and grandeur: a will and self-determination that is so extreme it can be pathetic and self-destructive; the politics of gender (what does it mean to be feminine?); race (what does it mean to be nonwhite? what meanings are imposed on us if we are nonwhite or if we aren't?); and class (how does the struggle to make a living, to be economically viable in American society, affect how we see ourselves?) How do we struggle for the self-improvement of something that often doesn't need to be improved, against a sense of worthlessness that comes from a position that is—for most of us—economically insecure? What lengths will we—like female bodybuilders—go to shape a career and shape our bodies as a reflection of this, to "achieve" in the area of our bodies if we can't do it elsewhere, to make ourselves *appear* more powerful than we might really be in our day jobs and our daily lives, to do what it takes to make it economically? What do we do to our bodies to make ourselves appear successful in an increasingly image-driven culture? Image, success, and power—all these issues, central to so many of our lives, come into sharp focus through the lens of female bodybuilding. It is a discussion that—as it was in the case of the repeated flaming and bickering and guts-to-the-wall debate in an Internet discussion group, Femuscle, devoted to female bodybuilding—remains volatile and controversial.[10]

Female bodybuilding—as a practice, a way of life—can be understood existentially as a problem of meaning that intimately engages the dominant culture's, and those who have struggled to be valued by it, most central problems.[11] As a former scholarship athlete and a bodybuilder of eighteen years, I have, although not always consciously, organized my life around that understanding and around the meaning and healing I was able to forge in my life through athletic participation. Personally, I have a great deal at stake in my arguments. Although traditionally personal investment has been said to cloud the objectivity of a writer's argument, I believe that the fact that I have lived this book, struggling with and critically reflecting on the issues presented in it, allows me to put that struggle on display: the thinking through, the uncertainty, the awkwardness where the logic stutters, the places where the narrative starts pursuing its own course through the weird complications of daily life. Ardent and devoted in my belief that the muscular female body—mine and others like it—is a kind of sanctuary, a kind of cultural safe space where the old questions of sexism and female nonvalue need not apply, in response to a changing cultural context and to feminist criticisms of such beliefs, I began to question the value of my daily pilgrimages to the gym and seriously interrogate their meaning.[12] *Bodymakers* is the result.

RESISTING EITHER/OR

I have a point of view that seeks out shadows, spots over the sun, monsters, the ugliness that lies in wait just under the smooth surface of an aesthetic, any picture, any image, any goal that presents itself as purely ideal and good. I am compelled by contaminants, the ugly things, the contradictions that mark the pretty pictures up. The *pharmakon*, from Plato, the poisoned cure, seems to describe so many things. In literature, movies, the things we do with our lives: Dorian Gray's ravaged face underneath the decorous lines, the hidden face of Mr. Hyde just waiting to erupt from Dr. Jekyll, the collapsing faces and damaged arteries and chests under the smooth plastic of the new aesthetic surgeries, the used-up joints and vulnerability to disease inside bodies that look perfectly built, the hidden histories of alcoholism and abuse shattering the pictures of so many perfect American families. Nothing was ever as it seemed, so I could never leave anything alone. I was always told I saw glasses half empty, not half full: the critical way of looking at things Christina Hoff Sommers calls "unwholesome and divisive" in her attack on second-wave feminists.[13] In my lifetime, permission to speak about ugly has swung between extremes, from enforced cultural silence (you don't speak about such things) to an obsession with public confessions (the talk-show circus) and back, so that part of the cultural conservatism so pervasive today is a returned injunction to silence. Civil, women's, and gay rights struggles gave legitimacy to public speech about ugly (Courtney Love: "There is no power like my ugly"),[14] about hate

speech and sexual harassment and rape and abuse and the way social institutions work systematically to devalue and negate human dignity and
worth for lots of people. While ten years ago speaking out about experiences of violation and criticisms of social structures that help produce
those experiences was encouraged, largely because, as Ann Jones writes,
"the rise of the women's movement in the 1960s and the antirape movement
in the early 1970s provided encouragement and a forum for women to
speak about violence in our lives,"[15] today speaking out about such things
is called "old hat" or "whining." But I'm not going to whine. I'm going to
talk about monsters.

Bodybuilders, male or female, aspire to be monsters, to become the dictionary definition: "one unusually large for its kind; extraordinary and often
overwhelming size." They want to stand out, have no one take them at face
value. They act out and build in their own bodies the American cultural
love affair with individualism, turning love into obsession. As Sam Fussell
puts it: "It's saying, or rather screaming, 'More than anything else in the
world, whatever it takes, I don't want to be like you. I don't want to look
like you, I don't want to talk like you, I don't want to *be* you.'"[16] But *female*
bodybuilders can't be *just* individuals. They construct themselves under
the double bind of conforming to the strongest ideas about what it means
to be feminine, a woman, a girl, which do not involve big biceps or thighs
but rather big breasts and small hips. The strange hybrid of the fitness ideal
that evolved in the eighties—a more muscular, toned, worked-out body—
and standard ideas of the ideal female form—big breasts, long hair, feminine features—created a contradictory body ideal that is mirrored in the
continual crisis over femininity in women's bodybuilding. So on the one
hand, bodybuilding as a sport values monstrosity—one of the highest
compliments that can be paid to the male bodybuilding physique. On the
other hand, however, women should be monstrous but also feminine, which
means not monstrous. The pendulum swings from year to year about just
how muscular the ideal woman bodybuilder should be, and while there was
greater tolerance for bigger women in the late eighties and early nineties,
the movement now is toward smaller women, at least in terms of their representation in magazines. Even more graphically, the growing popularity of
fitness competitions, which are more like beauty pageants and include both

Bodybuilder Sue Price: Women acting out the American love affair with individualism in an ad for a protein supplement. (*All Natural Muscular Development*, May 1997)

swimsuit and evening gown rounds, threatens to return body competitions to very traditional definitions of the feminine. While bodybuilding competitions consist of compulsory muscle poses and an individual routine meant to showcase that muscularity, fitness competitions showcase women with much smaller muscles and emphasize beauty over athleticism, reinstituting much more limited possibilities for the female form. But bodybuilders, as distinguished from fitness women, use their bodies to depart from as well as incarnate the norm, and are a attack as well as a defense. Like other "monsters" in the contemporary scene, like third-wave feminism, bodybuilders can be seen to use contradiction to create a new way of being for themselves.[17]

"It is not conceptualizing reality, but realizing concepts and materializing ideas that interests [Americans]," French sociologist Jean Baudrillard writes in *America*. Perpetually inventive, definitively postmodern, rather than coming up with a concept to describe what's around them, Americans come up with a concept first and then make it into the reality around them. According to Baudrillard, an example of this strange American practice is our treatment of our bodies: the point is not to *have* a body in America, but to *create* one according to your ideal image and to spend a lot of money doing it. Nothing, including our bodies, is a fixed, set, natural, given ("Be all you can be"; "Just do it").[18] And nothing more clearly demonstrates bodily pliability *and* determinacy, immateriality and materiality and the contradiction between them, than does bodybuilding, particularly the women's version. Female bodybuilders create bodies in which so many contradictory cultural meanings are gathered that it is impossible to reduce the female body and the femininity associated with it to one particular, natural, unchangeable thing. In the female bodybuilder's arms, back, breast implants, and carved-up thighs, traditional images of the female body are put forward and changed at the same time, pointing to some of the most dangerous contradictions facing female bodies. Female bodybuilders show how those contradictions—between, for instance, hard bodies and soft ones; masculine bodies and feminine ones; bodies that seem like you can't mess with them and bodies that seem like you can; bodies shaped by hours and hours of hard work or by plastic surgery and bodies that are dull and shapeless and fat; bodies that own and create themselves and bodies that are created by someone and something else; bodies that act upon others and bodies that are acted on by others; bodies that are made through technology like weights or surgery and bodies that refuse those things—are part of us all, both sides of the equation in us.

Since political activism in the contemporary context is perhaps best practiced though a war of images, an inclusion of both of these sides is something third-wave feminism assumes. The Riot Grrrl movement in music, for instance, was characteristically third wave because it centered around the production of rock music and zines, and combined equity feminism, gender feminism, and poststructuralism with, as Crystal Kile writes, "an analysis of oppression that also plays with images." [19] Her example is the Riot Grrrl appropriation of the Hello, Kitty image—the blank, innocuous kitty without a mouth, who covered the pencils, lunchboxes, and notebooks of many American girls in the eighties. "Hello, Kitty," Kile writes, was the "obscure blankness . . . the muffled, muted girl we were before feminism." Hello, Riot Kitty (with her anarchy teddy bear) is the Riot Grrrl appropriation of that image so central to many girls' socializations, taking a marker meant to promote innocuous niceness and transforming it into a symbol of rebellion against the idea that girls should be inconspicuously quiet, selfless, and nice. Through zines like *Upslut, Inner Bitch, Girl Fiend,* or *The Adventures of Big Girl,* young Riot Grrrl feminists take negative stereotypes about women and girls and make them empowering. Female musicians have further turned stereotypes against themselves by writing loaded words like "whore" on their arms with Magic Marker while performing. Playing on the old convention that says proper femininity does not exhibit itself on stage, these women anticipate arguments that might be leveled against them in the form of unconscious assumptions about women performers, and they make those assumptions explicit, part of their performance.[20] Female bodybuilders can be seen to use contradiction in a similar way, calling attention to assumptions about women and weakness and incompetence by building a body that says otherwise. As a third-wave feminist bodybuilder and writer, I hope to make these contradictions part of a performative activism in these pages.

What does it mean to be a female bodybuilder? Is bodybuilding a sport or an aesthetic, and how might it be seen as a form of activism? The female bodybuilder jangles the code of symbols that signal "girl" because she's got these shoulders, man, and oh! what a back, and did you see how much weight she just pumped up? But whoa, she's hot: "It is with hollow eyes but a glad heart that I write this letter. I've been staring upon the pictures of Lei Lani for days now and still cannot comprehend or fathom the degree of intensity and hard work that it took to develop the greatest women's physique of this age"; "Sharon Bruneau is dangerous and gorgeous. She exudes sex appeal with class"; "The pictorial of Ericca Kern was really breathtaking. What a beautiful work of art!"; "Dinah Anderson, who is 43, looks better than women half her age." And the female bodybuilder isn't just a body. The July 1996 *Flex* ran a feature profiling a number of women who bring these contradictions together, beauty and "gray matter," as the article put it, women bodybuilders who are also NASA flight directors, nurses, Yale medical school graduates, mothers, technical engineers, lawyers.[21] If American women are tired of the superwoman syndrome, if hours put into slinging iron at the gym comes on top of long work hours and the hard work at home, who would want it? Isn't the avocation of female bodybuilding just creating another unrealistic expectation for women to hold, adding pressure upon a sea of pressures already barely navigated? Yet more and more women are heading to the gym, and more and more women love it and won't give it up.

Why bodybuilding, why now? Much like the female flesh it hopes to make over again into a better version, bodybuilding has historically been something that both fascinates and repulses most Americans. Women's bodybuilding, a late addition, arrived at the time of Title IX, which mandated equal funding for men's and women's athletic programs. It arrived just after affirmative action and legislation against discrimination in the workplace was fully implemented, just after equal numbers of women began to attend college and occupy the workplace. It arrived when women began to get athletic scholarships and take up weight lifting as part of their training. It arrived when movie heroines were becoming stronger, like Sigourney Weaver in *Aliens* or Farrah Fawcett in *Extremities*, as well as when the first movie about female bodybuilding, *Pumping Iron II: The Women*, was released. It arrived at a time when more statuesque models, like Christie Brinkley and Cindy Crawford, began to take up all the print space in

Vogue and *Cosmopolitan* and *Glamour*. It arrived when violence against women had reached unprecedented levels.[22] It arrived as concepts like battering, abuse, rape, eating disorders, sexual harassment, and violence against women became part of the collective national consciousness. Female bodybuilding became part of a self-medicating cure that helped heal bodies split apart by violence.

The sport was at its height—the early nineties—at a pivotal moment in feminist history, when gender roles and cultural tolerance toward progressive change were renegotiated once again. Chapter 2, "Building Backlash: Doing Bodybuilding and Feminism in the Time of the New Right," explores the bodybuilding-versus-fitness debate in light of this history of women's bodybuilding and the contemporary political context. In 1994 Newt Gingrich took over the House, and Republicans came to rule both House and Senate, along with attendant attacks on affirmative action and stepped-up legislation against abortion. Feminism was blamed (again) for the decline of family values. In an amazing historical reversal, the radical right appropriated the rhetorics of choice and self-determination from political progressives, and turned the liberatory languages of feminist, civil, and gay rights in opposition to freedom and choice. This appropriation used the label "politically correct" to halt progressive change. The term took progressive movements that had been liberatory forces for many individuals previously denied freedom and choice, and it represented those movements precisely *as* limitations on individual freedom rather than as the agency of that freedom. In the popular culture of this period, *Disclosure*, *To Die For*, and *Little Women* were box-office hits, the first two vicious critiques and even parodies of female ambition and the third encouraging its restraint. The year 1994 marked the increasing audibility of conservative feminism, with Naomi Wolf's *Fire with Fire*, Katie Roiphe's *Morning After*, and Christina Hoff Sommers's *Who Stole Feminism?* appearing to wide media acclaim. Pundits—conservative feminists among them—did all they could to discredit second-wave feminist critiques of sexual objectification, rape, battery, and sexual abuse. These arguments exacerbated the policies of the Reagan-Bush years, in which, as Ann Jones writes, "programs to aid battered women and abused children [were] cut back or canceled altogether, like so many social programs."[23] The assault on feminist arguments was the subject of the three books mentioned above, and many others, on the grounds that feminist cultural criticism—not anything actually happening in the world—made women into victims when really they are active agents.

In the context of these larger cultural forces, 1994 marked the growing popularity of women's fitness competitions and a heightened criticism of large female bodybuilders. There was also a turn from representing women bodybuilders as competitors and athletes to representing them as primarily sexual, as is seen in soft-porn pictorials and centerfolds of female body-builders. This practice began in 1994 in *Flex* magazine, which is known as the hard-core bible for bodybuilding insiders. In the industry as a whole the dominant representational codes shifted from sport to sex for the women, with no corresponding shift for male bodybuilders. *Flex* picked up on political-correctness rhetoric and used it in defense of its soft-porn pic-torials. All these cultural factors influenced the shift away from women's bodybuilding and toward fitness by neutralizing feminist critique that might be directed against that shift, and promoting a facetious idea of individual choice and power central to other conservative cultural agendas.[24]

As shifts in bodybuilding so graphically document, ideas about mascu-linity and femininity, ideas about race and what it means are determined culturally and change over time. Chapter 3, "Zero: Raced Bodies, Mascu-line Voids," looks at contemporary constructions of masculinity and race, and how these constructions affect bodybuilding. The chapter puts forward some of the differences in men's bodybuilding, discussing how it is a prac-tice that exposes masculinity as a fragile structure as much as bodybuilding shores masculinity up. The chapter then turns to a discussion of the way contemporary representations of race, such as those found in the J. Crew catalog, inflect the way race functions in bodybuilding, how traditional ideas about race and gender work together to affect the ways we construct, experience, and see the built body.

The role of photography in constructing how we see and interpret is the subject of chapter 4, "Hard Times: The Pornographic and the Pathetic in Women's Bodybuilding Photography." This chapter explores the question of pornography in the representation of women's bodybuilding, advocating not the red herring of a censorship or pro-sex position but rather an exami-nation of the multiple levels of meaning one can use women's bodybuild-   **1 5** ing to read. These meanings include sexuality but explore even more basic questions of identity and experience, such as agency, cultural valuation, vulnerability, and proximity to violence.

Female bodybuilders take up space. Their bodies are armored. They say "I am here I do exist my outlines are fixed you can't mess with me, mess any openness around 'cause I'm already here and I'm saying it." Female bodybuilders are disturbing because they stand against the abject openness associated with traditional femininity and give themselves some borders, a reality stark as a stone. Maybe this is what the labels "gross," "monstrous," "ugly," "unfeminine" are about. Chapter 5, "Loving Mr. Hyde: Rethinking Monstrosity," looks at the movie *Mary Reilly* and its retelling of the Jekyll/Hyde story through a woman's eyes in order to suggest how the monstrosity of female masculinity might be reconceptualized to explore the possibilities bodybuilding offers as a response to abuse. The bodybuilder's body can be a reassertion of presence, a suture, a demarcation between outside and in that you can rely on. It is a solid demarcation—claiming ownership of one's own body, insisting on its boundaries and that others respect them—that can serve as a form of healing for those women who have experienced some form of violence. The shift from bodybuilding to fitness competitions threatens this healing by explicitly shifting the emphasis in and motivations for bodybuilding practice from strength and self-determination to sex appeal, a shift from an activity that is done for self-development to an activity that is done to please others.

If we agree with Ann Jones that "women and children have an *absolute right* to live free from bodily harm," and that all women have "equal opportunity to emotional and economic self-sufficiency," then the shift from bodybuilding to fitness marks more than a historical development or a superficial trend.[25] That shift represents another, even more subtle way that the gains of the second-wave women's movement, which helped ensure that very equal opportunity, is jeopardized. Like the attacks on affirmative action and cutbacks in programs to aid battered women, which can be directly seen to affect equal opportunity, the shift from bodybuilding to fitness jeopardizes the chance that training with weights will be utilized by women for the primary purpose of physically, emotionally, and mentally strengthening themselves.

Similar to providing a way of coping with physical violence, bodybuild-ing provides, for women, a chance to take part in the classically American obsessions with individual empowerment and sovereignty. It can be seen as a third-wave feminist practice that grows out of that part of the second-wave women's movement which extended opportunities for individual develop-ment to some women. Chapter 6, "American Girls, Raised on Promises: Why Women Build; or, Why I Prefer Henry Rollins to Beck," develops connections between the female bodybuilder and the rock star by way of Georges Bataille's concept of sovereignty. The chapter explores how con-temporary popular music provides the illusion of sovereignty—tradition-ally associated with masculinity—to its listeners of both sexes, and how bodybuilding is a practice that creates a similar sense of self-ownership and power in its practitioners. In this way, female bodybuilding can be seen as revolutionary for women even as it simultaneously functions as a cul-tural strategy of containment that can divert more overtly activist aims.

It is no coincidence that the decline in female bodybuilding and the turn to fitness competitions occurs at the same time as discussions of violence against women are labeled "victim feminism," and are turned against and dismissed. Yet the problems remain in our lives. They continue. Body-building is one way of negotiating those problems, one way of taking the responsibility and active agency so often called for in criticisms of feminist discussions of domestic violence. Bodybuilding is a form of healing, one way of physically and psychologically creating a safe space in which one is neither weak nor a victim. In a positive cultural context sympathetic to feminism and women's rights, bodybuilding can function as an alternative form of embodiment that helps women overcome gender-related issues that range from eating disorders to battery and sexual abuse. Because it so pow-erfully helps us to live, bodybuilding must be kept alive. We must take it back from the representational strategies that would reduce it to monstros-ity or sex, and redefine it as the opportunity for self-actualization that it can be. Monster, feminist, and babe, the contemporary female bodybuilder is a third wave realization of second wave women's activism. She is an Ameri-can girl raised on the promise of equal opportunity and self-realization who is doing her very best to claim it.

2

Building Backlash

Doing Bodybuilding and Feminism

in the Time of the New Right

Racks fitted with steel plates: ten pounds, twenty-five pounds, thirty-five, forty-five. Metal racks: two-tiered for squatting; a platform and backrest for pressing legs. Benches: metal, plastic, foam; welded at thirty-five–degree angles. Metal racks with pulley cables. Racks stretched horizontally along the walls. Mirrors. The curve of a tricep, curve of a thigh. Bodies, mostly men: oversized sweatshirts, pants, leather belts and black fingerless gloves. Striding the floor shoulders back, chins high: bodies with dominion. Music with a feral beat, the steady clank of metal plates: the free-weight section of the gym. A pause. On a single weight bench, one woman presses a hundred eighty-five pounds from her chest, the focus of all eyes: "How long have you been lifting? Do you compete?" It's the one place she can really stride: power, collateral, confidence, pride, the pleasures of exceeding what women are expected to be.

But it is not sheer power that generates awe. It's the contradiction. Her body that presses one-eighty in defiance of expectations of female weakness is also a body corrected to aesthetic norms: curved breasts, tight butt, firm thigh. Hence the valuation, admiration. Tight glutes and abs take sometimes violent self-correction: treadmill, Stair Master, pounding the street, two hours out of every day. The workout itself at least an hour, pounds and reps, fierce concentration. Resent distractions from outside: friends, social activities, work. Anxiety over tortilla chips, grams of fat on every package. Engineered food and herbal diets, the endless stare into the mirror, rage against a surface made too smooth by an extra percentage of subcutaneous fat. Day by day, hour by hour, rep by rep, piling the iron on heavier every week, injured back, compressed knees, distorted joints. Admiring looks, the awed questions, the requests for advice—assurance no one else will sport such an impressive physique. Sense of power, its appearance.

Appearances of power. In 1991 Susan Faludi's best-selling book *Backlash* documented ways in which political advancements made by women in the U.S.—usually white, middle-class women—had been met by a pendulum swing on the cultural barometer.[1] Faludi describes some of the ways in which the dominant culture adjusted itself to neutralize women's gains in areas like equal opportunity in the work force, while simultaneously preserving the appearance of these gains. Faludi's book exposed the manipulative basis of the media construction that equality has largely been won, an idea that has little to do with the material reality of most women's daily lives. That was 1991. In 1994, Naomi Wolf, whose 1991 bestseller about the devastating effects of internalized cultural standards of femininity brought her national prominence, wrote a follow-up, *Fire with Fire*, which seemed to be a direct repudiation of her original claims. In *Fire with Fire*, women "lack a psychology of female power to match their new opportunities."[2] Opportunity and equality are there, Wolf and a long list of other power feminists like Camille Paglia, Rene Denfeld, and Christina Hoff Sommers argue, women just aren't taking advantage of them, and are instead repeating tired old clichés about sexism and objectification.[3] Wolf's book and others like it act out the very cultural tendency that Faludi named a few years before: the tendency to claim equality and blame any evidence that suggests otherwise on women themselves.

19

Attack of the Pod-Fems

I am a feminist. Unequivocally. Despite the current feminism-as-victim rhetoric, I am a feminist because feminism has empowered me. Like millions of women before me, it has given me a way to understand my life and what I have seen, experienced, and felt as something that didn't happen just to me. It helped me to understand issues that now have names because of feminism, issues largely unspeakable and undocumentable because they did not have names or because they were loaded with the it's-your-problem-you-provoked-it mentality when I experienced them, previously discredited "girl" issues like low self-esteem, parental battery, sexual harassment, rape, eating disorders, exercise addiction. Because of feminism I could speak about them and read about them, see them as intimately connected to larger, structural problems rather than purely as isolated, personal pathologies, something that had happened only to me (and I should be ashamed of it) or flaws and problems that were products of my or my family's individual weaknesses and aberrations. Feminism has given me a way of working through and with those issues, connecting those issues and myself to the larger culture that provides the context for their meaning and my experience. It has allowed me to feel and be nonpathological. It has humanized me, given me back a sense of dignity and personal worth in a way that nothing else could.

And yet, at least since 1994, feminism has been dismissed and degraded precisely as personal pathology, and feminists as a bunch of crazy women with warped views of the world trying to impose them on everyone else. Issues like sexual harassment and abuse and rape are once again being silenced, and speaking about them is dismissed as "talk-show confession" or "exhibitionism." Christina Hoff Sommers, who calls herself an "equity feminist" and whose work *Who Stole Feminism?: How Women Have Betrayed Women* was funded by the Olin Foundation, attacks prominent feminist academics she calls "gender feminists" as "a lot of resentful and angry women . . . spread[ing] their divisive philosophy and influence. . . .It was . . . clear to me that the bitter spirits they were dispensing to the American public were unwholesome and divisive."[4] Sommers's charge of "unwholesomeness" is particularly indicative of her stance, one quite common today, evoking images of feminism as a pathology and disease better stamped out. Webster's defines *unwholesome* as "detrimental to physical, mental, or moral well-being: unhealthy; corrupt, unsound; offensive to the senses, loathsome."[5]

Feminism detrimental to well-being? Offensive? Loathsome? This is clearly not the feminism I felt had given me a lease on life, a chance to feel valued and included in a culture previously devoted to my exclusion from public life. No, Sommers's feminism, and feminism for many right-wingers like Rush Limbaugh, who often quotes from Sommers's work, is a feminism of distortion, defined against "true" perception. "I believe," Sommers says, "that how these feminist theorists regard American society is more a matter of temperament than a matter of insight into social reality."[6]

That "temperament" seems to verge on the hysterical, for, Sommers writes, "the feminist ideologue testifies relentlessly to how she has been sinned against. Moreover, she sees revelations of monstrosity in the most familiar and seemingly innocuous phenomena."[7] A feminist, then, according to Sommers, a growing chorus of younger voices like Rene Denfeld, Naomi Wolf, and Katie Roiphe, and various media caricatures like Rush Limbaugh's notorious label "femi-nazi," is someone who sees the world from an inaccurate, exaggerated, overly sensitive perspective, and who tries to impose that inaccuracy and her own sense of personal injury on everyone else. A feminist is not "objective," what she says is not "true" but is rather the product of her own isolated and distorted perceptions.

In a time when a female news reporter on National Public Radio prefaces her discussion of a successful female filmmaker with the comment, "She's one of those rare women who still calls herself a feminist," Sommers's charges have got to be taken seriously. If I am one of these rare women, then, who still calls herself a feminist, and for whom feminism doesn't match the charges, how, in the context of these charges, can I write about feminism, or any other subject, in a way that won't be open to charges of extremism, ideologism, attacked for lack of "objectivity" and reason, or dismissed as another "mind-numbing exposé of the evils of male culture"?[8]

Although she never explicitly addresses these debates, Sommers writes from the point of view of traditional social philosophy, a point of view that has been rigorously questioned in the last thirty years all over the United

States, Europe, and Australia, with the advent of poststructuralism—what opponents call relativism. That she does not address some of the most important conceptual developments and debates of the last thirty years is related to her failure to consider the work of a "younger generation" of feminists not in the Roiphe/Wolf model, who grew up with and were educated by these debates. Sommers presupposes a fixed, discernible truth out there that can stand as the watermark by which all ways of thinking are judged. She makes reference to a "feminism that reveres great art and respects truth," and speaks of "legitimate feminism" and the importance of "objectivity," criticizing feminists who "have little faith in the Enlightenment principles that influenced the founders of America's political order." She wants women to join with men to "contribute to a universal human culture," and says gender feminism leads "inappropriately" leads away from this universality through its distortions of "reality": "The New Feminists are a powerful source of mischief because their leaders are not good at seeing things as they are."[9]

In poststructuralism, "seeing things as they are" is dependent upon the point of view you are seeing them from, and this standpoint depends on variables like your race, your social class, your gender, your sexual orientation. This is a different concept from the "standpoint theory" Sommers mentions—the idea that "being oppressed . . . make[s] one more knowledgeable or perceptive."[10] Sommers's rhetorical move here is one characteristic of much contemporary right-wing discourse on political correctness. Questioning traditional concepts like truth or universal human nature becomes in this discourse a claim for special privileges or handouts. Conceptually, however, poststructuralism questions ideas about truth, objectivity, or nature on a much different basis, one that reveals how the discourse of political correctness has taken the terms of poststructuralism and turned them back on themselves, using its most basic precepts to defeat it. For what poststructuralism argues conceptually is not that membership in a minority group gives one higher truth status, but rather that truth is a relationship of competing discourses that are provisional and that change over time, and are related to questions of power—whose word holds more weight when. Sommers's claim that in feminist discourse "being oppressed . . . make[s] one more knowledgeable or perceptive" is a clever turn of the universalist screw so that what is, in feminist discourse, actually a claim for recognition, legitimacy, and value of a particular point of view becomes instead a bid for power that masks Sommers's own bid for power under the powerful guise of the universalist norm that actually represents the interests of a particular few.

Sommers's own allegiance to truth and objectivity as independent universal standards is undercut everywhere by assertions that are indisputably the product of a particular point of view, to which there are many opposing points of view. To choose only one of the most obvious, her assertion that "there is no radical militant wing of a masculinist movement" shows that the assumptions informing her method of interpretation of contemporary cultural movements differ greatly from the points of view of many who would interpret Rush Limbaugh and Pat Buchanan, not to mention Robert Dornan, precisely as a "radical militant wing of a masculinist movement."[11]

Whose point of view is closer to objective truth, then? What are the standards by which this distance might be gauged, and who determines them? As Joan Wallach Scott puts it,

> if there was any doubt that the production of knowledge is a political enterprise that involves contest among conflicting interests, the raging debates of the last few years should have dispelled them. What counts as knowledge? Who gets to define what counts as knowledge? These are difficult problems. . . . Those who would deny the existence of these problems . . . are not without their politics; they simply promote their orthodoxy in the name of an unquestioned and unquestionable tradition, universality, or history. They attack those who challenge their ideas as dangerous and subversive, antithetical to the academic enterprise. . . . The cry that politics has recently invaded the university . . . is itself a political attempt to distract attention from the fact that there [is] more than one valid side to the story in the current debates about knowledge.[12]

The debates about feminism are part of the debates about knowledge, and the rhetoric of universals Sommers employs throughout her book to undermine feminism is symptomatic of parallel political attacks from the right on curricular reform, affirmative action, multiculturalism, or any discourse that addresses "politicized" questions of power, authority, and structural, institutional inequality.

Because the mainstream media and right-wing speakers have taken **23**

Sommers seriously, promoting her version of feminism as the only accurate version, we as feminists of a very different stamp need to take her seriously. In order to do so, I will provide a brief and necessarily schematic summary of her positions. Sommers splits feminism into two camps, and two camps only: equity feminists and gender feminists. She defines equity feminists as those who "stay within the bounds of traditional scholarship and join in its enterprise." She defines gender feminists as those who "seek to transform scholarship to make it 'women-centered.'"[13] These definitions prove inadequate to the work she does later in the book when she conflates gender feminists who "seek to transform scholarship to make it women-centered" with poststructuralist feminists who have been influenced by the work of Michel Foucault and others—feminists whose work, coming from poststructuralism as it does, is vastly different from what Sommers calls "gender feminism." Her definitions exclude the most prevalent and exciting work that has happened in feminist theory in the last ten years, and that has been the subject of the most vigorous debates.

As anyone at all familiar with feminist theory would recognize, the kind of rigid consensus Sommers insists gender feminism employs simply has no basis. To name just three collections among hundreds, complicated debates about connections between and problems with connections between poststructuralism and feminism are theorized in Linda J. Nicholson's collection *Feminism/Postmodernism* or Marianne Hirsh and Evelyn Fox Keller's *Conflicts in Feminism*, and, more recently, in Seyla Benhabib, Judith Butler, Drucilla Cornell, and Nancy Fraser's *Feminist Contentions*.[14] What Sommers seems to regard as gender feminism—taken from her examples, feminism that is separatist and dedicated only to women's ways of knowing—instead of functioning in alignment with or being basically the same as poststructuralist feminism, actually couldn't be more different. In addition to the fact that these definitions presume an academic feminism and disregard the popular, an important group of feminists not accounted for by this polarity between equity and gender feminisms—myself among them—are young feminists who grew up with equity feminism, got gender feminism in college along with poststructuralism, and are now hard at work on a feminism that would combine elements of all three along with greater attention to intersections among race, class, gender, and other aspects of our multiple identities than Sommers's definitions would allow for. One good example is Rebecca Walker's inclusive activist feminist collective Third Wave, whose mission statement reads:

> Third Wave is a member-driven multiracial, multicultural, multisexuality national non-profit organization devoted to feminist and youth activism for change. Our goal is to harness the energy of young women and men by creating a community in which members can network, strategize, and ultimately, take action. By using our experiences as a starting point, we can create a diverse community and cultivate a meaningful response.[15]

Third Wave makes the inclusion of persons of various genders, sexualities, nationalities, and classes a top priority, and combines elements of equity feminism and gender feminism in a grass-roots feminism (which Sommers says doesn't exist because gender feminism has killed it off) that still fights for equal access, equal pay for equal work, but also seeks to transform the structures young people would be working within.

Most jokes and complaints about the academy and poststructuralism have to do with its "incomprehensibility," or what Sommers refers to as the "law of intellectual fashion . . . Parisian determinism . . . whatever is the rage in Paris will be fashionable in America fifteen years late."[16] In addition to her conflation of drastic differences between gender and poststructualist feminists, she plays the academic-fashion card here and suggests that feminist theorists who use thinkers like Foucault or Jacques Derrida are like Elinor and Marianne Dashwood in Emma Thompson's 1995 movie version of Jane Austen's *Sense and Sensibility*. In the scene where Marianne and Elinor attend a big ball, the elite women who are at its center sneer at Marianne's and Elinor's country fashions—unfashionable imitations that are behind the times, not the real thing. Or, to use a more contemporary example, feminist theorists who cite thinkers like Foucault are like teenagers who still think the early nineties grunge fashion of baby-doll dresses with combat boots is hep. This way Sommers participates in a traditionally masculinist devaluation of anything culturally coded feminine (like fashion trends) as not serious, and suggests that not only is postmodernism and postmodernist feminism not serious, but is also behind the times, passé.

This is not to argue that postmodernism doesn't have its problems; it has been criticized from the left as well as the right. Katha Pollitt, for instance, in a review of the film *The People vs. Larry Flynt* for *The Nation*, argues that "only a postmodern academic could seriously propose that a skin magazine offers a serious challenge to 'state power.' How many divisions has Larry Flynt?"[17] Pollitt highlights the ways in which some facets of academia, intoxicated with rhetorics of agency and choice, end up seeing "disruption" and "subversion" everywhere, creating a set of discursive conditions that make any kind of systematic thought or critique suspect. But as Susan Bordo writes, "There are other choices than pining for Reality with a capital 'R' or tripping on plurality(s) with a postmodern '(s).'"[18] A third-wave feminist praxis would strive to perform a kind of hybrid thinking that contains elements of both, focusing the lens of a "critical media studies" on disruption as well as containment.[19]

But why should the average American reader, who may not consider herself or himself feminist, care about debates in feminism? What is at stake for readers outside of the academy, or even in it? What does feminism have to offer young women and men, our next generation of cultural workers of all kinds? Because there is so much cynicism in the air associated with the terms "feminist" or "activist," because the right has been so skillful at using the rhetoric of feminism against feminism itself, and because second-wave feminist concepts have come to seem foreign to a generation of women and men who grew up in different cultural conditions (including some acceptance and implementation of feminism), we need to find a way to show how and why feminism matters, how it speaks to conditions today. Third wavers are products of all the contradictory definitions of and differences within feminism, lived contradictions Sommers's account of feminism doesn't even begin to touch.

WHAT FEMINISM'S GOT TO DO WITH IT

Antifeminist, political-correctness rhetoric aside, the "backlash" that Faludi named in 1991 has intensified. Nowhere is this more clearly marked than in contemporary developments in the sport of women's bodybuilding, whose history can make sense only in the context of bodybuilding in general. The first publicly acknowledged bodybuilder—"the founder of bodybuilding"—was Friedrich Muller, whose stage name was Eugene Sandow.[20] Sandow became prominent in the last decade of the nineteenth century. Promoted by Florenz Ziegfeld, Jr., as the world's most aesthetically developed physique, Sandow served as a model for famous photographers and sculptors, and did a world tour of weight-lifting and posing performances. His popularity helped shift public attention from the idea of strength to the idea of aesthetic muscular development, setting the stage for male bodybuilding, in which strength is not the focus. Sandow himself organized the first physique competition in London in 1901. Sandow's chunky body, lack of striations, and undeveloped pectoral muscles made him a far cry from bodybuilders today, but he was the first to focus public attention on the idea of physical development. This idea and his promotion of it spawned companies like the York Barbell Company that were the precursors of the vast empire of contemporary fitness industries. Sandow's contests started a chain of other contests that officially became part of sporting history in 1940, when the Amateur Athletic Union (AAU) sponsored the first Mr. America competition. This contest led the way to the establishment of the International Federation of Bodybuilding (IFBB) in 1947, and the Mr. Universe competition in the early 1960s. By the late sixties the contest was renamed Mr. Olympia, and it remains the most important bodybuilding contest to this day. To insiders, the Mr. Olympia trophy is still affectionately known as the "Sandow."

By contrast, women's bodybuilding did not get under way until late 1977, when such cultural forces as the women's liberation movement, affirmative action legislation, and the development of women's sports had initiated a wider public acceptance of strong, athletic women. In 1977, Ohio YMCA director Henry McGhee established the United States Women's Physique Association (USWPA) and sponsored the first bodybuilding contest for women. The winner was Gina LaSpina, whose long-limbed, soft-stomached, stringy-muscled physique marked the characteristics of the first wave of women's bodybuilding: skinny women with some scraggly muscle tacked on, women whose bodies did little to challenge accepted notions of masculinity and femininity. Others followed McGhee's lead, and contests became more frequent. George Snyder's "Best in the World" was held in 1979. Modeled on beauty pageants, this contest, like others of this period, **2 7** required the women to pose in high heels. Promoter Snyder marketed the event as a "beauty contest for women in good shape," and competitors were asked not to flex their muscles lest they appear too "intimidating" or "unfeminine."[21] But Carla Dunlap-Kaan, who was later to become Ms. Olympia, had other ideas, and started a mass rebellion in which competitors kicked off their heels and began hitting front double-biceps poses. A month later the television show *Real People* profiled Laura Combes and Doris Barrilleaux, and featured a Florida contest, bringing the sport national attention. Women's bodybuilding began with women kicking off their heels in a grand statement of self-empowerment and claim to compete as real athletes in a real sport.

Lisa Lyon, who was the first female bodybuilder to get widespread national attention, won the first Women's World Bodybuilding Championships in 1979 in Los Angeles. In addition to television, magazine, and newspaper appearances worldwide, Lyon served as the model of the first photography collection devoted to a female bodybuilder, Robert Mapplethorpe's *Lady: Lisa Lyon* (see chapter 4). Lyon's body is one of the best examples of the first wave of women's bodybuilding: aesthetically balanced, muscular in a smooth way, communicating not so much a transgression of gender but its development. Lyon and others like her (such as first Ms. Olympia Rachel McLish) built bodies that were in alignment with body ideals expressed in popular culture in the early eighties: bodies "positioned," in Laurie Schulze's words, "in a more normative regime. . . . Sleek, athletic female bodies . . . are the new markers of feminine sexuality, desirability, and status."[22] Lyon's body was the size and style of some of the fitness competitors today, clearly worked on but still minimally developed, lacking the density and sheer bulk female bodybuilders would develop ten years later.

Larger bodybuilders of the first wave—Laura Combes, Kay Baxter, Lori Bowen, and perhaps especially Bev Francis—paved the way for the body that would become widely accepted by the end of the eighties. This body had comparatively so much more muscle mass, vascularity, and striations that it made first-wave bodies look tiny, and Francis was the first to build this kind of body roughly eight years before its time. Francis, a powerlifter, switched to bodybuilding in the early eighties and constructed a body with so much muscle mass and so little body fat that from the neck down it really was gender indeterminate. Her body was the focus of the controversy over femininity that raged in *Pumping Iron II* and that remains a crucial question in the sport to this day. In the movie, Francis's body was posed as the counterpoint to McLish's beauty-queen good looks, perceived by many as an example of the threat women's bodybuilding can pose to traditional notions of femininity. While Francis finished a humiliating eighth in that contest although she was clearly the most muscular, her body set a standard of possibility for women that would reach ascendancy in 1990, when the densely muscled Lenda Murray was crowned Ms. Olympia. The early nineties marked female bodybuilding's second wave, an unprecedented period in the development of the female form when really big women were the norm. Then came 1994, and the explosion of fitness contests and the rise of the soft-porn and swimsuit pictorials.

To Big or Not to Big

Perhaps because of the turn in women's bodybuilding toward larger women and more developed muscularity, the fitness competitions that were initially seen as not athletically serious—a kind of entertaining fluff for the amusement of male audiences—gained popularity shortly after female bodybuilders got huge. Although they began in the late eighties, fitness competitions did not develop a wide following until 1994, and they were not added to the Olympia competitions until the Fitness Olympia in 1995.[23] Debbie Kruck, an early competitor, sees fitness as an avenue for women who don't have the genetics to achieve the amount of muscle mass professional bodybuilding had begun to require by the late eighties: "Only a very few women have the genetics to become competitive at the highest levels of bodybuilding. . . . My problems in developing enough muscle mass for bodybuilding [led me to] try fitness competition, which . . . allowed me to combine training and diet with the interest I've always had in dance, theater, and performance."[24] Whereas bodybuilding competitions consist of compulsory muscle poses and a choreographed routine that emphasizes muscularity, the fitness competition, modeled on the Miss America pageant, has swimsuit, evening gown, and interview rounds as well as a choreographed routine that emphasizes gymnastics and dancing ability, and

29

tests of physical fitness such as a timed test on the Versa-climber. The degree of muscularity achieved by a fitness competitor is significantly less than that of a bodybuilder, although competitions still require intensive training and dieting.

The bodybuilding/fitness debate often sets the two against each other. Bodybuilding proponents declare that fitness is not a serious sport but is rather girlie entertainment that caters to prurient adolescent fantasies, and is a diversion from the serious business of bodybuilding. In an article addressing the bodybuilding-versus-fitness debate, Chris Aceto writes,

> [In] *Ironman's* January '96 issue . . . the mag's writers ask the nicely loaded question "Who is sexier: female bodybuilders or fitness competitors?" Allow me to rephrase that: "Who is sexier: an athlete or a *Playboy* model? Is Martina Navratilova or Jackie Joyner-Kersee sexier than Anna Nicole Smith?" I am sure that both of the aforementioned world-champion athletes, whose goals are to defeat all comers, couldn't care less! Are Dorian Yates and the rest of the Mr. Olympia lineup as "hunky" as the guys on *Melrose Place*? [25]

By equating female bodybuilders with "world-champion athletes" like Navratilova or Joyner-Kersee, and fitness women with *Playboy* centerfolds, Aceto makes the controversial argument that bodybuilders are real athletes while fitness competitors are not. By defining bodybuilding as a sport rather than a question of sex appeal, Aceto calls into question the whole argument—still hotly debated in bodybuilding circles—about whether it is good for the sport for women to get too big and thus lose their femininity. By reframing the issue as sport, bodybuilding as an act of doing (building a body) rather than a question of appearing (not building too much so as to appear feminine), he effectively derails the common knee-jerk reaction that is based purely in limited definitions of aesthetic femininity. But he also negatively reaffirms what Susan Douglas refers to as the catfight—by continuing to play female bodybuilders and fitness competitors off against each other.[26] Aceto further undermines solidarity between bodybuilders and fitness competitors, participating in an either/or debate that may, because of wider public acceptance of fitness, contribute to the downfall of bodybuild-

No limits on femininity? A fitness woman, circa 1997. (Ad for No Limits Sportswear in *All Natural Muscular Development*, May 1997)

ing as a competitive sport. The recent move by the International Federation of Bodybuilding to cut the Ms. Olympia prize money from $115,000 to $60,000, while raising the Fitness Olympia prize money from $25,000 to $60,000, as well as the move to stage the contests on the same night, shows an erosion of bodybuilding and the ascendance of fitness at the institutional level. Although the IFBB later decided to restore the Ms. Olympia prize money, it is clear that fitness threatens to upstage bodybuilding in the near future.

Any discussion of bodybuilding versus fitness necessarily invokes the category of femininity, particularly in a sport like bodybuilding where traditional ideas of the feminine are in question. Since the first women's bodybuilding contests, the most controversial point in judging is just how far a woman's body should be allowed to stray from the dominant cultural feminine ideal of smallness and delicacy. Underlying that ideal is a complicated psychology, perhaps given voice most graphically by Octavio Paz:

> The person who suffers [violence] is passive, inert, and open, in contrast to the active, aggressive, and closed person who inflicts it. The chingon is the macho, the male; he rips open the chingada, the female, who is pure passivity, defenseless against the exterior world. . . . When we say, "Vete a la chingada," we send a person to a distant place. Distant, vague, and indeterminate. To the country of broken and worn-out things . . . Her taint is constitutional and resides . . . in her sex. This passivity, open to the outside world, causes her to lose her identity. . . . She is no one; she disappears into nothingness, she is Nothingness. And yet she is the cruel incarnation of the feminine condition.[27]

The feminine is a crucial category in women's bodybuilding, where many debates about judgment standards are framed by the imperative that female bodybuilders not lose their femininity. When the bodybuilders with reconstructed femininity—defined as smaller muscles, facial beauty, and large breast implants—are the ones who win contests and lucrative product endorsements, it is safe to assume that a measure of this femininity will be pursued, that women will struggle paradoxically to incarnate Nothingness, the open, since for this they get rewards.

Such an incarnation is tangible today in the turn against the sport of women's bodybuilding that I read as symptomatic of a return to more traditional gender roles and reduced possibilities for women. The fact that fitness women are more marketable, and that therefore many bodybuilders are leaving the sport for fitness—such as standouts Michelle Ralabate and Sharon Bruneau—reflects a clock turning back to notions of the feminine like those Paz so lyrically traces. The widespread exposure and public praise that fitness women receive function to reinstate a narrow definition of femininity that reduces it to sexuality since fitness women are almost uniformly portrayed as sexual rather than as athletes, even though they may be very good athletes.

The creation of a gender differential like that described by Paz—male invulnerability and closedness; female vulnerability and openness—is one effect of the sexualization of female athletes. That differential defuses the anxiety raised by physically powerful and competent women. If femininity is redefined from its traditional (white) associations with delicacy and weakness, many female athletes fear the loss of approval, acceptance, and love that acceding to this norm brings them. As Chris Holmlund writes of *Pumping Iron II*, "The overwhelming majority of the female characters . . . from the bodybuilders themselves to the one female judge, fear that a redefinition of femininity will entail the loss of love, power, and privilege." Most bodybuilders work hard to reassure potential doubters that they are still feminine, even if they have muscles, and the visual code that reassures a viewer on this point has come to be understood as sexuality. Photographers and filmmakers create images of female bodybuilders that, in Holmlund's words, "function to defuse rather than provoke male and female spectators' anxieties about muscular women by fetishizing women's bodies and by making them the objects of heterosexual desire."[28]

Holmlund is describing the filming practices characteristic of *Pumping Iron*, made in 1984 when bodybuilders were considerably smaller. It is not surprising, then, that in 1994 when *Flex* started to run its "Power and Sizzle" pictorials featuring women who were now much more muscularly developed than the women in the film, this practice was proportionally heightened. Each month, hypersexualized images—women in leather bras, high heels, lace gloves, red fishnets, holding guitars, riding wooden horses—of the female bodybuilders are accompanied by quotations attrib-

3 3

uted to the women themselves that insist on their sensuality. They further-more insist that they are completely responsible for creating their bodies and their look, that their sensuality is their essence, and that sensual appeal is in fact their goal in bodybuilding. The following is just a small sample. Drorit Kernes: "Who says that female bodybuilders are not sensual and sexy?" Laura Creavalle: "You can be sexy, feminine, and muscular. I feel sexier today because I am responsible for how I look." Latia Del Rivi-ero: "Muscle on a woman can be shocking, even formidable-looking, yet it also can be alluring and appealing. . . . In designing my own body through iron, my goal has been to create an unnervingly sensual appeal." Sue Price: "The red lingerie covering the muscle heightens my sense of sexual power. I'm feminine but I'm strong; I'm a woman but I'm not weak." Skye Ryland: "Thanks to bodybuilding . . . I feel more alive and sexy than ever be-fore. . . . If people think that I look like a man because of my training-enhanced muscularity, what they really need to do is . . . assess their own fears about masculinity and femininity." Six-time Ms. Olympia Lenda Mur-ray articulates the confusion quite nicely when she says, "There has been some controversy in the past few years about whether or not some of the photos I've posed for are 'too sexy.' This is really ironic, because it wasn't long ago that people were claiming that highly muscular women weren't sexy at all."[29] The *Flex* layouts focus on making female muscularity sexu-ally attractive, and the discussion has stayed on this level. Because analy-sis of the photos has been put in terms of whether they are too sexual, or even pornographic, this detracts from the question of context: that these are female *athletes* who are photographed sexually—the context is athleti-cism, not sex.

Female bodybuilders, perpetually under the eyes of the femininity po-lice, are continually pushed toward more traditional ideas about gender, and part of that recuperation is accomplished precisely through this strategy of making highly muscular women sexy. Each month, "Power and Sizzle" tries very hard to sell the equation between muscle and sex. The statement in-cluded at the beginning of every pictorial reads:

Women bodybuilders are many things, among them symmetrical, strong, sensuous, and stunning. When photographed in competition shape, repping and grimacing or squeezing out shots, they appear shredded, vascular, and hard, and they can be perceived as threatening. Offseason they carry more body fat, presenting themselves in a much more naturally attractive condition. To exhibit this real, natural side of women bodybuilders, *Flex* has been presenting pictorials of female competitors in softer condition. We hope this approach dispels the myth of female bodybuilder masculinity and proves what role models they truly are. [30]

There are some conceptual problems with this sexualization, however, contradictions the magazine does its best to paper over. The idea that bodybuilders should be role models sets up its practitioners as examples of ideal femininity. As such, unnatural masculinity has to go, and the women are expected to construct themselves more in terms of the feminine norm— that is, softness and openness.

Paradoxically, according to *Flex*, women bodybuilders are unnatural when they are in competition shape, when they have reached the goal and end of the bodybuilding process. What are they "threatening"—perhaps the idea that gender is "natural," that the "real, natural side of women bodybuilders" is "softness"? To reveal that masculinity is a set of characteristics that women can possess as well as men? While bodybuilding fanatically relies on the rhetoric of self-determination—that you can, in Sam Fussell's words, "defy both nurture and nature and transform yourself . . . you can become the person you dream of being"[31]—the *Flex* pictorial contradicts that dream for women, who are not allowed to have masculinity, which, despite visual cues that say otherwise, can be for women only a "myth." Despite the bodies women manage to create, the text says, they are really soft, "naturally attractive." Hardness is a pose: these women really are women after all—soft, feminine, sexually available, corrected to cultural norms. But is this really all women are, all women can be?

In the late nineties, at least 80 percent of the top women bodybuilders in the U.S. have gotten breast implants. The most recent and visible example is Ericca Kern, who got implants in 1996 and was only then featured in shots that show her chest whereas before her chest was never visible. Women like Kern do so to replace the breasts that are naturally lost through the process of bodybuilding, since the attainment of a chiseled physique means that breasts, which are primarily composed of fat, become very small. All of the women who have appeared in the *Flex* pictorials have implants. "Natural feminine softness"—surgically constructed. The silicone expanses under Debbi Muggli's massively muscled chest give the futuristic vision of the cyborg an ironic embodiment, even as the section on "shapely breasts" in one of Cory Everson's recent books begins with a discussion of implants, as if shapeliness is not possible without them.[32] The paradox of female bodybuilder femininity exposes the idea of the natural body for the treasured mythology it is. The *Flex* pictorials seem frantically concerned with reinstituting these bodies as women's bodies as defined in traditional ways: soft, vulnerable, open. Perhaps this is not the way, however, to promote female bodybuilding as a sport. Many women bodybuild precisely for the reason that it allows them to exercise characteristics culturally labeled masculine: integrity, precedence, physical strength.

The bodies of fitness women don't present much challenge to traditional definitions. Fitness proponents see fitness as a competition for women whose bodies, due to the lower level of muscularity, are more attainable and desirable for the average woman and the men who ostensibly look at her. The focus has clearly shifted from sports to looks, and with tangible effect. Today bodybuilding's top women, having achieved unprecedented competitive size, are once again slimming down to the diminutive feminine ideal and are putting back on the high heels they kicked off a decade and a half ago, largely because fitness competitors are generally seen as much more marketable than bodybuilders. As a result, many women have switched from bodybuilding to fitness because it is much easier to get endorsements and widespread exposure. As longtime bodybuilding photographer Bill Dobbins writes in an Internet posting, "There was a time when women bodybuilders were all over the magazines but couldn't get a break with the NPC [National Physique Committee] and IFBB judges. The reverse is true nowadays. The judges have pretty much accepted the idea that women can be as big and muscular as possible as long as they conform to the accepted overall aesthetic standard of bodybuilding, but now it is the magazines that have turned their backs on the competitors."[33] The bodybuilding magazines, which are the main outlet for bodybuilders' exposure outside the industry, have taken a conservative, reactionary turn from their coverage of female bodybuilding in the mid- to late eighties and early nineties, which focused on the women as strong, revolutionary athletes. Now most of the muscle magazines have stopped featuring female bodybuilders at all, preferring to show fitness women instead, and the magazines that do still feature female bodybuilders follow *Flex*'s format and feature them in swimsuit, lingerie, and nude-centerfold pictorials, focusing on the women as fantasy objects for the viewer.

Industry insiders make no secret of the fact that the new trend in naked or near-naked pictorials in the muscle magazines that feature mostly fitness women has boosted circulation even more than expected, and that this boost is their purpose. In the logic of commerce and marketability, giving the people what they want means giving them naked muscle women of whatever shade (one layout in *Flex* featured the proverbial male fantasy of blond twins) who will use their tightened glutes and implanted pecs to stimulate and titillate the viewer.

This practice is rarely questioned, even in the bodybuilding subculture. Whenever questions about such layouts were posed on the Femuscle Forum, the Internet discussion group devoted specifically to female bodybuilding, there was an instantaneous chorus of "It's pure marketing; sex sells" offered as substantive analysis of this form of pictorial presence. One participant, though, e-mailed the editor in chief of *Ironman* magazine, asking why the coverage of female bodybuilders was suspended in preference of fitness women, and received the following response:

> From our surveys we've determined that our female readers want to look more like fitness competitors than Lenda Murray, and that our male readers want to look as big as possible. So we give men hardcore bodybuilding and we give the women profiles and routines from fitness competitors. . . . As for extended profiles on the "big" women, those are few and far between. If the demands of the market change, so will *Ironman*. Our job is to give the majority what they want.[34]

Give the people what they want, just never ask why they want what they want. Why exactly is it that women want to look small while men want to look as big as possible? Why doesn't the market support big women? Something that never appeared, except in private e-mails between individual women, and drew only one response when I posted it to the general list, was some analysis of why sex doesn't sell the other way around—that is, why similar pictorials featuring the male bodybuilders fail to grace *Flex*'s and other bodybuilding magazine's centers.

That sex is the point of women's bodybuilding and fitness has become the accepted industry standard. The August 1996 issue of *Playboy* magazine, for instance, ran a pictorial called "Hard Bodies" that featured many fitness competitors, and all of the major muscle magazines have featured the same women, arguably in more sexual poses than did *Playboy*. Writing in *All Natural Muscular Development*, John Romano points to the degree to which the bodybuilding industry has gone toward the sexualization of the sport by arguing that the *Playboy* spread was *less* sexual than the pictorials that currently run in the muscle magazines:

> One swimsuit issue this year was obviously directed squarely at the Al Bundy/Tim Allen crowd. Top fitness babes twisted into lascivious poses; pertinent bodyparts straining provocatively against sheer wet cloth, looking up at you with a tawdry little pout. It's definitely got nothing to do with bodybuilding. . . . We compared [*Playboy* and the *Ironman* swimsuit issue]. And you know what? *Ironman* was unanimously voted most provocative. . . . How the girls were portrayed was far more, shall we say, arousing? The naked girls were just naked. Is that the way it's supposed to be—like, that's why nudity is considered art? Because its purpose is intended to appreciate the artistry of the ultimate human form, rather than exploit sexuality? Hmmmm, I thought that's why we had swimsuit issues.[35]

If bodybuilding industry magazines have taken on a sexualized focus that surpasses that of *Playboy*, it is clear that there has been a shift industry-wide from the presentation of female bodybuilders as athletes who also have a dimension of sexuality to the presentation of fitness women who are primarily sexual. In terms of how women themselves negotiate these conditions, marketability ensures that many women will construct themselves and be happy to have themselves constructed sexually since this in turn ensures their individual financial success. But in terms of the larger cultural picture, this individual success works to reinforce traditional definitions of the feminine—pliability, sexual access—that affect many women.

This is not to say that these women should be blamed or that they shouldn't develop their own careers because that development may hurt other women. It is to point out that those of us whose careers do not involve posing in magazines should employ what Douglas Kellner terms a "critical media literacy" and be conscious of how these representations are working, and choose whether to construct ourselves according to the terms that the magazines propose.[36] What the subculture of female bodybuilders who do not compete does with the dominant cultural representations is key. For some of us, individual success may rest more in the construction of the "myth of female bodybuilder masculinity" in our own lives, a myth which gives us confidence, strength, and a sense of integrity and place. To the extent that the spectacle of female masculinity—evident in our bodies— threatens the unquestioned basis for unequal power relations between the sexes, for the purposes of our lives, success may in some ways depend on our ability to attain some measure of traditional masculinity, thereby gaining the respect of, and being taken seriously by, those around us.

In dominant culture, however, success is usually connected to the exhibition of traditional femininity. The same competitors who posed for *Playboy* are also featured—at very high salaries—on syndicated television workout shows that run on most local cable stations. ESPN2's *Fitness Beach*, broadcast at 11:30 a.m., is an example of how fitness competitions and competitors can lend themselves to reactionary constructions of gender. Like its sister programs, *Body Shaping* and *Flex Appeal*, *Fitness Beach* features women working out in bathing suits, aerobicizing by the Jamaican shore or lifting very light weights. Power is definitely not part of their aesthetic. Zoom shots continually focus on cleavage, and the overall look of the program very much resembles the swimsuit edition of *Sports Illustrated*. The emphasis is on sex rather than athleticism, sex appeal rather than fitness, instead of some combination of the two.

By contrast, Cory Everson's *Gotta Sweat*, broadcast every morning immediately preceding *Fitness Beach* on ESPN2, contains much more of what Douglas Kellner would theorize as both resistance and containment. The show is mixed gender, with both men and women performing the exercises. Men consistently train with much heavier weights than the women, but they also participate in the aerobic portions of the show and do all the same exercises. Everson herself, the six-time Ms. Olympia just before women's

Affirmative fitness: Competitors for the Ms. Galaxy title pose with the owner of Hot Skins, a clothing company, in a positive representation that primarily emphasizes athleticism. (*Hot Skins Bodywear Catalog*, Spring 1997)

bodybuilding turned toward extensive muscular development, was and is fairly muscular. Everson, who combines breast implants and a lean, feminine look with significant deltoid, bicep, and pectoral development, is an example of reconstructed femininity that is accessible and not alienating to the average woman, but whose body suggests a strength and activity that is more than pure sex.

Choosing Your Chains

For the most part, however, contemporary developments in the bodybuilding and fitness industries mark a return to traditional gender roles, making
cultural limitations on female possibilities sexy once again. Even though
women's bodybuilding is a very young sport, a recent *Ironman* article asks
whether fitness competitions will wipe women's bodybuilding off the map.
Deemed more natural because the competitors do not take steroids, wom-
en's fitness competitors certainly do come closer than bodybuilders to the
dominant feminine ideal, although it has always been part of women's

bodybuilding to enact that ideal along with its disruption. It is the approximation rather than the disruption of that ideal that makes fitness so popular. The advent of the fitness competition definitively shows that soft curves and hard bodies is the new feminine ideal, and represents to most a more acceptable female body than the more masculine, heavily muscled bodies of the female builders. As Susan Bordo writes, "Viewed historically, the discipline and normalization of the female body . . . has to be acknowledged as an amazingly durable and flexible strategy of social control," and the shift within the industry from women's bodybuilding to fitness is an example of this normalization.[37]

The illusion of choice—I choose to construct my body as a fitness woman rather than as a bodybuilder—tries to make acceptable what can otherwise be seen as degrading. Messages are sent on at least two levels. The first level is that of a culture that has lived through twenty years of the second-wave women's movement, and is well aware of feminist critiques of pornography and female objectification, and is also aware of the conservative turn against such critique, heralded by, for instance, *Esquire* or the *New Yorker* approval of the new, sexy feminist who loves high heels and finds them empowering. (Current media caricatures of feminists make me feel it is necessary to emphasize here that I am not critical of either high heels or sex.) The pod-fems discussed earlier are part of that turn, and their arguments are used to discredit feminist critique. Such discrediting discourse functions to make seem acceptable sexist practices that are not acceptable from a mainstream standpoint informed by feminism or racial analysis. These practices are made acceptable (the thinking might run) through an appeal to self-determination and control offered in the guise of stereotypical sexuality, which, as the first law in the land (We love sex!), is sure to mitigate the objections of all but the most strident feminist viewer. The second level is to resexualize the image of a female body that might not immediately be accepted as sexual since it is muscular, to make that body acceptable to an audience with conventional notions of gender that define *female* as unmuscular and weak. Read together, the mixed message functions to contain any chance the muscular female body might have to get a little respect, unless it is read critically. The point of analysis is to create a critical media literacy equipped to deal with this kind of complicated message so characteristic of dominant culture today. This kind of literacy allows a woman (or a man) a true choice, a more informed basis on which to decide how exactly to how to respond to the images, and how to construct herself.

The history of women's bodybuilding can be read as a history of more general political gains and decline, a text on which the history of the politics of race, gender, and power is played out in graphic visual form. Currently, like the myth of the femme fatale in the general culture, the illusion of personal power that bodybuilding confers covers a darker reality of a power transformed through the subject's eager orchestration of her own containment. In the late nineties, shifts in women's bodybuilding and shifts in feminist discourse in the mainstream media are two interdependent cultural forces that can lead women to participate eagerly in activities not in their best interests. But what is the history of these shifting forces? What made women become bodybuilders? What made women feminists? Why are those words—"female bodybuilder" and "feminist"—threatening?

So many ways to turn human beings into ghosts, deny them existence, a place. Sara Evans attributes the explosion of the second-wave women's movement to women workers in the civil rights movement, who "were important but invisible," often doing the organizing while the public recognition was given to men.[38] Often ghosts fight, struggle to be visible. If enough fight together there are civil rights, gay rights, women's rights. Visibility produces results. There was a brief period when female bodybuilders enjoyed wider acceptance through the late eighties and early nineties, a period when it looked like cultural ideas about femininity and masculinity might have broadened enough to allow women visibility in a different way. That difference, however, like theories of multiculturalism that argue for the valuation of and respect for nonwhite, non-Western perspectives, is under attack from a variety of angles today.

The normalization that would erase that difference is usually masked as diversity and choice, and female bodybuilding's biggest promoters make use of this familiar strategy. In the September 1994 issue of *Flex*, bodybuilding's biggest magnate, Joe Weider, responds to the demand for fitness women by evoking precisely this rhetoric. "The all-embracing purpose," he says, "for all the bodybuilding contests I have launched over the years is to present as wide a range of physiques as possible." The advanced degree of muscularity that top female competitors have achieved is suppressing that "range." "I want to steer women's bodybuilding in a more inclusive direction," he says. "Female bodybuilding has evolved to the point where the leading competitors at the Ms. Olympia contest possess breathtaking muscularity. However, not all women bodybuilders can duplicate that extremely muscular look." As a result of this exclusiveness, Weider instituted the Fitness Olympia in order to, as he puts it, "involve those women who present a leaner, more streamlined look than the more muscular, more genetically gifted women." This will, Weider writes, "give the general public a truer guide to the full range of physiques that weight training can offer." [39]

Weider's language evokes a paradoxical inclusiveness. Competition, by definition, involves exclusiveness, so to steer women's bodybuilding in a "more inclusive direction" is to undermine the very foundation of the sport. As is so often the case in the contemporary context, here the rhetoric of choice ends up enacting a rhetoric of standardization. There is certainly no talk about making men's bodybuilding more "inclusive" by adding subdivisions to the Mr. Olympia for men who "present a leaner, more streamlined look than the more muscular, genetically gifted" men so that the "general public" can have a "truer guide to the full range of physiques that weight training can offer" men. What Weider's language of diversity obscures is that what he is actually including in the repertoire of female bodybuilding is the conventional femininity that female bodybuilding used to help question, disturb, make more "inclusive." After all, which body type has traditionally functioned as the ideal standard: Nancy Kerrigan's "lean musculature" or Tonya Harding's "thick, muscular thighs"? It is no coincidence that the slender, big-breasted Rachel McLish and Cory Everson were more popular female bodybuilders than the thickly muscled Bev Francis, and what Weider seeks to reinscribe is a conventional femininity only momentarily disrupted. He is using the rhetoric of exclusion to include the very standard of femininity that has functioned to exclude large female bodies of any kind from its parameters. He wishes to include what has always excluded, to reinstitute a center that has never been at the margins. Under the guise of providing a "wider range of physiques," he reinscribes the small, lean, compact female body as the standard.

One thing that makes this reinscription so effective is that the negative turn against women's bodybuilding is often voiced by the women themselves. Kiana Tom, a fitness woman who has one of the most popular body-shaping shows on ESPN, writes that early in her fitness career she had to ask herself, "Would I opt for the sometimes bizarre world of female bodybuilding, or go the more mainstream—and healthy—route to female bodysculpting?" The first full-page shot of Tom in her book *Kiana's Bodysculpting* presents a body with no obvious muscularity. The delicate, thin lines of her arms extend upwards from the shot's focus: her deep cleavage. Her soft eyes and smile are accommodating to the viewer, and her body reaffirms an expected picture of bicepless diminution. She voices a perspective heard more and more frequently in the muscle magazines and elsewhere today: "I decided to stick with what I liked—the lean, feminine and muscular look instead of the more masculine, muscle-bound image that the female bodybuilders convey. Women should aspire to a sleek, toned and feminine appearance." [40]

What Kiana's emphasis on choice obscures is that masculinity and femininity, much like the shaped bodies under discussion, are cultural prescriptions which generate everyday practices that in turn orchestrate a body's adherence to norms. Women "should aspire to a . . . feminine appearance" because a feminine appearance, defined as diminution and weakness, helps to maintain existing power relations. As Gloria Steinem writes in *Moving Beyond Words*, "very different groups of men come together in their belief that women are supposed to be weaker than men; that muscles and strength aren't 'feminine.'" [41]

The argument for femininity and against muscle and strength is yet another facet of the culture wars, related to calls for a return to traditional curricula and attacks on affirmative action, reproductive rights, and any kind of identifiably feminist or other civil rights rhetoric. In this cultural context, female agreement with reactionary arguments about gender is very lucrative. Yet traditional correlations between femininity and weakness are used as justification for gender inequalities of all kinds, from the second-shift mentality that makes women responsible for domestic work to entrenched assumptions about femininity, weakness, and capability. So while power feminists and fitness women may be riding the tide of gender reactionism all the way to the bank, the actual image the fitness women convey works all the more powerfully to create images of inequality in the popular cultural imagination. Margo Napoli, for instance, with her huge breast implants and little girl gaze in the 1995 swimsuit issue of *Muscular Devel-*

opment, does little to inspire a view of the female body as anything but packaged to a standard that is relentlessly reactionary. Under the guise of individual achievement and choice, fitness women and power feminists alike are arguing for the idea that women, as femmes fatales, can use sex appeal for power. But what actually happens to a femme fatale, to a woman who succeeds in her seduction, her creation of a physique that approximates desirable feminine norms?

Frequently quoted speakers like Camille Paglia, who are marked as the new feminists, the less repressed, more progressive thinkers, argue for femininity and its power to control men. Restating very old arguments, she says, "The femme fatale expresses woman's ancient and eternal control of the sexual realm."[42] We don't need tougher legislation for equity or against domestic violence, we don't need affirmative action in the public sphere, because women control private relations through their control of sex. Feminist thinking that addresses rape and sexual harassment is now "victim feminism" according to writers like Katie Roiphe and Christina Hoff Sommers, and feminism—not sexual violence—makes women into helpless victims.

That such positions are marketed as the new feminism helps one to read current trends in female bodybuilding. These trends are another indication of the cultural shift away from a progressive politics that sees women's bodies in some light other than their ability to attract or control men, to an acceptance of that old status quo mandate, currently marketed as alternative, liberated, and new. Again and again women bodybuilders are quoted as saying that they feel powerful *because* they feel sexy, a very different concept of power from that utilized by male bodybuilders, perhaps best expressed by Arnold Schwarzenegger.

For Arnold, bodybuilding is about space: power, domain, prerogative, the physical space his body takes up, and the precedence granted to it in the world. Arnold poses on top of a hill, filling the frame, towering above the mountains. The density of his muscularity establishes dominion over unbounded territories: this land and all that is around it is his. His rhetoric matches his masterly pose. As a teenager in the early sixties, he feels stifled in Austria, and wants to get to America: "'I've got to get out of here,' I kept thinking. 'It's not big enough, it's stifling.' It wouldn't allow me to expand. There never seemed to be enough space."[43] Arnold's body is liter-

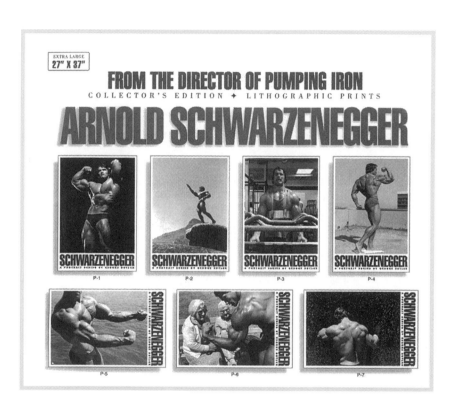

Taking space: Arnold as the "unacknowledged legislator of the world." (Ad in *All Natural Muscular Development*, May 1997)

ally his medium of expansion. And for Arnold (a man with a goal) girls and women, femmes fatales, "get crossed off [his] list" no matter how much sexual power they may have because they are a distraction from the goal, something that "might hold him back." Arnold and Camille agree that woman, the feminine, holds back. According to Paglia, "Men are biologically impelled outward to flee from woman. To make a world separate from women. That is the basis of civilization. . . . The artist [creates because] he is swerving from women's power and dominance."[44]

Arnold creates power and dominance by narrowing his life to training. "Whatever I thought might hold me back, I avoided," he said. "I crossed girls off my list, except as tools for my sexual needs."[45] The success of his fitness endeavors are dependent upon separation from others, and from precisely those kinds of relations that Paglia argues give women power. By contrast, Kiana Tom experiences embodiment very differently. Compare Arnold's statements to hers, describing her fitness regime: "I was driving everybody crazy by bringing baked potatoes with me for casual drives around Westwood, eating nothing but low-fat, unprocessed foods, drinking nothing but bottled water without sodium. I was too one-dimensional. I believe that women need to strike a balance in their lives. Balance breeds success."[46]

Arnold's bodily construction is dependent upon social norms that equate masculinity and power with physical size. His body is constructed not to appeal to viewers sexually but to stand for his ability to take over the world. Kiana's bodily construction is dependent on cultural norms that expect her to accommodate to others, to be not too "one-dimensional." She feels she has to change and become more "balanced," which means other-centered, not "driving everybody crazy." She succeeds by responding to their demands. For Arnold, the opposite holds true. Ignoring the demands of others, retaining an unbalanced, singular focus, brings him success. Kiana Tom succeeds by slimming down, contracting, becoming more pleasing to others. Arnold's expansion provides a sense of possibility for other men, inspiring the question, to use Sam Fussell's words, "What if I made myself a walking billboard of invulnerability like Arnold?"[47] Precisely that message spreads Arnold across the international imagination, forever the relentless Terminator.

FEMINIST/BODYBUILDER MONSTERS:
REVOLVING DOORS, SHRINKING SPACES

Like the scene in the film *Natural Born Killers* (1994) where serial killer Mallory Knox screams "I'm a new woman now" after she has offed both her parents, feminist rhetoric in the contemporary scene is often appropriated in a way that neutralizes feminist threats to the status quo, or feminist rhetoric is used as an example of monstrosity, a word often used to describe bodybuilders. For a man, "monster" is a compliment. For a woman, "monster" means not feminine, ugly, deficient, out of control, too much. Mallory accedes to an independent, "feminist" position by becoming a killer, making feminism seem out of control and inherently dangerous, much the way the earlier rash of movies like *Basic Instinct* and *Fatal Attraction* demonized the career woman. It is in the context of a cultural turn against more progressive ways of thinking about and constructing female embodiment and empowerment that James Cameron's *Terminator II*, with its female power aesthetic, can be most effectively understood. The film is an early example of a growing conservative unease with the concept and concrete evidence of flexible gender boundaries and bodily norms. Because the muscular female body exhibited by Linda Hamilton touches so directly on questions of the cultural construction of femininity and the female body, constructions directly related to and serving as a barometer of cultural politics of gender, the movie reflects a parallel to the recent developments in female bodybuilding just discussed. These developments can be read more broadly as the indication not, as Naomi Wolf would have it, of a female power or cultural capital reaching ascendancy, but of female ambition under attack in popular culture.

The conflation of muscles, new norms of sexual desirability, and monstrosity is perhaps best exemplified by Linda Hamilton's character Sarah Connor in *Terminator II* (1991). In the early nineties Hamilton's power physique stood as one of the most culturally valued female forms. As Susan Bordo writes, "My male students (as well as my female students) literally swooned over Linda Hamilton's fierce expression and taut body in *Terminator II*."[48] But what is elevated in terms of sexual valuation is also simultaneously devalued. Bordo wrote this in 1992, just before the conservative turn. In 1995, movies like *Disclosure* or *To Die For* take the illusion of female power, both desired and feared, and directly equate it with evil, with the destruction of family values and society at large. Demi Moore's crazed career woman, planning corporate raids on the Stair Master, and the brutal parody of female ambition in Nicole Kidman's stop-at-nothing small-town media personality are later versions of Hamilton's muscular mother with a mission. The first frame in *T2* in which we see Hamilton focuses on Sarah doing pull-ups, the camera zooming in on her biceps. Her expression is that "look of grim determination" which Sam Fussell uses to describe body-builders in the California gyms;[49] her body is composed of taut ropes of muscle. A body with potential for violence.

As the sequence proceeds to locate her in a mental institution, with a voice-over from her doctor explaining Sarah's "delusional architecture," another close-up shot gives her eyes a crazed, animalistic look that complements her disordered hair. She is constructed as resisting male institutional authority; in the hall, male orderlies bring women who make gestures of resistance back into line. Her first spoken lines are the ironic "Good morning, Dr. Silverman. How's the knee?" delivered with an air of grim hatred; the doctor loses his professional authority momentarily and winces with embarrassment. So while the filmic narrative initially posits Sarah as a heroic female resistant to specious institutional male authority, the conflation of that resistance with hysteria, violence, and monstrosity that continues throughout the movie begins here.

In a second sequence, Sarah plays the good mother when asking to be moved to minimum security, making the emotional appeal, "You have to let me see my son . . . please . . . he's in great danger. He's naked without me." When this doesn't work, and the doctor tells her he knows how smart she is and that he has "no choice but to recommend to the review board that you stay here another six months," she looks sad for a moment and then suddenly transforms into a fierce monster with clenched teeth and distended lip, using the power of her muscled physique to jump across the desk and strangle him while a freeze-framed videotape image of her face with that same crazed expression flickers in the background. The next sequence shows Sarah escaping the restraints that strap her to her bed, picking the lock on the belt around her waist, and flinging off wrist cuffs. Soon she is padding kinetically through the halls, hair tied back and biceps poised, shoulders defined, a taut assailant who bloodies the guard with vicious, repeated blows to the head, a ninjette with a billy club incapacitating her male adversaries with blows to the chin, chest, knees. She takes the doctor hostage and advances through the hospital with a drain cleaner–filled syringe and fierce commands to "Back off, don't move, don't fuck with me."

Although *T2* offers a new sexualized female ideal, it presents that ideal as dangerous: the bad mother who is ultimately unimportant in saving worlds, whose fierceness served its limited purpose, whose hysteria when dealing with the computer wizard almost blows the whole deal, and whose feminist rhetoric is contained by her son. In a critically much-discussed scene, after Sarah reproves scientist Dyson for using his (male) creativity to build hydrogen bombs rather than to give birth to human life, her son, John, cuts her off with the comment, "Mom! We need to be a little more constructive here." Sarah in her self-assertive difference from the feminine norm is clearly not "constructive," and the now familiar feminist sentiments she is given to speak aren't seen as "constructive" either.

Instead, being "constructive" in this film means returning to the knowable, the already known, the certainty of fixed definitions. *T2* is an instance of the early nineties cultural imperative, as Susan Jeffords puts it, to "offer, in place of the bold spectacle of male muscularity and/as violence . . . a self-effacing man, one who now, instead of learning to fight, learns to love."[50] This self-sacrifice is, however, no reversal of conventional gender roles. To the contrary, Jeffords argues, it is the ultimate form of masculinity, the very thing that will save masculinity's "termination": "What greater and more powerful act of *individual* self-determination can there be than the *rational*, willing, and determined decision to end one's own life . . . being the generator of the human future?" Since the film plays off the new, fully mechanized terminator against the embodied, muscular old one, who cannot feel sympathy for the "good" old Terminator, Schwarzenegger himself, tragically lowered to his destruction? In the opposition between old and new, muscle and machine, the film, for Jeffords, "manages not only to reveal the 'new' masculinity/father but to excuse the 'old' one as well."[51]

As the death of the "bad Terminator" dramatizes, *T2* marks a growing uneasiness with the postmodern concept of shifting identities, fluid bound- **5 1** aries, and changing roles. This uneasiness legislates against Sarah and her monstrous strength as well as the T1000. The T1000 has no need for the muscularity of the old masculine body since it is an indestructible machine capable of taking on any form. As such he (or it—gender indeterminate) is suspect: mechanization gone too far, presenting a frightening spectacle that can engender a nostalgia for the dated but more human good-old-bad-guy masculinity that is more familiar, natural. The "bad Terminator," like Sarah, is a monstrosity, a horrific consortium of shape shifting dramatized in the closing scenes of the movie where he becomes a floating scream, a floating face of dissolving metal, compromised parts, a face that floats away. The dangers of unfixed identity, *T2* argues, are that you will suffer, and your identity will float away. An early example of an argument that resembles typical mid-nineties attacks on postmodernism/poststructuralism within the academy, in *T2* borders are better; fixed, knowable identities are best.

The threat of shape shifting is effectively contained in the filmic narrative through the agency of Schwarzenegger, the "good Terminator," the good old bounded masculinity now softened, capable of self-sacrifice to a higher good. "Is he dead?" John asks, looking at floating bits of T1000 residue in the red, apocalyptic soup. "Terminated," Arnie-as-Terminator replies, and we are reassured—but with the hidden price that Sarah's alternative femininity is "terminated" as well. Arnie's heroism, his knowable masculinity, has restored order. His is the sacrificed body we mourn for, producing an audience affinity with, as Jeffords writes, "the reproduction of masculine authority . . . through the affirmation of individualism."[52] In the end, Sarah's resistance—exemplified by her muscled body—is trivialized. Her physical presence, aligned with the stereotype of the hysterical woman out of control—opposed to the more humane, controlled violence of the Terminator, who learns from John to injure, not to kill—marks a woman who is violent, misguided, dangerous. Muscular male bodies are good, muscular female bodies are bad: the filmic narrative strives for a reproduction of traditionally gendered bodies that is mirrored in contemporary body-building rhetoric. Although Hamilton's biceps started a national personal-training craze, the movie itself works to discredit her character.

The cultural construction of the body is often a process of self-correction to norms. But it is also often the self in negotiation with norms, and the

Linda Hamilton as Sarah Connor in *Terminator II*: Biceps that were
more than a fashion statement. (Copyright 1991 Tri-Star
Pictures, Inc.)

women who wanted biceps after they saw Hamilton were doing more than conforming. Through their response, they created a new ideal that had an element of power to it. Like current tensions between conservative representations of gender in the bodybuilding industry that are counteracted by the subculture of women bodybuilders who often do their own thing with the representations, *T2*'s conservative message was undercut by women who experienced Sarah's character as the cultural authorization of female power in the world, and who developed their biceps as a personal statement of that empowerment. Female bodybuilders are an even more dramatic statement, and push the envelope of cultural expectations about femininity and aging, the equation between the female body and weakness, and cultural ideas about when a woman is no longer desirable and therefore visible.

But we also can, in our pursuit of social respect, end up acting out the very norms we began to reshape in the first place. Often, female bodybuilding begins in an attempt to close the body's peripheries, to create a boundary around what seems open because it has been broken. It's the late twentieth century. Welfare mothers are under the gun of the Contract with America, the rhetoric of genetic ties is used to control new reproductive technologies and reinforce a white nuclear family norm, organizations like the False Memory Foundation speak out against accusations of sexual abuse. The shift from bodybuilding to fitness, and from feminist critique to a power feminism that denies the validity and makes a mockery of that critique, may have deadly consequences. These shifts are disempowerments performed in the name of power. These shifts are taking away our chances to reactivate a sense of being that is eviscerated by abuse, our chances to close ourselves up, give ourselves boundaries, make ourselves resistant to abuse. Fitness women and power feminism are helping to put us back in the position of abuse—what feminist critique was helping us climb out of—and is telling us we're creating the abuse ourselves.

I am a feminist. I am not a victim. Rape and sexual harassment and childhood domestic abuse have been among the most formative experiences of my life. The two things that have most helped me not be a victim are bodybuilding and the feminism that encouraged me to speak. As Sara Evans writes of the experience of early women's movement activists who got their start fighting for civil rights, "There was the image of a woman who recognizes and names her own oppression and then learns to stand up for herself, breaking through patterns of passivity and learning new self-respect in the process."[53] Bodybuilding and feminism teach self-respect, but in the nineties they are under attack everywhere from *Flex* to the *New Yorker*; bodybuilders are compared to unnatural monsters and feminism to outmoded trends like mood rings. Feminists and bodybuilders (or feminist bodybuilders) are too loud, too depressing, too big. Seeking beauty, denying strength, women line up at the Stair Masters in the gym in pursuit of the hot fitness body, the corset and the Wonderbra have come back, implants and plastic surgery are presented as avenues to individual personal power, advertisements are fond of corpses, and what's called power feminism attacks the collective gains of the women's movement: How much longer will we believe it, how much longer stand by and watch the clock turning back, back, further back, while we stand by and witness the erasure of our worth taking place under the banner of increasing power and worth? How much is a woman worth dead?

Yet there is much going on in the culture that would keep us alive. While it may be the case that dominant culture—images seen on television, in advertisements, in videos, in political rhetoric—has shifted to the right, mobilizing a nostalgia for family values and those better times when there wasn't all that pesky women's rights, civil rights, gay rights rhetoric, and while it may be the case that the bodybuilding industry has shifted along with dominant culture in its call for smaller women bodybuilders who are of interest for their sexuality, rather than for the fact that they are athletes, on a populist level, people themselves are often acting differently. Within gym culture, they're not buying it. Gym culture and sports culture more generally are sanctuaries from the tyranny of retro images like the 1997 Mercedes ads that hark back to a fifties sensibility and outlook and plaintive pleas like Paula Cole's (ironic, but calling attention to the current mood) hit song "Where Have All the Cowboys Gone?" that invoke the happy times when men were men and went to work and women were women and stayed home and kept houses clean and devoted their lives to their children—images that turn back the clock and diminish us and our potential to do many things. Although sports sociologists may be right that sports culture is for the most part a rigid supporter of what have been labeled **55** masculine values (such as competitive individualism), that culture has, in many ways, been fairly open to extending those values and possibilities to women. There has recently been phenomenal growth in the popularity of women's sports, and that popularity is providing a powerful alternative to the diminished images of women circulating in the culture at large. Noncompetitive gym culture has been particularly good at providing an environment of equality and potential, a space where women can actively build not just their bodies but their senses of self and give themselves a way of combating regressive tendencies in the larger culture. Gym culture and women's sports have provided powerful sites for gender activism in the late twentieth century, when many traditional sites of activism have failed to capture the imagination and passion of young women.

W O M E N ' S   B O D Y B U I L D I N G   A S   A C T I V I S M

What does it mean to call something "activist" in the context of America in the late nineties? The question is an important one in academic circles, where it sometimes operates as a device to establish in groups and out groups by means of the barometer of authenticity—as in, "I'm a real activist and you're not." Paradoxically, the more restrictive the definition becomes regarding what counts as activism, the more likely it is an activity will be seen as inauthentic, effectively screening off large numbers of people who may have otherwise found a way to participate in the cause. This is a form of activist elitism that works precisely to deflate the very kind of mass participation or vigorous action the restricted definition of activism presupposes. A standard argument is that real activism went into decline in the eighties, when various regimes of self-improvement and acts of individual change came to replace mass demonstration and collective action, and effectively slowed any real political progress.

In an unpublished manuscript, Merri Lisa Johnson argues for the need to expand this argument and its traditional definitions of activism for the contemporary scene: "Conventional activisms—sit-ins and picket lines and open letters—do not work well in popular culture where entertainment and desire inform the marketability of ideas."[54] Activist strategies, if they are to succeed in bringing about widespread change, must above all be marketable, salable to the very groups of people who would conceivably mobilize to bring about change. Indeed, since in the nineties context our most basic desires and motivations may be in alignment with ideas and institutions which are traditionally defined as the oppressor (the desire, for instance, to *be* marketable, or competitive, or self-interested), these desires must be taken into account rather than ridiculed. These desires can be tapped and used in the service of activist praxis.[55] In addition to—*not* in place of—activisms that work to change laws, implement legislation, and affect hiring practices, reproductive freedom, and pay equity, rather than merely serving as the cultural co-option of potentials for change, women's participation in team sports and individual activities like bodybuilding can work to facilitate change particularly on the levels of perception and consciousness. One of the challenges third-wave feminism faces is how to take what Douglas Kellner refers to as a problematic "individualist activism"— the idea of the empowered individual whose activism doesn't go beyond self-development—and find ways to make that very individualism help other women, thereby becoming a form of activism.[56]

Incorporating this expanded definition of third-wave activism, I argue that female bodybuilding, whether competitive or noncompetitive, can be seen as a form of third-wave gender activism. On an individual level, one woman at a time, women change how they see themselves and their position in and relations to the larger world, and how they are seen by others. While this kind of change does not take the place of legislative actions like Title IX, which came out of organized efforts in the second-wave women's movement and made intercollegiate athletics a possibility for women that no change in consciousness could bring about, it is also true that changes in consciousness often lead to organized efforts for institutional change. As Mariah Burton Nelson argues in *The Stronger Women Get, the More Men Love Football*, a woman's participation in sports is a feminist act:

> Feminism is about freedom: women's individual and collective liberty to make their own decisions. For women, sports embody freedom . . . give meaning to the phrase 'free time.' Women find it, use it, and insist on retaining it. Their time for sports becomes a time when they free themselves of all the other people and projects they usually tend to. **5 7**

They become the person, the project, who needs care. They take care of themselves. For a group of people who have historically been defined by their ability to nurture others, the commitment to nurture themselves is radical.[57]

This radicalism, women's assertion of self through participation in sports in a culture defined by the assertion of self ("Live free or die!," as New Hampshire's state motto goes), a culture that claims self-assertion and self-determination as its definitive birthright, is the crux of a cynical double standard that assigned the for-self rights to one sex and a for-others orientation to the other, defining, by its own rhetoric (Live free or die!), the traditional female role as a kind of death. If we are to take our most fundamental American ideologies seriously while remaining aware of their limitations, sports for women is a way out of death-in-life, a tangible, daily path to freedom—the freedom from commitments to nurturing the development of others at the expense of one's own development.[58] But perhaps since a nation of for-self orientations would be a social impossibility and large numbers of men have been less than enthusiastic about taking on nurturing roles, social pressures to keep women in those roles are omnipresent, and have perhaps even intensified since 1993.

Rhetoric about latchkey kids, the rise in adolescent crime, drug addiction, and pregnancy blames career women, who have been, the argument goes, selfishly achieving for themselves at the expense of their families. Appropriating the self-achievement ethos and combining it with traditional roles, images of mothering are now combined with images of exercise. The ubiquitous advertisements such as the GNC ad that shows a woman runner pushing her baby stroller as she runs ("Look, you can develop yourself and still nurture others!"), are a good example.[59] Motherhood is (still) glorified as a woman's most important achievement of self, as seen in the deluge of media coverage that heralded Madonna's motherhood as the singer's "greatest achievement," or as, in the singer's own words, "the greatest miracle of my life."[60] The have-it-all mentality was one of the cultural reactions to women's greater participation in sports and careers, and that cultural prescription has intensified. An ad for the November 1996 issue of *In Style* magazine, for instance, features actress Jane Seymour with her baby twins in hand, proclaiming "We don't live a Hollywood lifestyle," with ad copy that promises "In Person with energetic Jane Seymour, who's successfully nurturing Dr. Quinn and year-old twins." Of course Mel Gibson isn't featured on covers with any of his nine children with copy about him "successfully nurturing" them, and if Billy Corgan (of the Smashing Pumpkins) ever has children, this—unlike the birth of Madonna's child—won't occupy a full week's programming on MTV or VH-1 (as indeed Michael Jackson's fatherhood occupied only a couple of days). Because nurturing others, particularly children, is still very much defined as a female role, women who have their partners go for a run with the baby stroller while they go find a pickup basketball game at the park or head over to the gym for some bench presses and cable flyes are, as Nelson puts it, "committing feminist acts."[61]

But probably the most convincing argument for women's bodybuilding as a form of activism has been, for me, the actions of other women in the gym. Many days I am approached by women who have watched me train, who tell me I am inspiring to them, and who ask for advice on their own training. Since I sometimes work out in a gym that doesn't seem to want to pay a staff of experienced trainers, there is especially little guidance for those who are just getting into the sport. I have become a de facto source of information about and discussion of their workouts, and it is their experiences, as well as my own, that have convinced me that bodybuilding can function as a basic—if unnamed—form of activism in many women's daily lives. I don't know how many times I have worked with women who don't think they can lift some small amount of weight—fifty-five pounds on the bench press, say, only to find, with my coaxing and encouragement, that they can actually press close to a hundred. I was surprised to find that I had imposed similar limits on myself when, upon training with a partner who urged me to do more than my standard weight, I found I could do quite a bit more. Unconsciously I had stopped at a certain point because I figured that it was good enough, a lot of weight—for a woman. I remember leaping up from the bench that day with an expanded sense of what was possible for me to accomplish in all facets of my life, not just the gym. I have watched other women expand with a similar feeling. I have seen them go out of the gym with their shoulders back and their heads held high, a little   **5 9** bit more confident about their positions in the world, a little less bounded by limits that they've internalized from years of absorbing cultural mythologies that impose drastic limits on women's strength and potentials. "I can't do that," they always say, but when they do—and they almost always do— the world opens up a little bit. They jump up with that shake of the fist, that "Yes! I did it!" which comes when you've faced some challenge and won. Their sense of themselves grows, visibly, on the floor of that gym, in their postures, the way they carry themselves, in the lines of their faces.

And so does mine. I don't know how much impact this actually has in their personal lives. I don't know whether it makes an abusive husband cut it out or if it makes women more assertive at work. I don't know if it makes them demand some respect from a supervisor or coworker, their kids, but I like to imagine that it does. I know that bodybuilding has done these things for me. One look at the way that I carry myself and most people's response is, "This chick don't take no shit." Like affirmative action, like Title IX, like job opportunity, and all the other things that more traditional activisms opened up, this has affected me in daily, concrete ways. Had those other things never happened, I probably would never have made it to the gym. But since I have, I'm here to stay.

3

Zero

Raced Bodies, Masculine Voids

In our culture, we simultaneously fetishize and disdain the athlete, a worker in the body. For we still live under the sign of Descartes. This sign is also the sign of patriarchy. As long as we continue to regard the body, that which is subject to change, chance, and death, as disgusting and inimical, so long shall we continue to regard our own selves as dangerous to others.

KATHY ACKER, "Against Ordinary Language: The Language of the Body"

MASCULINITY VANISHING

Bodybuilding has struggled for years as an outsider's sport, an activity of the margins. Its participants were seen as aesthetically extreme, as narcissistic freaks who preen before mirrors and worry incessantly about what they eat. Most public reaction was that of repulsion, and gyms were gathering places where covens of men and a handful of women wove alchemistic magic, turning ordinary flesh into bulging rivers of steel. But in the nineties, bodybuilding exists on the margins less and less. As copies of *Muscle and Fitness* sit comfortably next to *Good Housekeeping* at grocery store checkouts and shows like *American Gladiators* get top ratings, it is clear that bodybuilding occupies a more central place in a culture characterized by the very logic of human plasticity on which bodybuilding has always relied. Bodybuilding's movement from the margins to the center marks a crucial juncture in cultural constructions of gender, and its signification is radically different for male and female versions. Male bodybuilding may be read as a postmodern crisis of masculinity, the end of a master narrative once more fully believed.

In *Male Subjectivity at the Margins*, Kaja Silverman writes, "The implicit starting point for virtually every formulation this book will propose is the assumption that lack of being is the irreducible condition of subjectivity. . . . If we were in possession of an instrument which would permit us to penetrate deep into the innermost recesses of the human psyche, we would find not identity, but a void."[1] Bodybuilding is a spectacle that clearly reveals this void, which marks the vanishing point of masculinity and thereby the subject. It is from the standpoint of this void that male bodybuilding can be read as an example of constructions of the masculine position within popular culture, an example that reveals the fragility inherent to the masculine bulk. Bodybuilding makes visible the effort to create masculinity as a point of stasis you can count on, a bulwark above the frightening dizziness of chance and change. In its absurdity and extremes, bodybuilding reveals just how much of that stability is an act of will.

I will argue that male bodybuilding, in its deliberate, self-conscious construction of a particular bodily form, marks the limit point of the subject, the point where the fact that, as Silverman writes, "being has been sacrificed to meaning" becomes visible.[2] Bodybuilding is the material inscription of that sacrifice, a mode of compensation for a void. It is the substitution of something for nothing, the fetish that suspends the lack, the fleshly curtain that covers a void of essential self or identity. In the paradoxical binary codes that continue to characterize Western thinking, the body has represented lack of being while being is granted to the mind. In relation to these codes, bodybuilding scripts a paradox that is peculiarly postmodern: in bodybuilding that which has been represented as lack (the body) is substituted for a deeper lack (the fictive construction of subjectivity or being) in a gesture that simultaneously reveals and conceals that "lack of being is the irreducible condition of subjectivity."

Bodybuilding conceals the lack of being even as it reveals it. Since it is dependent upon a postmodern assumption of the plasticity of the human form, it marks postmodernism's intersection with consumer culture as represented brilliantly by, for instance, a series of Nike advertisements that appeal specifically to the existential sense of the deficiency of being in a gendered form. In an ad that ran in British *Vogue*, a line of ostensibly differently shaped women stand together with only a kind of Greek drapery covering their genitals. Appealing to the political context that insists on the validity of difference, the text of the ad reads, "It's the shape you're in, not the shape you are that matters." Assuming that what the shape is that you're in doesn't also depend on a hegemonic standard, that your shape allows you to take control and express who you are, the ad appeals directly to the postfeminist sensibility that women now have the choice to express who they are since they are no longer slaves to a cultural beauty imperative. Through working out in Nike products, the ad suggests, everyone, no matter how different, can look great and subvert hegemonic forms of beauty. The assumption of plasticity, control, and constructability seem to offer the consumer subject the chance to create something out of nothing, literally to create herself through the act of constructing her body, and this creation is a liberatory act that subverts traditional gender paradigms. The ad sells an illusory sense of empowerment and choice that depends on the female subject forgetting that the shape she's in also answers to the dictates of a very restrictive image, that the plasticity and infinite formability of her body answers to a particular script. While the ad copy plays to the idea that anyone can be healthy and fit regardless of body type, there is no striking diversity shown in the ad. All the women are white, and despite variation in breast size, all the women are thin.

Paradoxically marking a feminized position to begin with since it necessarily assumes a changeability masculinity would like to deny, as the ultimate form of self-creation, bodybuilding is also heavily invested in this rhetoric of empowerment through self-shaping. World amateur champion Achim Albrecht is characteristic: "When I look at these photos of myself, I notice how one line flows into another; how one bodypart complements another. I see the physique as a work in progress, and I have the control to decide where to take that work."[3]

In *Unbearable Weight*, Susan Bordo demonstrates how the postmodern characteristically assumes a plasticity that extends itself to both "the self" **6 3** and "the body" so that both are seen as constructions that can be created according to choice and individual will. The shift from endurance to constant change is a broad cultural indication of masculinity vanishing, and marks such often frantic attempts to reinstate it as those made by the Promise Keepers, followers of *Iron John*, and Howard Stern. If in postmodernism the rigid sanctity of the self breaks down into pluralistic possibility and fluidity, the notion of fluidity is used to bolster the notion of individual power and choice. If we no longer have an inner essence or self that will define us, the definition of our essence is left to us, offering us seemingly limitless possibilities and freedom from metaphysical determination. The popular deployment of postmodernist thought in advertisement offers an apparently endless array of consumer choice, a radical freedom from norms that doubles back and becomes an equally radical enactment of norms. This is what Bordo terms "our present culture of mystification—a culture which continually pulls us away from systemic understanding and inclines us toward constructions that emphasize individual freedom, choice, power, ability."[4] This appeal to individual freedom and choice serves to bolster the traditional construction of the masculine as being, which the very notion of plasticity, with its taint of femininity, threatens. If one is free to create what one is, this is a radical fantasy of being that covers the creeping, paralyzing anxiety brought about by its lack, and our apprehension of it, an apprehension that makes us into consumer subjects. In a consumer economy, it is a covert appeal to a sense of lack and an overt appeal to individual power that fuels the economic apparatus. You are free to construct yourself however you wish through the purchase of particular products and services, a self-construction that promises a power ardently desired. The desire arises from an apprehension of the fundamental deficiency of being, the plasticity that arises from nothing.

Perhaps more obviously than any contemporary phenomenon, bodybuilding relies on a radical notion of plasticity while that plasticity paradoxically functions to bolster the most fixed, traditional masculine norms. More than any other sport, it draws attention to the fact that masculinity is a masquerade rather than an unquestionable essence. As Chris Holmlund argues by way of Lacan in "Masculinity as Multiple Masquerade," for the masculine as well as the feminine "dressing up and display are essential. . . . 'In the human being virile display itself appears as feminine.'"[5] If display places one on the side of spectacle in the sense of film theory, and the spectacle is the position of the feminine, then bodybuilding for all its hypermasculine posturing visibly marks masculinity as both posture and literal physical construction. By definition, bodybuilding is a spectacle that performs the masculine; looked at another way, it is the masquerade of the phallus unveiled, stripped of its signifying power. Perched precariously on the balancing point between the slavish enactment of masculinity and its denaturalization and thereby deconstruction, bodybuilding is the fortification that will destroy the fortress. As Holmlund writes, "The ultimate threat of the masquerade may be that under the mask there is *nothing*," and it is the nothingness of masculinity that bodybuilding both reveals and conceals.[6]

It is for this reason that bodybuilding has until recently been marginalized by dominant culture. There is something unsettling to the fixed, naturalized conceptions of masculinity about nearly naked men posing, preening, stepping out into the realm of spectacle, deliberately making their bodies an exhibition. The most common reaction of those outside the circuit to pictures of bodybuilders is "Gross!" for the mounds of muscles so obviously artificial call attention to the fact that what is presumed natural—masculine muscularity and the images of power that accompany it— is a construction, a performance, an image put on that is unnatural almost to the point of physical death. In his theoretical, ethnographic study, *Little Big Men*, Alan M. Klein quotes a competitive bodybuilder who, after winning an international title, declared "When we're up there [on the posing platform], we're closer to death than we are to life."[7] Between the liver damage, cardiac irregularities, and radical mood swings (to name just a few) that are side effects of the steroids most internationally competitive bodybuilders take, and the debilitating effects of radical dieting and dehydration that bodybuilders subject themselves to before a contest, it is clear that the image of the hypermuscular masculine body which functions as a masculine ideal in the popular imagination is an image that has nothing to do with nature or anything inherent to masculinity and men. Bodybuilding exists on the fringes because it is extreme, and in its extremity can reveal much about the norm. Its very extremity points to the fiction **65** of masculinity. Given the foregrounding of conscious construction, if the muscular body is the physical embodiment of masculinity, masculinity is a construction in the most fundamental sense. Bodybuilding is masculinity performed and pushed to its furthest logical extension, a performance that, pushed far enough (as in the case of several of the sport's top competitors), results in death. Bodybuilding is the literalization of cultural norms of masculinity, and as such reveals the fictiveness of its figurative manifestations, such as the immediate equation in the popular imagination of masculinity, individuality, and power. As Klein writes, "The bodybuilder naturalizes the cultural claim that masculinity is bound up with large muscles. . . . Even in its excessive view of the male form, bodybuilding is, oddly enough, more mainstream than marginal. . . . By appealing to exaggeration, gender conventions are propped up."[8] Yet the contradiction is that if bodybuilding serves as a naturalization or prop for conventional definitions of masculinity, more than any other sport it is a prop that reveals itself as such.

It is interesting to note that at this point in history bodybuilding exists more in the mainstream than it ever has. A TwinLab ad featuring a bodybuilder runs on prime-time TV; male models in the magazines sport obligatory abs and pecs; there are at least five cable programs featuring bodybuilders; and memberships at gyms have never been higher nationwide. Arnold Schwarzenegger, who is considered one of the founding fathers of bodybuilding, is also one of the world's most popular screen stars. Sylvester Stallone, whose nice-guy softer movies flopped, reinvigorated his box-office ratings with a return to the hypermuscular physique in *Cliffhanger* (1993). He exhibited this physique on the November 1993 *Vanity Fair* cover, with the attendant description: "Sly's Body of Art—Sylvester Stallone muscles back into action . . . At 47, Stallone is flexing his muscles on all fronts: his body is bulging, his spirit is soaring, and his career is back on track." In the article, Stallone declares, "I try to go for tightness, tightness, tightness. Boom, boom, boom, you know?"[9] His booming tightness was rewarded with returned commercial success, showing a public veneration for bulging bodies that has not always been part of the norm.

So the question remains, Why now? What is it about the contemporary historical moment that would allow bodybuilding a more mainstream cultural acceptance? Beyond the norms of postmodern plasticity, bodybuilding in its mainstream manifestations helps to mark a masculinity in crisis, insecure of its status and even existence. If the postmodern is, to invoke Jean-François Lyotard, characterized by the failure of master narratives, particularly those in which the phallus is the center, the bodybuilder's flesh is a dramatic enactment of that failure. In the context of film stardom, Barbara Creed writes that Schwarzenegger and Stallone are "casualt[ies] of the failure of the paternal signifier and the current crisis in master narratives," and Yvonne Tasker comments on the paradox that arises from the fact that musclemen "self-conscious[ly] perform . . . qualities assumed to be natural."[10] In its more mainstream acceptance at this historical moment, bodybuilding may be read as the literalized version of "the crisis of the paternal signifier." While anorexia, another contemporary body practice that reveals a dominant cultural logic, may be read as a form of "gender passing" in which the female body tries to pass as male, bodybuilding marks the passing of the masculine norm itself.[11]

Bodybuilding reveals that the norm is fictive, passing itself off as natural, and the passing of the norm in terms of its cultural precedence and prerogative. With the exception of cultures like that of ancient Greece, at earlier historical junctures the physical perfection of the male body was not an essential focus. The current construction of the male body as spectacle makes masculinity visible in a way that reveals its constructedness, so that even as bodybuilding seems to incarnate hypermasculinity it marks its passing away. In this sense bodybuilding may be seen as a form of *aphanisis* or fading of the masculine subject, its slippage in the moment of its constitution.[12] As Tasker notes, "In Lacan's concept of male parade . . . the accouterments of phallic power, the finery of authority, belie the very lack that they display. In a similar way the muscular male body functions as a powerful symbol of desire and lack."[13] The male bodybuilder reveals the desire for a secure masculinity and the lack of such security simultaneously.

In his ethnographic analysis, Klein found this desire and sense of lack characteristic of the bodybuilders he studied. Feeling that they are failing to enact prescriptive masculinity or that they fall short of dominant cultural standards, contemporary bodybuilders often follow the logic of Charles Atlas and build their bodies in order to bolster a masculine identity experienced as deficient. Egotism exists side by side with its opposite, self-abasement. "Coexisting," he writes, "with the narcissistic ideal . . . in fact embedded in it, is the self-loathing that equally characterizes bodybuilders."[14] If masculinity has traditionally been equated with individuality, identity, and being, the desire for this being as well as the sense of its loss can be seen as a primary motivation for most bodybuilders. The first chapter of former Mr. Olympia Frank Zane's book *Fabulously Fit Forever* is entitled "Bodybuilding Womb to Tomb." Describing his early motivations, Zane writes, "I always felt I could do better on my own. . . . Here was a sport I could do myself without having to rely on anyone else."[15] The language of "womb to tomb," along with the emphasis on self-reliance, marks what Klein analyzed as a problem repeatedly articulated by bodybuilders in their conceptions of masculinity: "the need to separate from the mother . . . a complex of attributes that stems from a fear turned to the denigration of women." Zane's initial attraction to the sport, that of not "having to rely on anyone else," marks the kind of connection anxiety that characterizes an uncertainty of being, the fear of slippage from a concretely defined and embodied masculinity into the chaotic indeterminacy of something else. "I would argue," Klein writes, "that men use their bodies defensively, by which I mean that the body can be consciously constructed in such a way as to give the appearance of hegemonic masculinity to compensate for a vulnerable, weak sense of a man's self . . . [a] 'protest masculinity' designed to conceal the powerlessness that most of these people fear is theirs."[16]

Zane writes that "muscular growth is often motivated by a desire to overcome a sense of inferiority by armoring the body with a protective layer of muscle. The process of 'bodybuilding as character armor' or body armoring begins since it fulfills a need to cover a lack of confidence or feelings of inadequacy." While Zane and other bodybuilders probably would not consciously connect that "sense of inferiority" or "lack of confidence" to a postmodern crisis of masculinity, the end of a master narrative formerly more fully believed, there does seem to be a defensive reaction to a perceived threat that characterizes bodybuilding language. The title page of the July 1995 issue of *Flex*, for instance, extols the virtues of "shock sets" and promises advice from "a noted mass monster," while articles in the March 1994 issue of *Muscle and Fitness* promise techniques to get your body "hard, ripped and tight" and to "zap the back with a laser," and a "three-prong attack" for shoulders. Biceps are referred to as "guns," and good shoulder development as "destroyer delts." The language of body-building is the language of violence, and the object of that violence is one's own body. Bodybuilders like Zane explain this with the idea that "destruction is the first step in the process of creation," but the pervasiveness of attack lingo signifies the kind of hostility that can only arise from fear that one doesn't measure up.[17]

For many bodybuilders, this fear seems to stem from an uncertainty about identity, a desperate need to distinguish oneself from the undifferentiated "masses" who, through lack of individuation, would deprive one of identity. Arnold Schwarzenegger writes:

> You have to make a decision what you want to be in life. If you want to be a genius or something special, then you have to sacrifice a lot. From the age of ten, I wanted to be the best. I thought I had been born in the wrong country. All I wanted was to leave Austria and come to America. And when I got here I would not be one of the masses.
>
> I get the most satisfaction out of things not everybody experiences. . . . I want to be the best and I'm perfectly willing to go through anything to get it.

Arnold associates the ability to "be something special" with not being "one of the masses." He gets "satisfaction out of things not everybody experiences" precisely because they are different and not everybody experiences them, and he sees being "the best" as made possible by the act of sacrifice, the willingness to "go through anything." To return to the Silverman formulations I began with, he is willing to sacrifice being for meaning since his immense being has significance only as meaning, and, following Lacan, forms his identity through differentiation, the split that confers identity but also its loss. The "sacrifice" Arnold alludes to is the sacrifice of ordinary activities and relations with others. He asserts, "I'll do those things I missed [later]." "If you want to be a champion," he writes, "you can't have any kind of negative force coming in to affect you. So I trained myself for that. To be totally cold and not have things going through my mind."[18] In his desire to eliminate negative forces that would deter him from his goals, the meaning and distinct identity he seeks, he makes himself "totally cold," cutting himself off from the distractions of daily life in the human community in order to achieve a form he has decided is the only thing that is meaningful, that will give him the identity he feels he otherwise lacks. Being is sacrificed to meaning so that Arnold in effect vanishes (and becomes visible) at the moment of his self-constitution as champion, individuated other. Because both the lack and the meaning are fictions, effects of the linguistic split in which the subject is constituted, there is only precariousness and uncertainty either way—even for, as he was called in bodybuilding circles by a nickname that attempted to incarnate solidity and presence— the "Austrian Oak."

Bodybuilders seem to rely on strict individuation to confer a sense of presence. In *Muscle: Confessions of an Unlikely Bodybuilder*, Sam Fussell writes, "The shock value is all. It's saying, or rather screaming, 'More than anything else in the world, whatever it takes, I don't want to be like you. I don't want to look like you, I don't want to talk like you, I don't want to *be* you.' . . . I hated the flawed, weak, vulnerable nature of being human. . . . The attempt at physical perfection grew from seeds of self-disgust." [19] The fear of being like others is the fear of *being* others, and the fear of being others is the fear of nonbeing, the "flawed, weak, vulnerable nature of being human." If one is the same as everyone else one would not exist, if existence is conceived of in terms of identity and identity in individuation. Both Schwarzenegger's and Fussell's rhetoric situate a paradox that bodybuilding makes particularly visible. If bodybuilding is the attempt to transcend weakness and being human (as the pervasive rhetoric of the body as machine would suggest) so that the attempt brings bodybuilders closer to death than to life, what stands as the quintessence of life, identity, and achievement is simultaneously its erasure. The attempt at transcendence is generated in an anxiety about lack of being, an apprehension of the void of subjectivity and the anxiety that absence engenders. But the subject is absent or void precisely because it is defined as individuation, and the act of individuation is necessarily a fiction conferred by language. It is the definitions of the subject and masculinity that are problematic, creating the paradox of voids and meanings. Through acceding to meaning one creates a void, and the apprehension of that void generates an anxiety about absence. The anxiety about absence and its manifestations in bodybuilding prove, however, that there is something rather than nothing, since an emptiness cannot be anxious.

REGRESSIVE FLESH: BODYBUILDING AND THE REPRODUCTION OF RACE

To a certain extent, however, intellectual speculation about presence, voids, and lacks remains a privilege for those who haven't historically been figured as a void or lack—that is, this form of speculation may mark a privilege of white masculinity. As many theorists have discussed, the Cartesian mind/body duality which inaugurated modernity generated its own structure of presence and lack of which racist discourse, particularly in the nineteenth century, made powerful use. For if the mind was the privileged term and the body its degraded other, and the mind was gendered masculine and raced white while the body was gendered feminine and raced black, this system of signification instituted a powerful cultural logic whereby presence—self-ownership, integrity, sovereign individuality—was indicated by mind, and ostensibly, then, by the lack of body. I mean "lack" in the sense that the body was not seen as an important consideration for white men but rather as something that, by virtue of their superior intellect, they had supposedly transcended. Conversely, metaphysical lack—lack of self-ownership, integrity, sovereign individuality—was figured as the presence of body, and the presence of body was culturally conferred by an emphasis on how much the body supposedly held sway over and determined the individual. Those individuals whose bodies were said to determine them were gendered female and raced nonwhite.

According to this dominant cultural logic that ran through slavery and its legacies, in America black masculinity in particular is embodied, associated with physicality, while white masculinity is transcendent, associated with the mind. This system of signification has a profound impact on social relations. Bell hooks writes, "Since male power within patriarchy is relative, men from poorer groups and men of color are not able to reap the material and social rewards from their participation in patriarchy. In fact they often suffer from blindly and passively acting out a myth of masculinity that is life-threatening."[20] Because black men in particular have been constructed as primarily physical, as beasts of burden with bestial sexuality, acting out machismo (which for white men is seen to reflect natural dominance and self-ownership) has only colluded with that stereotype. Of the characteristic ways machismo is acted out in sports, Richard Majors argues that "contemporary black males often utilize sports as one means of masculine self-expression within an otherwise limited structure of opportunity," but that this "emphasis on athletics . . . among black males is often self-defeating, because it comes at the expense of educational advancement and other intellectually oriented activities that are integral aspects of the dominant forms of masculine power and success today."[21] Former athlete Kenneth L. Shropshire makes the case that traditional assumptions about intellect and bodies underlie racist practices in the sports industry, where progress for "African-Americans in or striving for management and other 'power positions' in sports" is severely limited by "the spirit and racism of the past."[22] Because mind/body codes still underlie much of what transpires in contemporary culture, to follow a bodily oriented activity instead of an intellectually oriented activity is to confirm old assumptions if you have traditionally been figured as embodied.

Perhaps the pinnacle of embodiment is visually figured by the enormous bodies of bodybuilders, sprouting muscle and striations from every seam. Black male bodybuilders in particular fall under the stigma of intersecting codes of race and gender. Hooks writes that "representations of black men in mass media usually depict them as more violent than other men, super-masculine (television characters like Hawk and Mr. T)."[23] Given the dominant cultural association between the muscular black male body and animality, violence, lack of restraint but also the "super-masculine," which, as hooks points out, tends to provoke both fear and fascination in white audiences, the black male bodybuilder is a priori framed by these ideas. Like his female counterparts in the bodybuilding world, it is assumed under this framework of assumptions that he is just naturally more muscular and doesn't have to work as hard to attain his muscular stature. Muscularity, however, like most genetic attributes, is on a continuum. Some women are more muscular than others. Some blacks are more muscular than others. Blacks are not always more muscular than whites. Men are not always more muscular than women. But physical embodiment and muscularity are naturalized in the dominant cultural imagination as a priori black, and the hypermasculinity that the bodybuilding body encodes is coded more sexually for a black bodybuilder than is that of his white counterparts.

This has often been the case in representations of black male bodybuilders. While these bodybuilders are mostly not sexualized by the camera and staging like the women are, they cannot be entirely detached from a long racist history that has equated black males with the body, manual labor and omnipresent sexuality, an equation that denied them rationality as well. Hence shots of white male bodybuilders may strike viewers as a bit more strange, out of place, more freaky since they are so embodied, such visceral representatives of carnal flesh, when tradition tends to forget white male bodies, focusing instead on their rational minds. One pictorial in *Flex* magazine in October 1994 of Aaron Baker embodies this mostly unspoken set of cultural assumptions. That those assumptions are always there, framing how we see, contributes to why the images of Baker seem particularly to embody stereotypical ideas about the hypersexuality and physicality of black men while images of white bodybuilders such as Achim Albrecht signify differently.

In a September 1994 pictorial, "Magnificent Muscle," Albrecht is posed on a rock next to a caveman club and a lion's skin, but this comes across more as a photographer's cheap ploy than any primitive bestiality inherent in Albrecht himself.[24] Baker's pictorial, by contrast, simply titled "Baker," opens with a diptych, the first in color, the second in black and white. He wears the same leopard-skin thong in both shots, which is unusual for a male pictorial. Men are usually featured—as Albrecht was—in solid-colored briefs. The leopard skin, combined with the heavy neck chain featured in the first shot and the pose—seated in a chair, shot from the front but head turned in profile, body straining off to the side—are untypical of pictorials featuring men, which rarely use props of any kind, and usually have the bodybuilders strike competition poses. The second shot of Baker on the chair is surprising since it so clearly has nothing to do with competition. Like the characteristic pictorials of the female bodybuilders, this shot features Baker first as a sexual male, and second as a bodybuilder. His full lips, pushed out in profile, the way his body is frozen in a particular line to put emphasis on his leopard-skin crotch, all posit him fully as subject to a sexual gaze. While his body is not posed in such a way as to communicate "Do with me what you will," it is posed in such a way as to posit Baker as a sexual being—again, not a negative thing in itself, but in the context of bodybuilding conventions, unusual for men. The accompanying text, in white letters blocked by red and placed in strategic stripes across the photo, reinforces this: "An incredibly developed pro [across his chest, just above his nipples] Aaron Baker is finally starting to get noticed." The whole idea of notice, spectacle, is given particular inflection by the pose— the notice Baker is getting or is supposed to get in relation to this picture is the notice of sexual interest. The remainder of the pictorial has him striking uncharacteristic poses—down on one knee holding onto a sword; head down and arms flexed, knee bent to emphasize his hips; again down on one knee with his hand resting on the other, light falling on the leopard skin. It seems Baker is down on his knees quite a bit, while in most bodybuilding pictorials the men are standing. These down-on-his-knees shots form a real contrast to the two more standard competition-type poses included in the pictorial (in these shots the leopard skin is replaced by a black brief), which are the fifth and sixth images in a series of eight.

Flex also reinforces the conflation of black bodybuilder bodies with their sexuality in an interchange that provides an interesting twist on the whole gender and race iconography debate. The "Talkback" department in the May 1994 issue was full of letters debating the "Power and Sizzle" pictorials, both positive and negative. One of the negative letters—making use of quotes from *Flex*'s mission statement at the beginning of each pictorial— asserts, "We do not need another magazine that perpetuates the stereotype that women are supposed to be 'soft, unstriated, shapely, and sensual,' while men are supposed to be big, strong, and powerful. In my opinion, the only way you can redeem yourself is to publish an article of equal length depicting male bodybuilders as 'complete, multidimensional human beings' (i.e., naked on a bearskin rug)."[25] As if in response to this letter, the magazine editors include, centered on this particular page, a photo of black bodybuilder Daryl Stafford, shown in a pose much like the letter's author describes. Since none of the letters in the column refer to him, this can be the only conceivable reason he appears on this page. The photo poses Stafford in a black thong bikini, shot from behind, bent over an incline bench, on which he rests his left knee. He is performing a triceps kickback, an exercise that necessarily elevates the buttocks since you have to put one knee up. The focus of the photograph is on his buttocks and his back, and framed as it is, it is undoubtedly sexual—Stafford is constructed as the object of the viewer's gaze. Photos of male bodybuilders framed in this particular way rarely make an appearance in *Flex*; when they do, if the subject of the unusually sexualized photo is black, this cannot be divorced from the history of representations of black masculinity that present black men as bodies rather than minds.

If black masculinity tends to be sexualized, the ways female sexuality and cultural definitions of femininity are constructed according to racial codes has a similar and exacerbated structuring effect on the representation of female athletes. As the work of Beverly Guy-Sheftal, Nell Irvin Painter, Sander Gilman, and many others has shown, late nineteenth-century definitions of femininity that invoked women's physical fragility, lack of interest in sex, and an inability to work outside the home were racially based. Working in the context of a broadly expanding imperialist ethos that evolved, among other things, from British imperialism in Africa and slavery in the United States, black women and white women were placed in the same social context like never before, and that proximity necessitated ideological justification for the social roles assigned to each. Medical and scientific communities stepped in to fill the breach, offering biologically based theories to account for the white female role as wife and mother unfit for work in the public sphere, and for the black female role as domestic laborer.

Sociologist Elaine Bell Kaplan argues that the historical definition of femininity in the U.S. is constructed specifically in reference to race and class:

> The definition of *femininity* in this country is class-bound. Because the "feminine" attributes of helplessness and delicacy can apply only to a comparatively small number of females of the dominant class, the mass of women are compelled to undertake many forms of strenuous and "unladylike" activity. And when one thinks about the image of black women

as strong workers performing chores usually reserved for men, the issue of race becomes important as well. . . . "Feminine" women did not work at all. Today the swelling ranks of white, middle-class women in the labor force challenge that notion, but the idea that black women are tough, strong, and "macho" lingers on.[26]

These cultural ideas obviously have significant implications for bodybuilding, which, as I have repeatedly argued, is more concerned with maintaining the femininity of its practitioners than it is with developing as a sport. If the historical definition of femininity was dependent on delicacy and it was only possible to attain delicacy by not working, it was only possible to be feminine, by this way of thinking, if you were upper class and white. Bodybuilding is by definition strenuous and unladylike, so perhaps even more than most sports it struggles to attain an upper-class white femininity through its aesthetic ideals of delicacy and grace. One need look no further than the Rachel McLish/Bev Francis controversy to see the primacy placed on femininity as small-bodied and delicate rather than bulked up—the Nancy Kerrigan/Tonya Harding rivalry in skating reinforced these norms for figure skating as well. Given the historical association between black women and strength, there would be two strikes against any black female bodybuilder trying to compete in the femininity category.

Women's sports historian Susan Cahn has shown how, throughout the twentieth century, support for women's sports or women in sports has waxed and waned according to how feminine a given sport was seen as being. A significant part of public support, or lack thereof, is related to how the dominant cultural definition of femininity is construed by reference to stereotypes about race. Cahn documents a struggle within such sports as women's track and field, which had a majority of black athletes, from the early twentieth century through the 1960s. These athletes struggled under a public stigma of mannishness that promoters of the sport had to work hard to disclaim, and since historically black women were seen as less feminine, that battle was doubly difficult. The work of selling women's sports like track necessarily involved a fight against the double stigma that black female athletes faced. It is a fight that promoters of bodybuilding face today. Bodybuilding moguls who are trying, like earlier track and field promoters, to gain some feminine respectability for their sport, have tended to feature white, blond women much more often than black women.[27]

Track and field for women grew out of a thriving network of community meets that initially were located in working class and black neighborhoods in the twenties and thirties, generating a growing interest that culminated in the addition of women's events to the Olympics. Much like the public discussions of female bodybuilders today, the development of women's track and field raised a debate in which "an assortment of critics attacked women's track by raising the specter of the mannish woman." "In the eyes of her detractors," Cahn writes, "the 'wholly masculine' female track athlete became a freak of nature, and object of horror rather than esteem."[28] This is strikingly similar to the language used in descriptions of and protests against female bodybuilders today. John Romano, for instance, writes in the March 1996 issue of *Muscular Development*, "These days you see women on stage in dire need of a third gender classification. Apart from Lenda Murray's awesome genetics, and Sue Price's unspoiled beauty, the line-up at this year's Ms. O was appalling. I couldn't even look at some of them. And I'm not the only one."[29] Often "objects of horror rather than esteem," the female bodybuilder is less horrific the more closely she approximates the white feminine norm.

Cahn documents how such sanctions against track and other "mannish" sports were inflected racially and given support by the scientific community:

> The charge that sport masculinized women physically and sexually resonated with scientific and popular portrayals of mannishness and sexual pathology among black women. . . . The myth of the "natural" black athlete lent further support to . . . the myth that people of European descent were cultured, intellectual, and civilized, while those of African heritage were uncivilized beings guided by physical and natural impulses . . . convert[ing] black achievements into evidence of racial inferiority.[30]

Although it has been driven underground, the same logic sometimes still surfaces today in discussions of female bodybuilders. The myth of the natural black athlete is visible in discussions of six-time Ms. Olympia, Lenda Murray, who is black and who is constantly referred to in terms of her "awesome genetics," as John Romano does above. Although women of color don't seem to be accused of mannishness any more than their white counterparts, they are hypersexualized in ways that recall nineteenth-century associations between masculinity and sexual voraciousness, the counterpart of which was a desexualized white femininity, Freud's frigid women. In a generalized framework that attempts to make female bodybuilding acceptable to a larger public by sexualizing it, the sexual images of women of color are repeatedly kinkier than those of their white counterparts. As hooks writes, "In a white supremacist sexist society all women's bodies are devalued, but white women's bodies are more valued than those of women of color."[31]

Contemporary portrayals of female bodybuilders provide good examples of how race is an issue that always informs a conservative deployment of gender. A recent *Flex* magazine pictorial featuring Sharon Bruneau, a professional bodybuilding competitor better known for her model-like good looks than for her muscle, situates these issues in a way that is overdetermined. Bruneau, a former model, has recently quit bodybuilding in order to compete in fitness shows, stating that the sport was going in a direction—more and more women competing with a great deal of muscle—that she did not want to follow. Always one of the smaller competitors, she makes statements that both provide an inaccurate assessment of standards for women bodybuilders and reflect a frustration with consistently placing lower in top contests than her more massive counterparts. The *Flex* pictorial picks up on her mass-market appeal, including shots that are reminiscent of the Victoria's Secret catalog: Sharon in a sheer, red, patterned bodystocking, curled up on a sofa, holding a cat. Sharon in a satin and lace g-string, buttocks elevated by a footstool, arm and hair flung out behind her: "*Playboy* with a woman bodybuilder," as the guys in my gym referred to it.

Shot by Bill Dobbins, Bruneau's "Trained Beauty" pictorial ends with a striking image of Sharon, poised with a spear, amulet bones about her neck, and clothed in fringed cloth meant to evoke tribal dress. She looks straight at the camera, arm and chest muscles flared by her grip on the spear, lips pouting and legs flexed. A dark Farrah Fawcett mane is artfully tousled to curl between her eyes and wind gracefully down her back. While the written theme of the pictorial is the heightened sensuality and thereby strength, self-determination, and well-being of women bodybuilders in general, this particular shot is accompanied by a quote which reads "I am particularly proud of my Native American heritage to which this photo pays homage." Race and gender stereotypes intersect in a way that seems almost too over-determined here. That the pictorial is titled "Trained Beauty" and that these words occupy the space between her poised legs call attention to not just her weight training but to her training in evoking particular images, here of the Pocohontas-type princess, while the image claims connection to a natural "heritage" that Bruneau is "proud of." Yet whose heritage is this? Bruneau is constructing an image almost laughable in its stereotypical configurations, so patently the point of view not of her heritage, but rather of the white male photographer who frames her in all the old references to natural sensuality, state of being, and dress represented as the primitive. The unintentional irony that it takes training to evoke this particular vision of racial being intersects with the irony that it also takes training not only to build this particular body, which is evoking old notions of the natural or native body, but that nativeness also intersects with cultural notions that women, by their natures, are more embodied. Dobbins's image of Bruneau trains the viewer to accept three overlapping senses of otherness—the feminine, the muscular, and the racial—as a new brand of feminism that celebrates the sensual, and that turns all forms of otherness into the same old recognizable thing. Bruneau's body, trained to evoke particular associations that have the potential to cross boundaries between old categories of male/not-male, muscular/not-muscular, white/not-white, and mind/body, does not end up crossing boundaries because it is framed in this particular way.

Bodybuilding magazines like *Flex* that still showcase female bodybuilders seem to be very inclusive, equal-opportunity employers when it comes to the women whose T and A graces the magazine's center. But the images are racially coded. Flex has covered all the bases: Native American (savage beads), Asian (geisha heat), Caucasian (plastic blond-girl sex), and African American (just hot sex). The feature of Lei Lani, for instance, chooses

Asian as the flavor of the month, and presents a pictorial that brings together stereotypes of the exoticized female other in obvious ways. Ironically entitled "Mastery," the pictorial presents a mastered body that, rather than asserting the individual self-determination it markets and proclaims, is a testament to just how much the female body is designed to specification, effortlessly incorporating exotic deviations like muscle from the beauty norm. The images in the pictorial present Lani in a repertoire of stock seductive poses. Shot next to the ever-present pool, image one poses Lani with hands on a deck railing, towering against what looks like a very blue sky. Her muscles are pronounced, especially through her shoulders, biceps, and triceps, and the tight flex of her pectoral muscles makes her left breast implant look particularly like a balloon. Her chin is lifted so you can't see her eyes, but they appear to be closed, inviting the gaze but not looking herself. The other shots clearly have her eyes closed and mouth open, one on blue tile next to blue water shot from above focusing on her implanted breasts, which she pushes up from underneath with a muscular arm, red bathing suit strap slipping off her shoulder, while the next shot has her stretched out on her back, which is arched, on a white lounge, arm above head. The word "mastery" appears again above her outstretched arm. A full-page shot follows: eyes closed, mouth open, strap slipping, this time with "Mastery" on the upper left, along with the direct quotation "Being muscular allows me to feel sensuous and sexy, sometimes even daunting and masterful," which appears to the side of her arched back and inclined head.

If these shots present Lani in the "do-me" images that are typical for female bodybuilding pictorials of women of whatever race, the centerfold particularizes Lani's race, adding the exotic component to enhance the sizzle. Upright this time, legs spread widely across a rock, Lani's head (eyes closed once again—what do this woman's eyes look like?) is shot in profile, light falling on her high heavily rouged cheekbones and purple-shadowed slanted eyes, her mouth open in what looks like, given the arch of her lip and the particular tilt of her body and head, preorgasmic pleasure. Her left arm stretches to the top of her head, elevating her chest, which is covered this time by the primal native bikini, complete with tatters and beads. She's the do-me-I'll-please-you primal woman, pure sex with a sadomasochistic twist provided by her muscle. The ubiquitous "Mastery" appears once more in the upper right-hand corner, although in typical post-modern style, it seems to have no referent unless it refers to how the camera masters Lani's muscle, framing it with all the cultural stereotypes that historically have functioned to make women powerless, not powerful.[32]

The last image in Lei Lani's *Flex* pictorial gives us more exotic booty. Lani is posed again from the back, her head turned over her right shoulder, lips pursed, eyes shaded by the bangs of her auburn-brown bob. Her arms are propped on a shelf of stone, and her prominently framed buttocks emerge from thigh-high bubbling water. The obligatory native thong splits her buttocks, two strings arching across the top of her hips. The geisha bob, lips, and seductive posture suggest nothing so much as erotic fantasy, a muscular maiden of the islands, accommodating, ready to gratify any viewer's sexual whims.

Sexualization in these pictorials is racially marked, and disturbingly mirrors nineteenth-century constructions of differences between black and white women. Sarah Bartmann, designated the "Hottentot Venus" in 1810, was used, as bell hooks puts it, "as evidence to support racist notions that black people were more akin to animals than other humans."[33] Bartmann served as a repository for the brute, expendable matter that white culture feared and disowned in itself, making the black female body a repository of "blank darkness," of materiality, changeability, and mortality that the white female body could then be distanced from. As Sara Evans points out, the white female body could then be used to figure "cultural ideal[s] of beauty and 'femininity,' which by inference defined black women as ugly and unwomanly."[34]

In descriptions of Bartmann extensive attention was given to her buttocks. These buttocks and the "animalistic" sexuality they stood for in contemporary iconography were then taken as a synecdoche for the whole woman, for her essence. Today, in a supposedly postcolonialist, postfeminist, postmodernist late twentieth-century American culture, the iconography of that earlier tradition continues in the representation of black women bodybuilders who are often identified with the same body parts as Sarah Bartmann.

The biography section of Dobbins's *Women* describes Sha-Ri Pendleton: **8 1**

"Sha-ri has what many consider to be the best track physique of all time. But certain of her body parts attract more attention than others. If her physique is superior, her glutes are unique. Even top female bodybuilders like Lenda Murray, hardly deficient in this area, admit that 'Nobody's got a booty like Sha-ri.'" [35]

Two shots of Sha-ri embody the assumptions articulated in the biography. One, a shot from behind, focuses on her buttocks, or "glutes," displayed on a marble column. The shot draws the eye to the rounded contours, lightly sweating, directly in the center of the frame. Lighting and perspective ensure that the gaze will return to her "booty." A second shot positions Sha-ri with her buttocks elevated, crouched like a predator, lips drawn into a snarl. If Pendleton is both animalized and reduced to her glutes, the invocation of Lenda Murray's tacit support is doubly problematic, because Murray, whom Dobbins dubs "hardly deficient" in booty, is also black. In photos throughout the collection, Murray is herself exoticized in familiar racialized ways.

No white women in the collection are exoticized through images of animality and references to the primitive, although they are, by posing with snakes, constructed in reference to Eve, that old female standard, a pairing that conflates femininity with whiteness. Nor are white women singled out in terms of their body parts. Instead they are defined in terms of their connections to men. The photograph of Kim Chizevsky, the white woman positioned in what most closely resembles Pendleton's predatory pose, maintains a clear distinction. The blond, compliant Kim looks much less fierce, due to a gaze and facial expression more softly sensual, open. Her image is accompanied by a biography written mostly in Kim's own voice. She says, among other things, "I was doing aerobics in a health spa, and I met my future husband, who was a bodybuilder . . . so bodybuilding has given me a lot—not only a career, but a husband as well." Both biographical sketches follow traditional assumptions about race and gender: black women are reducible to their booties; blond white women are reducible to their husbands. Plantation rhetoric, nineties style, under the guise of achievement and self-determination for these female bodybuilding stars.

Both in similarity and by contrast, a recent *Flex* pictorial featuring former Ms. Olympia Cory Everson also shows the reproduction of disturbing norms about race and gender which are marketed as self-determination. The spread poses Cory, with her breast implants, in soft focus, standing nude in a swath of white tissue, with pouting lips and downcast eyes. This classical image of romanticized white femininity is contradictorily inscribed with the rhetoric of white masculine presence: "Muscle has taken me to places I never could have dreamed of. It's given me confidence, presence, and marketability."[36] As facetious as the notion of presence ever is, the facetiousness is at least triply layered here. Cory's picture, featuring little muscle, much more resembles the conventions of soft porn. It is clear that the "presence" she refers to is the presence of marketability, and that marketability is dependent upon constructing herself according to the very conventions of femininity that make her nonpresence, that idealize her as a fantasy being-for-(nonpredatory)sex, and it is a fantasy that is racially inscribed. Props like tissue paper and bubbles are characteristic of the centerfolds of white women, and suggest idealization rather than immediate access, while native spears, tattered bikinis, and cages are used as props for Asian, Native American, and Chicana women, hinting at a higher degree of savagery and thereby animalistic sexuality. This is a sign system that is reproduced in other cultural contexts, and to similar effect.

CONSTRUCTING AMERICAN COOL: RACE AND GENDER IN J. CREW

The racial tropes that bodybuilding publications reinforced in 1995 had startling resonance with tropes circulating in mass culture.

The dawn of 1995 marked the return of the old in the guise of the new, a new Republican Congress, layouts in *Vogue* magazine proclaiming that retro rules the runways, showing fashions reminiscent of a fifties prom dress and corseted fifties-style jackets from Donna Karan (touted as a "feminist designer), and *Vogue*-like layouts in the bodybuilding magazines showing the top competitive women bodybuilders in high heels and rubber dresses, skating skirts, bustiers. Meanwhile, in academic circles what had been known as feminist theory was surpassed by discourses about race, and in the mass media third-wave feminists proclaimed the power of individual achievement for women in the possibilities for material success.[37] Discussions of sexual harassment were represented as retrograde whining, and backlash movies like *Disclosure* (which featured a sex-crazed female boss as the harasser) were top box-office draws.[38] John Singleton's *Higher Learning* represented feminist movements on campus as ineffectual and naive. On the MTV music scene, macho throwbacks Frank Sinatra, Tony Bennett, Tom Jones, and Johnny Cash were marketed as alternative hip. Clearly race and gender were prominent topics in the national imagination, but no representations were quite so blatantly marked as the J. Crew catalog mailed in early January 1995, with only a fifties-style v-neck sweater on the cover and the text "A New Beginning 1995" in small letters at the bottom of the page. I could have chosen any number of cultural examples to demonstrate these points, but J. Crew, the arbiter of middle-class cool for twenty- to thirtysomethings across America, is a particularly good barometer of dominant cultural trends. In the J. Crew spread, cultural meanings hinted at elsewhere become bold statements: the white male standard is what is definitively, authentically *in*.

J. Crew is arguably the hippest mail-order catalog for the twenty- to thirtysomething set, with a distribution and circulation that targets most homes in this market. Since the mid-eighties their business has boomed. The catalogs themselves set standards for dress at the forefront of every fashion movement from eighties polish to nineties back-to-basics to grunge. Similar to the MTV aesthetic, these catalogs present the image of a carefree, down-home but hip and alternative life-style where no one wears makeup and everyone is pictured at home in repose or just out of bed but looks casually glamorous anyway. These are people with character, with soul— the images say—casual but unfailingly hip, not done up but physically striking. J. Crew constructs an ethos for the nineties combining the basics with an upwardly mobile life-style underscored with the trappings of ease. Linda Evangelista got her start in the J. Crew catalog before she ascended to the supermodel stratum, and recently Lauren Hutton has appeared in many layouts as a testament to the agelessness of cool. J. Crew always evokes both permanence and cutting edge, as if the vanguard of the new is dependent upon an endless recirculation and evocation of the past. Like T. S. Eliot, who in "Tradition and the Individual Talent" argues that for the poet, "not only the best, but the most individual parts of his work may be

Good stuff: Fashioning standards in J. Crew. (*J. Crew Catalog*, January 1995)

those in which the dead poets, his ancestors, assert their immortality most vigorously," [39] in the J. Crew catalog individual essence and character, the very best of American character, is represented by and dependent upon connections to older images, a deference to the basics, the strengths, the standards that made the American character what it is or most wants to be. The catalog makes it clear that the standard of integrity, essence, to which all must strive, despite the sexiness of some cultural deviations, is that of the white male. A new standard that is a very old standard.

The first image in the "New Beginning 1995" catalog is that of a Waspy-looking white male, dressed in exercise gear and a respectable-but-slightly funky haircut on the ground doing his preexercise stretches. The rhetoric of new beginning was everywhere in the media since the November 1994 elections, but exactly what was constructed and presented as new? In the catalog as elsewhere, the new seemed all too disturbingly familiar. The background is white light reflecting off the pavement; he's placed in front of a wire-mesh fence. The photo takes up a page and a third. The remaining two-thirds of a page is very dark by contrast, heavy granite pillars on two sides extending vertically into complete blackness with horizontal bands of dark shadow extended between them, alleviated by horizontal stripes of sunlight striking the ground in between and receding in perspective so that the figure of a black man, shot from behind, appears to be running into a series of boxes, each smaller than the next. He is tiny in contrast to the pillars and the white man in the image on the facing page, measuring about an inch and a half. He's running, away from the camera; you can see no part of his face.

The next human image occupies an entire page, and features a black man playing a trumpet, eyes closed, brow furrowed, lips pursed, dressed in a J. Crew twill button-down shirt with its sleeves rolled up, and laced up with a striped tie. The man's naked forearm occupies the foreground of the picture, and head, chest, and shoulders occupy so much of the page that the top of his head is cut off. There is no writing on this page. The facing page includes the text, in heavy boldface black letters, that reads "soulful." Underneath, in smaller letters, is the text "searching. Subdued. Reflective. Resonant. The color and mood of winter . . . with thoughts of spring some-where in the mind." In the context of the previous two images, this text is indicative of an underlying set of assumptions that this page alone would not make clear. The stereotypical association of "soulful" with a black musician is obvious, evoking images of the less complicated truths of simple souls whose connection to the body and emotional experience is more immediate than that available to their more sophisticated, cerebral white counterparts. But the evocation of searching, subdued, reflective, resonant that follows may or may not be intended to indicate a thoughtful sophistication. Yet these "thoughts," much like the thinking brought about by the foregrounding of race and racism in the national consciousness through events like the Clarence Thomas confirmation hearings and the O. J. Simpson trial, the Rodney King beating and the L.A. riots, are part of "the color and mood of winter." We are moving beyond that now, beyond that deadness, coldness, and into the new, the much more congenial and desirable "thoughts of spring." Part of the "New Beginning 1995" may be the getting beyond or forgetting of the unpleasant cultural problems reflecting on race foregrounds. We are moving, the images suggest, back to the springtime of whiteness where the white male body stretches out across the page with all his prerogative and purpose, into the "spring," the renewal of white male supremacy in which the black man resumes his diminished status running into continually shrinking boxes.

The next image is that of a young black male intellectual, dressed in an off-white J. Crew sweater and khakis, eyes straight to the camera but patient and kind, cheek resting in the palm of his hand. There is no written text on the page except that which describes and prices the sweater. On the table where he leans sits a white coffee cup and the ubiquitous trumpet. He embodies an image of difference that J. Crew presumably accepts, is happy to represent as the norm. Except. Except the boldface text on the facing page, and the next image. The text, under the forty-eight-dollar wool roll-neck sweaters: "Some stuff's been around for a long time for good reason. Consolation, and bone-warming comfort." Innocent enough on the surface of it. But read in the context of Toni Morrison's argument, in *Playing in the Dark: Whiteness and the Literary Imagination*, that the American character is based on, defines itself against, "conveniently bound and violently silenced black bodies . . . the projection of the not-me. . . . Nothing highlighted freedom . . . like slavery," the images and text of J. Crew **8 7** reflects much more. To pretend to racial neutrality and equality, as the catalog does here, is to "allow the black body a shadowless participation in the dominant cultural body."[40] The most valued features said to make up the American character, those of individuality and masculinity, independence and freedom, are dependent upon groups of others who don't have individuality, masculinity, independence, or freedom—namely women and African Americans. The J. Crew catalog looks back to a simpler time of integrity and meaning, a time when women couldn't vote, own property, or get a divorce and when African Americans were slaves: "Some stuff's been around a long time for good reason. Consolation, and bone-warming comfort." What better "consolation" for a lack of confidence or definitive identity, what more "bone-warming comfort" could one be assured of than the presence of others who were not free? Could not be independent? The text here, accompanied by the images, is about much more than sweaters. The catalog evokes the formative moments of America when the white male was the standard of being and everyone else the deviation, the not-that.

Representations of gender were similarly reactionary. After a couple pages of shoes we encounter the first image of a woman, a full-page shot of Lauren Hutton on a couch in jeans, socks, and a J. Crew sweater, balancing a newspaper and popcorn. She's got a fistful of popcorn in her hand, and she looks at the camera with a bit of bravado like she's been caught in the act and is daring anyone to call her on it. The text here, in bold, white letters, reads "shared." Underneath, in smaller print, is "case in point: men's sizing, a specification, not a limitation." Like the earlier images that posit the white male as the standard against which deviations are measured, here the catalog proclaims that men's sizing for both genders is a "specification" or choice, rather than a "limitation."

Hutton continues to function as the model for the unisex clothes, as well as the white representative of all women, posed on the next page with "man's three best friends, Murray, Max [dogs] and the J. Crew Henley." Even though it is Hutton, a white woman, who stands in for the unisex, the old language that presumes a male subject is used to subsume her under the category "man." A white woman appropriating his position is commented on in the next photo: Hutton seated on a pail, elbows on knees, baseball cap in her hands, and a text that reads, "He frowned when she borrowed it. She never did see him again." He doesn't want her to "borrow it," whatever "it" is, and the ambiguity of "she never did see him again" suggests either a desertion on her part or a desertion on his—either an act of agency and appropriation on her part that leaves him behind, or a punitive refusal on his part to engage with her if she borrows the guise of the masculine, effacing her difference by imitating him just as the fact that she stands in for all women renders women not like her invisible.

Hutton has clearly borrowed his positioning and privilege. On the next page, eating an apple and with her hand over her mouth, dressed in what looks like a man's button-down shirt, jeans, and boots, the text across Hutton's chest reads, "In the Spring, a young man's fancy . . ." Here she is either being positioned as a young man with particular fancies, tastes, that J. Crew clothes fulfill, or she is meant to evoke the image of a "young man's fancy," that of sexual innocence, naïveté, gentle interest and consideration. Or both. The tousled hair, and the Eve-like wiping-the-apple-juice-off-of-the-mouth pose, combined with the boyish clothes, suggest a transgressive gesture in the act of wearing the clothes, as well as a subversion of age codes. And if Hutton evokes the forbidden here, the forbidden knowledge of the older woman, or the transgressive gesture of appropriating masculine attire (and thereby power), the very association of transgression with a woman wearing male clothes suggests a gender distinction that marks reality and presence as his space, and the gesture of appropriation hers. Throughout this section, the clothes, although offered as unisex, are "all in men's sizes."

Such contemporary cultural representations both parallel and inform the controversies in bodybuilding. Discussions of steroid use, for instance, focus on women inappropriately appropriating male hormones, and looking too much like men. The gender disruption J. Crew plays with here is seen as a real threat in bodybuilding, and every attempt is made to accentuate sexual difference. If J. Crew shows how the white male is still taken as standard, the study of male bodybuilders shows how this standard is often maintained. The J. Crew catalog reveals the sophisticated and subtle ways dominant culture is working to reinstitute that standard under the guise of inclusiveness.

As I discussed in chapter 2, in the bodybuilding industry contemporary deployments of the rhetoric of inclusiveness often function to put reactionary ideas about gender and race front and center, again. When Joe Weider writes that he added a fitness competition to the Ms. Olympia because it provides an outlet for women who are less genetically gifted than the women bodybuilders, he is making a claim for inclusiveness, but the very act of adding fitness to bodybuilding marginalizes bodybuilding and diverts focus away from its gender disruptions and back onto normalized femininity: women in swimsuits and evening gowns doing quarter turns for the judges. A similar rhetoric of inclusiveness was employed to do away with affirmative action in California: affirmative action, according to this view, gives special preference, and we have to be inclusive.

Like much of contemporary culture, J. Crew doesn't just sell clothes. It sells us a way of thinking as well, sells the white male standard as reassuring, comforting, a return to home, to safety, to what *is*. Two years later, January 1997, even the pretense of including difference or raciness is gone. The models are white, white, and more white, as boring as the fifties Kansas housewife clothes on the agenda this year when, according to *Vogue*, the "new look" for spring is dowdy "grandma" skirts that properly cover the knees. This rhetoric, these images, do something. Through an appeal to the hip, to each individual's desire to be included in what's going on in the world around her, they do the serious cultural work of selling particular versions of the cultural horizon that consciously or unconsciously direct how we see, what we feel, how we behave. How art photography similarly works to sell meaning and how two different bodybuilding photographers offer two different versions of the cultural horizon that bodybuilding helps shape will be the subject of the next chapter.

4

Hard Times

The Pornographic and the Pathetic in Women's Bodybuilding Photography

Working the Image

Photography is the primary mode of representation for bodybuilders. While a few of the biggest names make marketable videos and a few contests are aired on ESPN, photography remains the primary means through which a woman's physical progress is documented and her body is presented to an audience outside of the gym. Newcomers to the sport begin their careers and build their reputations largely through pictorials in the muscle magazines, and the sale of pictures to the general public through the magazines or on the Internet is often a source of income. For amateurs or noncompetitive bodybuilders, the first photographs are often a tangible way of making the hours of training add up to something, and serve as a formal recognition of achievement—something like a college diploma.

For bodybuilders who have problems with self-confidence or body image, photographs can provide a more accurate, concrete sense of embodied selfhood than does the daily examination in the gym mirror. Despite the fact that the photo is an image not necessarily reflective of any bodily reality, constructed as it is through the photographer's formal senses of line and light and angle and his/her ideological sense of what constitutes a body of a particular race and gender, an image of oneself has a way of providing a concrete sense of one's own reality that may have been lacking before, a kind of this-is-me-this-is-what-I-have-achieved sense of being. As Bruce Chatwin writes of Lisa Lyon in his introduction to the collection of Robert Mapplethorpe photos of Lyon called *Lady*, Lyon considered herself "a sculptor whose raw material was her own body. Since this material was, in the long run, ephemeral, she was on the lookout for the right photographer to document it. 'A mirror,' she says, 'is not an objective witness.'"[1] Neither is a photograph, but to the bodybuilder, whose concerns about an insubstantiality of being, mortality, and personal distinction are often even more pressing than those same concerns for the average person, just having *something* to document your presence is a definite confirmation of presence.[2]

Yet the photograph may reveal more the fiction of presence than presence itself. As Chatwin writes of *Lady*,

> This book does not simply document Lisa Lyon: it is the work of the imagination—the visual counterpart of a novel, which, like all good novels, mixes fact and fantasy to reveal a greater truth. The photographer and his model have conspired to tell a story of their overlapping obsessions. Their glorification of the body is an act of will, a defiance of nihilism and abstraction, a story of the Modern Movement in reverse.[3]

Far from reflecting some objective reality, both the bodybuilder and the photographer actively shape their materials. But unlike the most widely accepted tenets of high modernism (which in their rejection of objective reality denied the body and its realities in preference for nonrepresentational abstraction), late twentieth-century bodybuilding photography presents the body as a work of art. Although it is itself an aesthetic sport, and bodybuilders claim to treat their bodies as the raw materials they shape into art, it is in bodybuilding photography that bodybuilding most directly meets the aesthetic.

The work of two bodybuilding art photographers—one better known and one less so—demonstrates two characteristic approaches to the subject. One, represented here by the work of Bill Dobbins, glorifies and naturalizes women's bodybuilding, and tries to sell it to the general public as a new form of sex appeal. Another approach, found here in the work of Bill Lowenburg, tends to focus on bodybuilding's most negative qualities, its absurdity, making bodybuilding even more alien to the observer outside the sport than it already is. Dobbins's work plays to the viewer, soliciting viewer identification with his subjects; Lowenburg's, on the other hand, solicits critical consciousness in the mode of dramatist Bertolt Brecht and strives for an alienation effect that makes the viewer reflect critically on the subject. While Lowenburg's work calls attention to bodybuilding as an explicit and often illusory method of self-construction, Dobbins tries to naturalize the image and present an essence of muscular femininity. Dobbins's work in particular is symptomatic of continuing cultural discomfort with texts, in this case bodies, that bring together images, desires, and lived forms of embodiment that are contradictory.

It is that discomfort, I will argue, that most jeopardizes women's bodybuilding and by extension the third-wave feminism it so exemplifies, especially since this discomfort is often managed by renormalizing female bodybuilders' bodies through photography that makes use of the formal strategies of pornography. It is this normalization—using representational strategies that align the female bodybuilder with traditional femininity and that attempt to erase her masculinity—that I take issue with here, not pornography per se. Since the question of pornography so often frames current discussions of feminist interpretation in general and women's bodybuilding photography in particular, it is crucial to explore the debate specific to bodybuilding as it is carried out on the pages of industry magazines and on the Internet. The angle of interpretation used to look at bodybuilding in general—whether you look at it as a sport, as an aesthetic, or as a lifestyle—often determines conclusions. The question of pornography is intricately bound up with those questions, and I examine them here as a way of framing the question of pornography in women's bodybuilding photography.   **9 3**

B ODYBUILDING AS S PORT , A ESTHETIC ,
OR L IFE - STYLE

In order for bodybuilding to function as a form of resistance, it must be seen as a sport as well as a possibly revolutionary aesthetic. The argument that female bodybuilding *is* a sport is necessary since most people respond to bodybuilders as aesthetic or sexual objects rather than as athletes. In an occurrence similar to those described by other critics who have done work on women's bodybuilding, a couple of years ago I took a tape of the 1994 Ms. Olympia contest to a professional for dubbing. Although I had not asked his opinion, upon observing the women's bodies on the tape, the video producer immediately informed me, "I just don't find that at all attractive," as if sexual attractiveness was the main point of or motivation for bodybuilding. For those who argue that bodybuilding is a sport, however, the issue of attractiveness is irrelevant. Arnold Schwarzenegger explains: "When women began competing in the late 1970s, a lot of people didn't like it. They didn't approve of women building muscle and they professed not to like the way these women looked. . . . Why women should be accepted as bodybuilders is not very complicated. Just as tennis, golf, volleyball, and basketball are sports that both men and women compete in, so is bodybuilding."[4] In this argument, imposing limitations on women's muscular development—as contest judges still often do—is like telling a marathon runner that she can't keep improving her times because doing so will make her unfeminine.

Taking a common position that marks the link between bodybuilding as sport and bodybuilding as photography, bodybuilder Heather Tristany makes the argument that femininity-as-sexuality should be used to popularize and promote bodybuilding as a sport. "There are ways," she writes, "that can potentially accelerate the social acceptability of female muscularity. Ultimately, this will require facing the challenge of creating an image of the female bodybuilder that is physically appealing, sexually exciting, and desirable." Female bodybuilders, she says, should "act like ladies" in order to help counter the masculine image—that is, they should wear only feminine clothes in public that don't show their arms and they should never act vulgar or swear. In order to create this image and help build public exposure and audience appeal, she argues,

> the common display of "hardcore" muscle shots for women should be avoided as standard practice when the target is the mainstream audience. . . . Frequent exposure of images that demonstrate the "heightened femininity" (exaggerated womanly lines) of women bodybuilders will ultimately stimulate greater public acceptance. As well, promoting feminine muscle in a manner that suggests sexual attractiveness creates an image for the average man and woman that muscle is an asset worth acquiring.[5]

Much like the retro-sounding advice columns that began to appear in *Cosmopolitan* magazine around 1993 that suggested women should not be too aggressive and call a man for a date because this would scare him off, Tristany's argument forwards several reactionary prescriptions regarding proper female behavior: Keep your body covered. Don't swear. Don't spit. Look sexy at all times.[6] Furthermore, Tristany assumes a logic of use value for bodybuilding that is foreign to some of the sport's most basic premises, as I discuss in the "Sovereignty" section of chapter 6. "Sexual attractiveness" should be used "to promote feminine muscle," by this logic, so that the average man and woman can be convinced that muscles on women are "assets worth acquiring" rather than being seen as pointless or as liabilities. By invoking the logic of commodities and use value in her attempt to argue for broadening the mass audience appeal of the sport, Tristany negates the possibility that bodybuilding functions as an activity in and for itself in the life of the individual who practices it. The possibility that bodybuilding functions in the lives of some individuals as a crucial space of sovereignty or self-ownership, where their actions are performed for the purpose of claiming a space in their lives for themselves and their own development, independent of the desires of others, is something that Tristany's prescriptive analysis would deny the sport's female practitioners, because what people think (according to this logic) is of greater importance than the women themselves.

A second common categorization—bodybuilding as aesthetics—relies on an analogy between the bodybuilder and his/her body and the artist and his/her raw material. As Dobbins writes, "The ultimate goal of . . . bodybuilding . . . [is to] achieve the ultimate aesthetic development of the body. They use muscle the way a sculptor uses clay, creating a muscle structure that is shapely, balanced, and well-proportioned.[7] When it approaches the body in this way, bodybuilding is a prime example of what Susan Bordo has named "postmodern plasticity"—the assumption that there are no limits to our possibilities for creating and shaping our bodies—one is what one makes.[8] Although there is often a mention of genetics as important in the determination of final form and the potential for degree of muscular development, the idea that hard work and the right supplements and/or drugs will allow you to make yourself into whatever shape you want is everywhere in bodybuilding rhetoric and advertisements. This emphasis on self-determination, the ability to overcome any external limits, is probably the single most important (and questionable) idea in bodybuilding ideology and is psychologically one of its strongest motivators.

Most often, it is because of the aesthetic component that bodybuilding is not considered a sport. Unlike other sports it most resembles, such as gymnastics or figure skating, which rely on judges' scorecards rather than a definite time or score, the primary emphasis in bodybuilding is how the body looks rather than how well it executes a set of jumps or gymnastic maneuvers. Dobbins writes, "The methods used to create a championship physique are athletic, but the goal is aesthetic. . . . Bodybuilders . . . use the stuff of muscle to express very specific aesthetic ideas. Bodybuilding is about beauty—although not necessarily the traditional beauty we accept in everyday life."[9] So while the training for a bodybuilding competition may be as rigorous or more so than the training for, say, a football game, or a marathon, those rigors are not what the bodybuilder is performing in the competition itself. Unlike other sports where you train by running and then run in a competition, in bodybuilding training and competition differ.

It is this division that marks discussions of bodybuilding as a life-style. Because you can train exactly like a competitive bodybuilder and yet never compete, when one speaks of bodybuilding one can refer to either extensive training with weights or to extensive training with weights followed by competition. Discussions of the bodybuilder life-style revolve around aspects of training, diet, and orientation, and need not necessarily refer to competition. Those who do compete—a small number of women—in some ways rightly tend to claim hierarchical authority, privilege, over those who don't. But because of representational strategies circulating widely in the dominant culture, including the bodybuilding industry, that attempt to counteract the challenge women's bodybuilding poses to traditional ideas about gender, it is on the level of lifestyle rather than aesthetics or the circuit of bodybuilding competition that bodybuilding is doing significant cultural work in the expansion of ideas about and practices of gender.

Because they so directly challenge traditional equations between the female body and nurturing, weakness, and dependence, female bodybuilders are even more striking examples of gender activism in play, and as such, are, from the perspective of dominant culture, even more in need of visual and rhetorical strategies that will normalize them in an attempt to contain their activist potential.[10] If something was not activist, if it was not *doing something*, there would be no need for counterrepresentations to contain it. Even media that attempt to sell female bodybuilding to the larger public (such as bodybuilding magazines and the film *Pumping Iron II*—whose movie poster advertised "a new definition of woman") are careful to present the women as women before women as athletes. Film theorist Chris Holmlund points out how *Pumping Iron II* was obsessive about always showing the female bodybuilders with their boyfriends or husbands, focusing on the women's heterosexual relationships rather than on the women themselves.[11] This is a common strategy. As Mariah Burton Nelson writes of female athletes more generally, "When female athletes are depicted, they're usually wearing short skirts or smiling. Commentators say approvingly, 'She's really strong *but still feminine*.'"[12]

Femininity, it seems, is synonymous with sexuality, or what used to be known as sex appeal, and issues raised about this form of representation for female athletes are likely to be met with one of the following questions: Sex sells, and what's wrong with success? What are you—one of those feminists who hates men and sex? What's wrong with sex? It's her body and she's choosing to put it on display, so how can you criticize her right to do that? These questions all ignore the crucial point that the criticism is not a **97** criticism of sex, or of marketability, or of personal agency and choice, but rather a criticism of the fact that sexualizing a female athlete—making sex rather than athleticism the focus—does some crucial cultural work of its own: it works to rewrite the iconography of power and strength that the female athlete represents. As Nelson points out, "Most critically, writers and broadcasters minimize female strength by sexualizing it." [13]

Sexualizing female athletes is linked to another counterrevolutionary representational code: "framing women as special athletes: female athletes. Through both text and photographs . . . women tend to be depicted primarily as women—genderized—while men are depicted as brave, successful, tough, admirable human beings." [14] Both of these tendencies are combined in the centerfolds in the bodybuilding magazine *Flex*, which I discussed in chapter 2. In addition to the female bodybuilder posed with props of femininity and sexuality such as veils, high heels, leather and lace, on one side, the centerfolds feature a straight competition shot of a male bodybuilder, sans props, on the other side. He is represented as a bodybuilder and athlete, while she is represented as a woman who happens to be a bodybuilder. In his case, his achievement is highlighted; in her case, her sexuality. *Flex* has been widely criticized as well as praised for this practice, and in the past has been defensive enough about it to deny me and other writers permission to reproduce the images in our work.

Such depictions have several consequences. First, and most obviously, they reinforce the tradition that if a sport is considered a woman's sport, the athletes are automatically not as serious or as good. Further, they instruct the viewer that no matter what else women may do, whatever else they may achieve, they are *still women*, and subject to all the traditional ideas about women and diminution. This undermines potential audience identification with female athletes as heroes. Second, these depictions are another manifestation of the for-self/for-others dichotomy described above. If male athletes are presented as just athletes, if no issue is raised about their masculinity or the fact that they are men, and if whether they are sexually appealing to women is not even raised as a question, then they are athletes for themselves and for their own achievements and are evaluated as such. If female athletes, on the other hand, are depicted as sexual

women first and athletes second, then this returns them to a for-others position in which the question becomes whether they are sexually appealing
to others rather than whether they excel at what they do (for themselves).
And third, because the photographs frame women as something other than
athletes even though they are ostensibly being photographed to document
that achievement, this can suggest that women train for the primary purpose of achieving a more sexy look. As Nelson writes of a photographic es-
say of Olympic swimmer Dara Torres that appeared in *Men's Journal*, "We
might think that she spends hours each day face down in a pool *so that she
can look like this*, wet and muscular and stretched open and laughing. Not
the reverse: that she has become stunning incidentally, because of her
commitment to athletic excellence." [15] Such representations further the traditional associations that emphasize activities (*what* they do) in men, and
appearance (how they look) in women, a being-for-self stance in men and
a being-for-others stance in women.

L O O S E N I N G   U P :   T H E   Q U E S T I O N   O F   P O R N O G R A P H Y

The most controversial aspect of the representation of female athletes, especially in photography, has to do with the question of pornography. In taking up this question, I would like to make it clear from the outset that
unlike antipornography advocates from, for instance, the southern United
States who have pulled the "pornographic" muscle mags from the shelves,
my critique of these images is not based on their sexual content. I've never
thought *Playboy* should be pulled from the shelves; I'm not a censor. There
is a market for pornography, and I don't agree with the procensorship feminism that calls for its eradication, controlled through legal measures, because I don't think censorship is an effective strategy. I am furthermore in
agreement with Ellen Willis, who writes, "The tendency of some feminists
to . . . define the movement's goal as controlling male sexuality rather than
demanding women's freedom to live active sexual lives, reinforces wom-
en's oppression." [16] At the same time, I am also in agreement with writers
who question the assumption that male sexuality is necessarily violent and

9 9

whose criticism of pornography centers around the fact that in pornography this is often the assumption.[17] But neither position is at issue here, for in its own context, in its place, I am content to let pornography be.

Where I am not content to let pornography be is in a bodybuilding magazine. I am not saying we should censor issues that contain pornographic imagery, but rather that we should come to a clearer understanding of what kind of cultural work the imagery is doing. Since bodybuilding very much promotes itself as a sport like any other, an equivalent would be putting Steffi Graf in a black lace bra, thong, and heels, and sticking her in the middle of *Tennis* magazine (or how about naked men sitting spread-eagled in the middle of *Golf Digest*?).[18] While it is true that bodybuilders of both sexes pose in competition suits that don't cover much flesh, it does not necessarily follow that this flesh need be sexualized, as it is not in most of the male centerfolds. Conversely, if there were equal opportunity sexualization, and male bodybuilders were pictured in the same way, the cultural message would be very different—progressive in some ways rather than reactionary.

There is not, however, such an equality of representation, for it is most often only representations of female athletes that make use of the conventions of soft porn in terms of framing, lighting, positioning, and props. As numerous nonpornographic depictions of naked Olympic athletes (such as those seen in *Life* magazine in July 1996) have shown, it is not the degree of nudity that is pornographic but rather the photographic conventions employed in the shot. Viewers are not responding to the bodybuilding pictorials by raising the question of pornography simply because many of the female bodybuilders are posing nude. What viewers are recognizing, without always articulating it, are the photographic conventions utilized in the creation of the image. Bill Dobbins explains that in terms of the staging of a shot and the final look that is achieved, "if you do photos that are glamorous and sexy but also focus on the athletic quality of the bodies involved, what you have are figure studies. If you shoot T & A, that's what you'll get."[19] It is the "athletic quality" that is lost in many images of female athletes, a loss that—through formal techniques and recognized conventions—presents the women's bodies as "T & A" rather than as athletic.

Sociologist Margaret Carlisle Duncan, whose research has long focused on gender, sports, and the media, explains that images of female athletes become pornographic when "they highlight women's hips, thighs, buttocks, breasts, crotches, when they offer viewers voyeuristic thrills by showing 'forbidden' sights, or when they show female athletes with certain facial expressions signifying sexual invitation."[20] Most of the images of women bodybuilders and fitness competitors that now appear in the muscle magazines—including some of Dobbins's work—have one or more of the features Duncan describes.

Images of muscular women are further characterized by techniques Chris Holmlund argues are employed in *Pumping Iron II*:

> In each sequence the images counteract the threat posed by muscular, active women by placing them in traditionally sexy, feminine environments (showers and pools). . . . *Pumping Iron II* positions women as fetishized objects of the camera's and the spectator's gaze far more than *Pumping Iron* does men. . . . The editing strategies, the framing and lighting, resemble those of soft-core pornographic films. . . . Though muscular, breasts and buttocks still appear as tits and ass.[21]

The *Flex* layouts often position women in just such environments, or in natural environments like the desert or North Pole—wearing leather or lingerie or heels or knee-high boots—while the men are photographed in the studio or the gym in their competition briefs. Criticisms of these images often make note of the very different techniques used to photograph and frame the male bodybuilders—and the implications of this difference, but the refutations of the criticisms never do.

Typical are the following three letters, which were written to *Flex*'s editorial staff and published in the "Talkback" column and which I quote significant portions of in order to give a sense of the terms of the debate:

> I'm writing in response to the female pictorials you print in each issue. I feel that picturing female bodybuilders nude is degrading, demeaning, and disrespectful. What is the world coming to when a bodybuilding magazine is the same as a pornography magazine? Why do you have to have these women appear in such provocative poses (straddling chairs, bathroom scenes, etc.) in order to see their beauty? You can tell just how

lovely these women really are by looking at them in their competition outfits. *Flex* magazine is a bodybuilding magazine, not *Playboy*. STOP WITH THE NUDITY.

After reading some of the complaints about your pictorials . . . I just had to write. I think that people who think your magazine has turned into *Playboy* apparently don't appreciate the wholesome looks of well-conditioned athletes. At contests and while working out, these athletes have bulging muscles and veins. Your pictorials of these women show a side of bodybuilding we rarely see. I think it *is* essential to let people know there is more to bodybuilding than just bulging muscles.

I am a 43-year-young married man with very strong opinions in favor of women's rights, and I firmly believe that a woman is entitled to act according to her passions, as it is she who is held accountable. Cory [one of the women in the pictorials] has a beautiful body that obviously reflects her hard, dedicated work. It is the frigid-minded women in today's society who, due to their own insecurities and jealousies, partially close the doors of opportunity for others. I say to these women, light a candle, turn on some soft music, pour a glass of wine, surround yourself in bubbles and loosen up![22]

The first letter, although argued from a critical point of view, obscures the issue and undermines the real force of the argument by framing the problem with the layouts as one of nudity rather than the formal techniques used to frame and present that nudity. While most of the *Flex* pictorials do meet Margaret Duncan's criteria for pornography cited earlier, particularly "show[ing] female athletes with certain facial expressions signifying sexual invitation," not all of the pictorials do this. Some of the pictorials, though nude, would qualify as what Dobbins dubbed "figure studies," and are not "degrading, demeaning, and disrespectful." By making her objection into a generalization about all nudity—"I feel that picturing female bodybuilders nude is degrading, demeaning, and disrespectful"—she sets herself up for the characteristic responses that follow. In a cultural climate where popular media has proclaimed and denounced the age of the victim feminist or new Victorian feminist (the feminist who supposedly hates men and nudity and sex if she criticizes sexual representations of women as degrading and demeaning), poisoning feminist criticism with the taint of a discourse that has been deemed passé, this writer's criticism will inevitably be met with responses like those that follow here, which themselves claim a feminist viewpoint and label criticisms like hers the product of frigidity. Had she not framed the issue as a problem of nudity, her subsequent points would have been more difficult to attack on this basis. For it is the way those nude bodies are posed, the expressions and props that accompany them, that is really the problem, as she goes on to say: "Why do you have to have these women appear in such provocative poses . . . in order to see their beauty?" This is a good question, but when she returns again to the issue of nudity per se she undermines this position: "STOP WITH THE NUDITY." It is quite possible—as indeed, a few of the pictorials demonstrate—to present a nude that is not pornographic.

Like the first letter, the other two in this series are typical. But they too make a generalization that obscures the underlying issues. These letters posit that viewers who criticize the pictorials—as the first letter seemed to—are objecting to pornography and nudity and sex per se, rather than objecting to these things specifically in relation to female athletes. This frames the debate, then, in terms of the larger debate about pornography, which also tends to fall into a generalized pro-or-con, for-or-against structure rather than a discussion that is contextually nuanced. The last letter in particular is situated in the context of a propornography stance that can at times be too simplistic. The writer tries to establish the authority to speak as he does by claiming an allegiance to feminism, a "man with very strong opinions in favor of women's rights." From that standpoint, though, he goes on to make statements that seem to exclude cultural critique from the purview of "women's rights" since his intention is to belittle that critique. According to this writer, "a woman is entitled to act according to her passions, as it is she who is held accountable," raising the question of responsibility and self-determination.

The *Flex* layouts, the writer seems to assume (as do many of the written texts that accompany the pictorials) are an expression of that self-determination, and furthermore, of hard work: "Cory has a beautiful body that obviously reflects her hard, dedicated work." This assumes that a critique of the pictorials is a critique of the women themselves rather than of **103**

the way they are framed, when the original letter that this writer was responding to was clearly critiquing the style of the pictorial rather than Cory
Everson herself:

> I'm writing in response to Cory Everson's pictorial. Being into bodybuild-
> ing myself, I have always looked up to her for inspiration, but I have to
> admit, I was appalled and offended to see your July issue. I truly think
> your magazine has lost its focus. I did a double-take because I thought I
> had picked up an issue of *Playboy* by mistake! And what's this—a bath-
> room scene with bubbles and all? Come on, do you really expect me to
> believe this is essential to bodybuilding? [23]

This letter does not criticize Cory Everson but rather the magazine itself,
specifically the mise-en-scène of the photographs and their pornographic
technique, which the writer, rightly, found strange in a bodybuilding context. The writer who responded to her letter assumed she was objecting to
Everson herself, and that her criticism of the magazine would somehow
limit Everson's opportunities: "It is the frigid-minded women in today's society who, due to their own insecurities and jealousies, partially close the
doors of opportunity for others."

"Chill," this writer seems to be saying, "You're just upset because you're
not as hot as Cory." His further proclamation that women who feel this
way should immerse themselves in the mise-en-scène that the pictorial
stages—bathtub, candles, bubbles—and "loosen up" is a thinly veiled
nineties version of the proto-seventies response to feminist critique: "Chick
just needs to have some fun." Women who criticize sexual representations,
in this view, are repressed and jealous of the woman being represented—
it is assumed that critics aren't sexual themselves, that they're not "getting
theirs," that they are somehow opposed to sex and pornography in general
rather than in specific contexts.

As Susan Bordo points out in a more nuanced discussion of the pornography debate, the issues involved are much more contextual than is usually
acknowledged on either side. The issue is not one of prosex feminists who
are for pornography or antisex feminists who criticize it. The problem is not
that sexual representations objectify women, but that the way the representation is staged communicates very particular messages (some suggest em-

powerment; others suggest subordination—all messages are not the same). According to Bordo, we need to approach the question differently, in terms of the *meaning* the bodies in pornography project:

> The old feminist fear of "objectification" seems inadequate to describe what is going on when women's bodies are depicted in sexualized or aestheticized ways. The notion of women-as-objects suggests the reduction of women to 'mere' bodies, when actually, what's going on is often far more disturbing than that, involving the depiction of regressive ideals of feminine behavior and attitude that go much deeper than appearance. . . . Often, features of women's bodies are arranged in representations precisely in order to suggest a particular attitude—dependence or seductiveness or vulnerability, for example. . . . We're not talking about the reduction of women to mere bodies, but about what those bodies *express*.[24]

Too often, what the bodies in the bodybuilding magazine pictorials express is sexual access, titillation, a being-for-others rather than a being-for-self. I am not arguing that it is always the case that such expression is negative, but that in the specific context of bodybuilding such messages undermine the revolutionary potential of female bodybuilders and athletes more generally. "Dependence or seductiveness or vulnerability" can be seen as "regressive ideals of feminine behavior" in the context of athleticism, which is a competitive realm in which sex is not the primary issue, and independence and invulnerability are crucial for winning. Naked, partially, or fully dressed, if athletic female bodies are coded in these ways, any body, including a muscular one, that is posed this way will communicate seductiveness or vulnerability. Conversely, nude or otherwise, posed differently—in ways that communicate power and self-determination, say—these poses would enhance the message of power that a muscular female body already sends. In this specific context, not always, pornographic representations are containment strategies. As Bill Dobbins writes, "When it comes to acceptance of female bodybuilding, I think what we tend to overlook is how revolutionary (and threatening) the whole idea of women with aesthetically developed muscles still is."[25] The *Flex* layouts, designed to promote such acceptance, often try to achieve this aim by presenting female bodybuilders in a porno-   **105**

Backstage access: Fitness competitor Monica Brant
in a milder version of conventions used in the
magazine pictorials. (*Hot Skins Bodywear Catalog*,
Spring 1997)

graphic light, neutralizing the more empowering message that the muscular body sends by positioning it in nonthreatening attitudes of seductiveness, openness, and vulnerability. I am not arguing against sexually appealing images, vulnerability, or openness in general—they are just out of place in an athletic context, in which they are doing cultural work, sending a counter-revolutionary message to the muscular female body's potentially empowering one.

Many, including academic writers on sports, are not in agreement with this position. Women's sports historian Allen Guttmann, for instance, concludes his book with a section on what he calls the "sports and eros" controversy. Guttmann argues that the erotic potential of the athletic body has been recognized at least since ancient Greece, and the contemporary feminism that argues against eroticism falls into a false either/or logic that defeats its own purposes. Why shouldn't we, he argues in a more sophisticated version of the loosen-up argument, appreciate both the athletic female body's eroticism and its athletic performance: "One can gasp at Katarina Witt's skill as a figure skater, shiver with delight at the beauty of her movements, and simultaneously be stirred by the erotic appeal of her gliding, whirling, spinning, leaping figure. Why not have it all?" The point he raises is a good one if we lived in an ideal world where all things were equal and eroticism, particularly female eroticism, wasn't so closely linked with social inequality, and if representations of both male and female athletes tended to follow the same conventions. "Why have so many radical feminists," Guttmann asks, "condemned the men who have admired physically fit women and their sports performances and why have they sought to discourage women eager for that admiration? Might they not, more logically, have demanded women's right to admire—and even to be erotically stimulated by—physically fit men and *their* sports performances?"[26]

As a female athlete who has gotten and enjoyed that admiration for many years, an admiration which has been important to me, I would hardly argue against this aspect of eroticism in sports. Furthermore, I am in complete agreement that it is pleasurable to "admire and be erotically stimulated by physically fit men and *their* sports performances." Most of my football-watching activity, in fact, consists in evaluating their bodies, searching **107**

for well-defined hamstrings and butts among the sea of fat-covered flesh.
Watching the 1996 Summer Olympics was extremely pleasurable, because
of what was for me the erotic beauty of the male sprinters. When British
sprinter Linton Christie was disqualified from the 100-meter dash because
of several false starts my heart went out to him, but the primary thing that
caught my attention was the incredible definition in his back and shoulders,
the deep carving in his abs visible when he tore off his singlet in disgust.
Some of the pole-vaulters had abs and biceps worth hours of watching. I
take great joy in the ability to look at men this way, and even consider, as
Guttmann implies, the ability to do so as an indication of the advancement
of feminist ideals within our culture.

This does not mean, however, that the representations of athletes are
equal, and that the men are now equally portrayed in terms of their eroticism. There are turns in this direction, such as the July 1996 issue of *Life*
magazine, which featured naked male portraits of powerlifter Mark Henry,
sprinter Michael Johnson, long jumper and sprinter Carl Lewis, diver Russ
Bertram, and the U.S. men's water polo team alongside naked fencer Sharon
Monplaisir, diver Mary Ellen Clark, sprinters Gwen Torrence and Gail De-
vers, heptathlete Jackie Joyner-Kersee, volleyball player Holly McPeak,
and Margo Thien and Nathalie Schneyder from the synchronized swimming
team.[27] In fact, with the exception of the water polo and synchronized
swimming shots, which contained elements of traditional gender-role ste-
reotyping, I found the photographs paradigmatic examples of the kind of
representation that could work to further ideals of gender equality. While
the polo team shot ("The Bod Squad," the good-natured boys-will-be-boys'
rebelliousness of fraternity pranks with the team members laughing jocu-
larly, standing completely naked except for the water-polo balls they held
in front of their genitals) and the naked synchronized swimmers ("Mer-
maids," splayed underwater, upside down in full waterproof makeup across
the America flag, arms crossed over their breasts and legs gracefully bent
to conceal their genitals) seemed to play to sex-role stereotypes, the other
shots were gorgeous studies of erotic beauty and athleticism. Men and
women were shot in similar ways, with similar lighting and positioning, and
in no case were the bodies positioned in the seductive I'll-do-whatever-
108 you-want postures so characteristic of the muscle magazines today.

The cover photo of Gwen Torrence, for instance (a figure study from the waist up), positions Torrence in profile, her arms in front of her chest, her hands clenched in fists, her head back and her eyes closed. The light falls on muscles in her shoulders, on her forehead and cheek, on her muscular chest and stomach. It is a strikingly beautiful shot, erotic but not necessarily seductive, for Torrence's body is not offered up to the viewer. It is instead self-possessed and self-contained, an object of admiration but not consumption. The power and grace of her muscular lines are beautiful, but it is clear that that beauty belongs to itself—it is there, irretrievably present, whether the viewer engages with it or no. Its sensuality is unquestionable but beside the point, there but not the main focus of the picture.

By contrast, the do-me photos (like that on the cover of the February 1997 swimsuit issue of *Flex*) beg for the viewer's gaze and sexualized response. The cover features fitness competitors Michelle Bellini and Karen Hulse, and bodybuilder Ericca Kern, arms around one another and provocatively posed rising out of a pool. A triptych of pleading flesh, the positions of the bodies—the curve of Bellini's and Hulse's buttocks, pushed out to form a straight line with their shoulders, bookend Kern, whose similarly extended buttocks rest against the curve of Bellini's stomach, Bellini's breast fitting into the indentation of Kern's waist—are deliberately sexual, their sensuality the point, not the by-product. Hulse and Bellini look directly into the camera and smile large smiles; Kern's lips are pressed into a sultry pout to match the Cleopatra-esque jeweled headdress. The colors, the angles, the lighting, all create a picture that asks the viewer directly to respond to it in a sexual way. Sex is the point, not athleticism, not these women as individuals. Any self-presence is subordinated to the sexual appeal, the direct address to the reader, the not-so-subtle yank at the groin chain that the picture performs. While pictorials of male bodybuilders in the magazines are repeatedly shot in the style characteristic of the *Life* feature, it is only rarely that pictorials of female bodybuilders and fitness women are shot in this style rather than in the style of pornography.[28] Because he publicly disavows photographing women bodybuilders in this style while his work sometimes seems pornographic, the work of Bill Dobbins reveals the difficulty of separating athleticism from sex in the popular imagination.

S C H I Z O P H R E N I C   L I B E R A T I O N :   T H E   W O R K
O F   B I L L   D O B B I N S

Just in time for Christmas 1994, Bill Dobbins, longtime photographer for
and contributor to the Weider bodybuilding magazines, came out with *The
Women*, the first book-length photographic study of women bodybuilders
since Mapplethorpe's *Lady: Lisa Lyon*. Mapplethorpe's work, published in
1983, shows just how far women's bodybuilding has come, for Lyon's body
is not muscular enough to count as a bodybuilder's by today's standards. A
normalized image of femininity, with her thinly muscled arms and legs with
little definition on striation, today Lyon seems like someone who works out
regularly but lacks the development of a bodybuilder.

Dobbins has a tougher subject. He tackles the contemporary scene,
striving to show "a cultural phenomenon without precedent—women attempting to develop the ultimate degree of muscle size, shape, definition
and proportion," and that "muscles on women can indeed be beautiful."[29]
Featuring a foreword by Arnold Schwarzenegger and published by Artisan
Press, Dobbins's book is marketed for mass public consumption. His aim
is to normalize the female bodybuilder physique, to orchestrate its image
in such a way that it will be appealing to a larger audience.

As I contended earlier, despite arguments that athletic bodies create
impossible new ideals for women, helping to create a wider audience for
female bodybuilding and encouraging more women to lift weights can be
seen as progressive aims. Yet this audience expansion is largely attempted
in Dobbins's work, as well as in that of many others, through stereotypical
sexualization, despite the fact that he is publicly supportive of female bodybuilders, and makes a distinction between what he does—"figure studies"—and what some of the other photographers do—"standard T & A."[30]
While I am reluctant to take issue with one of the few people in a position
of visibility in the bodybuilding industry who is willing to speak out in favor of female bodybuilders and who even articulates some feminist ideals,
there is often a split in his work. He does nude studies that are breathtak-
ingly beautiful and whose primary purpose is not to sell sex or stereotyped
views of femininity and race but rather the beauty of the athletic body. He
also does studies that—given props, angles, lighting, and point of view—

are sometimes stereotyped so much, making use of such clichéd sexual fantasies, that they might be taken as camp, yet clearly are not intended this way. Dobbins's publicly supportive, even feminist, stance is undercut by work that falls in the latter category and is indicative of larger cultural trends that employ feminist rhetoric for reactionary aims such as advertisements that proclaim a 'new woman for the nineties' who has returned to traditional gender roles.[31]

The stereotypical strain in Dobbins's work is even more disappointing when considered in the context of his interpretation of the turn toward blatant sexualization of female bodybuilders and fitness women in the bodybuilding magazine industry. In an Internet posting, he analyzes the inaugural swimsuit issue of *Flex*, which appeared in February 1996:

> As somebody who is a genuine fan of what Jerry Kindela has done with *Flex*, I was understandably disappointed in the recent swimsuit layout. It wasn't that the women used in the layout weren't beautiful or didn't have great bodies—both fitness and bodybuilding women—it was the quality of the photos, the poses, the overall sense that what I was seeing was, frankly, T & A jerkoff material. I've worked very hard over the years to photograph muscular women in such a way as to make them look attractive, aesthetic, and even sexy without compromising or apologizing for their physical development. The *Flex* layout, I thought, was a big step backward.[32]

To have a voice as influential as Dobbins speak out against this conservative turn in the bodybuilding industry, labeling it "a big step backward," is significant and could potentially help to affect what gets featured in the magazines with which he is affiliated, primarily *Muscle and Fitness* and *Flex*. That his analysis of the pictorial comes down to the layout's "poses, the overall sense that what I was seeing, was, frankly, T & A jerkoff material," marks one powerful dissident voice against the many voices that have accepted this turn uncritically. What I find confusing, however, when looking at the swimsuit layouts Dobbins criticizes and at some of his own images in *The Women* or in other *Flex* layouts, is what he thinks distinguishes his work from that which he criticizes. While many of his images clearly do not fall into the category of "T & A jerkoff material," due to the poses he chooses, the props that he uses, and the areas he emphasizes through lighting, I am not sure he can claim that his images always make muscular women "look attractive, aesthetic, and even sexy without compromising or apologizing for their physical development." Indeed, some of Dobbins's images, as I will show, work to neutralize what he calls the potentially revolutionary effect of female physical development.

Dobbins is inconsistent: sometimes his representations walk a similar line to the *Life* pictorials; sometimes they don't. The images that seem most transgressive are those without props, for the props Dobbins uses tend to situate his subjects in cultural contexts that are anything but transgressive. One propless shot in *The Women*, however—a pairing of Leilani Dalumpines and Drorit Kernes—is an aesthetically gorgeous piece of work that, while constructing the female body as both beautiful and sexual, also clearly emphasizes its strength and the beauty of that strength. Shot in black and white, the women are posed against a neutral background and foreground, a construction-paper text's surface made to serve as a reflector that mottles shadow and light in a way similar to how the light plays over the surface of the women's skin. The women are back to back, Kernes in the fore, linked by their muscular arms. They create a fantastic sculpture: human limbs intertwined and solid like some visionary tree. Dalumpines's straddled legs form the roots, framing those of Kernes, so that all that is visible of her body is her left forearm and facial silhouette, the back of a muscular calf on one side, an angulated hamstring and calf on the other, the lines forming an intricate triangular base to support Kernes. Kernes's legs, placed together, form a tripod extending from the flat plains of hip, stomach, and torso, breasts forming a perfect counterpoint to her muscularly separated shoulder, whose lines extend perfectly to the biceps on her right arm. Her head is turned in profile as well, the line of her jaw and delicate bone structure of her face the shaped equivalent of her musculature. The lines of the bodies are clean, even stark, an effect that is heightened by the black and white. The emphasis is on the beauty of the lines of the muscles, not the women's sexuality. They don't necessarily solicit the viewer's sexual response but rather his/her aesthetic appreciation: **112** these are beautiful bodies, needing nothing outside to complete them. Gorgeous, intact, invulnerable, whole—the image of female integrity created by Dobbins, while it may not represent the actuality of many women's lives, creates an aesthetic ideal breathtaking in its beauty, perhaps inspiring a sense in some of possibility and satisfaction that such a vision of female embodiment now exists, a welcome alternative in a culture that valorizes diversity and choice but often offers only standardized images to choose from.

At other points, however, Dobbins's aim is to take the "potentially intimidating physique" of the female bodybuilder and make it "attractive to males" in a traditional way. While making women bodybuilders attractive to men is not necessarily an antifeminist gesture (as I have repeatedly emphasized, contrary to popular media representations, "feminist" does not necessarily mean antimale or antisex), sexualizing female bodybuilders *in the particular way* Dobbins sexualizes them effectively subverts any disruptive potential of this new version of the feminine form. He writes that his intent is "to do photos that are glamorous and sexy but also focus on the athletic quality of the bodies involved," and this is an admirable aim, combining as it does the traditional with the new, an effective way of selling the new to a larger market.[33] But, crucially, as some of his own work has shown, there are other photographic methods than the soft-porn conventions Dobbins sometimes employs.

Despite the prominent triceps and striated glutes of his subjects, Dobbins sometimes creates all too familiar images of just-do-me femininity. "I am not strong," the women in his images cry out. "I just happen to look that way." Unlike his stated attempt to present "muscular women in such a way as to make them look attractive, aesthetic, and even sexy without compromising or apologizing for their physical development," many of his images beg forgiveness for muscle, and promise that despite appearances, these women are available to and malleable into whatever fantasy wants to mold them. For the images do appeal to stereotypical fantasies of all kinds: Erika Andersch—one knee up on the weight bench, face turned away and glutes in the air—gives the viewer rear access. Latia Del Riviero, standing in full rear presentation, grips handcuffs above her head. Suzan Kaminga, one leg in the air, arches back over a wooden horse, with the focus on her breasts, flat stomach, and leg spread. Debbie Kruck, in another rear presentation but shot from the side, is shown riding this same horse. Lenda Murray, **113** sleeping head down by the sandy sea, thong viciously splitting her buttocks. Dorothy Herndon and Debbie Muggli, in tattered black leather and chains. Debbie Kruck, again, on her back on the sofa, twisting her buttocks to the camera. Nikki Fuller, the cover model, in Viking breastplate and chastity belt, holding a thick steel-link chain. Laura Creavalle, leatherthonged in the stocks. Sharon Bruneau crouched naked behind a wooden lion, the lines of her body mimicking its pose. Diana Dennis with Egyptianstyle veils over her face and wire-mesh bra circling her breasts. Suzan Kaminga, back-arched over a mirror, the perfect image of self-satisfied narcissism. And on and on for a hundred twenty-two pages. Constructed and framed by these blatantly prurient references, the fact of the women's physical development seems very much beside the point.

Signature Dobbins, incorporating motifs that recur throughout his photographic oeuvre, include the woman-as-or-with-guitar. A *Flex* layout of Suzan Kaminga poses her next to a series of guitars, the lines of her body meant to mimic those of the instruments. Debbie Muggli's pictorial poses her in black leather and heels, electric guitar between her legs. A shot from *The Women* provides a naked frontal view, acoustic guitar held over one breast, head thrown back so you can only see only her throat. Two pages later, Leilani Dalumpines is shot from behind, golden spike-heeled legs in straddle position, a golden electric guitar extended from her left arm, amp in the background just on the other side of her left calf. Then there's that ubiquitous wooden lion and wooden horse, in both book and *Flex* layouts. In various stages of splay Sue Price is posed on it, Suzan Kaminga, Debbie Kruck, Sharon Bruneau . . . We get it, Bill, we get it, we really do.

When Dobbins publicly claims a very different intent and has furthermore created images like that of Leilani Dalumpines and Drorit Kernes analyzed above, one is left with a sense of confusion when faced with images like this. Why does he employ such traditional narratives if he is interested in more revolutionary ones? Why in pictorials like the November 1995 *Flex* layout of Ericca Kern does he combine beautiful, powerful images of Kern with images that are so traditionally cheesecake they are almost comic? The pictorial "Timid No More" begins with an full-page naked image of Kern turned in profile from the upper torso just under where her breasts would be to the bottom of her thighs just above her knee. The

S-curve of her back runs cleanly into the inverted **C** of her buttocks, from there to the solidity of her hamstrings and thighs. Her intercostal muscles, just under ribs, are clearly visible, and blend into the flat plane of stomach which forms a sideways **V** with the gradual hill of her quadricep. No question—this is a beautiful, strong, muscular body, in every way a positive image of what bodybuilding can do for women. But the rest of the pictorial is not shot in the same style. On the remaining pages, Kern is shown in white platform shoes with spike heels, with a matching two-strand pearl bracelet and pearl drop earrings, and in a couple of shots she is draped in a short, white diaphanous robe with white fur around the sleeves and collar. In one image Kern stretches out on a white bearskin rug, cuddling a large white teddy bear. Aesthetically as well as ideologically, the first image is compromised by the slight tawdriness of the others, and this compromise is characteristic of Dobbins's work as a whole.

Bodybuilding as a practice (how it's done) and discourse (ideas about how it's done, like those seen in photography) has a strange but forceful relationship to the idea of authority, to American hucksterism at its finest, and to what French psychoanalytic theorist Jacques Lacan calls "the subject presumed to know." Elizabeth Grosz summarizes this concept by saying that, for Lacan, "love is an investment in the other as the subject supposed to know."[34] In other words, desire is often motivated by the idea that an other has some answers we do not that could be valuable to us in some way, and our interest in that person has to do with the answers they might give us. Gyms are a beehive of people looking for answers, and the photographer is a particularly good example of the subject presumed to know, for a number of reasons. As the artist whose vision shapes the presentation of the body—since it is the artist who is in control, who has the power to make the body look good or not good—the photographer partakes in a long cultural tradition that venerates the artist as separate from and higher than his or her subjects. The artist occupies a hierarchical relation to that subject—he/she is the creative genius who takes the base matter and gives it shape, makes some higher cultural product from raw materials, unshaped nature. As such, the photographer performs significant cultural work, placing his/her subjects within a cultural context that gives them meaning, that interprets them for the viewer. While Dobbins declares positive intentions, and often produces work which lives up to those intentions, he also often instructs the viewer to shape women's shaped bodies in reactionary ways.

Waiting for Bodot: Bodybuilding Lowenburg Style

While Dobbins sometimes sexualizes the female bodybuilder in ways problematic for sports photography but in line with dominant trends in the industry, quietly and on his own, Pennsylvania art photographer Bill Lowenburg often desexualizes the female bodybuilder in such a way that her gender is incidental. Lowenburg has been chronicling Northeastern bodybuilding shows for years, building a massive archive that is an unforgiving testament to bodybuilding in all its hubris. The pictorial equivalent of Sam Fussell's 1991 industry exposé, *Muscle: Confessions of an Unlikely Bodybuilder*, Lowenburg's work is relentless in revealing that which his subjects would probably most like to keep hidden: bald ambition, tearing insecurities, and the terrifying and comical emptiness that Samuel Beckett once chronicled, in a very different context, in the modernist classic *Waiting for Godot*. Like Vladimir and Estragon, Lowenburg's subjects are waiting for the big break, that indescribable something that is will endow their lives with purpose and meaning. Bodybuilding is their Godot, a reason to get up in the morning, a way to make some scratches on, as William Faulkner put it in *Absalom, Absalom!* "the blank face of oblivion to which we are all doomed." [35]

The visual performative of so much modernist despair, pathos, grand ambition, and insecurity, Lowenburg's work sometimes partakes of a high modernist vision, or at least some characteristic features of that vision. His stance in relation to his subjects is that of the aloof master, "examining them through an attitude of detachment," the one who has not gotten sucked in, who knows better and has resisted. "I'm not laughing at them," he writes, "but neither am I buying the ticket." [36] In characteristic modernist style, he refuses both the mythologies of bodybuilding and public acclaim for himself: "Sometimes people who hear about my bodybuilding project . . . get all excited about the possibility of it becoming a well-known book. . . . I just stopped caring about it in those terms. If I did care about it I'd be just another believer in the myths about photography, not to mention bodybuilding, rather than one who is aware of them, and examining them through an attitude of detachment."

Lowenburg is a maverick in the contemporary context. While he is fully aware that "an attitude of detachment" is itself a mythology, this mythology has powerful effects on the choices he makes in his work. Stalwart in his repudiation of the postmodern ideological fetish defined by Slavoj Zizek ("I know, but all the same"), Lowenburg's austerity and refusal to produce images the public would be likely to consume ("My work is virtually unmarketable, and that's pretty much OK with me, . . . I have a job, a good one," he writes) relies on the modernist caveats about the detachment of the artist as a necessary condition for the production of high art. Yet the images he creates are so startling, so revelatory of the absurdity of his subjects, the viewer can't help but empathize with them. While it would be easy to speculate that Lowenburg is alienated from his subjects in the same way much of high modernist work in photography and other arts seems alienated from teeming humanity, the very strength of the absurdity in Lowenburg's images creates an empathy that is missing from many modernist texts. Lowenburg's aim may be the revelation of the absurdity of life, and the absurdity of bodybuilding as a pursuit—be it the male or female version— but that very absurdity creates a bond with the viewer that is irresistibly moving. Strangely cold, his work nonetheless *humanizes* in the deepest possible way. A true gender maverick in the way in which he levels cultural conventions of sexual difference, Lowenburg's is a genderless world where ghosts pose in costumes of masculinity, femininity, or just plain egotism. One photograph—of a woman who competes on an amateur level in both bodybuilding and fitness—puts conventions of masculinity and femininity on display in a way that denaturalizes them. An experienced poser, the woman smiles for the camera with the hollowness of beauty contest poise, achieving the standardized femininity that is aware of itself being looked at and presents itself to solicit that gaze. She is confident that she will receive approval, striking the pose with such ease that it becomes clear she is detached from it: she knows she is striking a pose. The pose does not define her. Masculinity—defined as the source of the gaze—is captured by Lowenburg through the inclusion of an onlooker, who watches her posing. The camera catches his look, interested but appraising and a bit **117**

Seeing yourself being seen. (Photograph by Bill Lowenburg)

skeptical, his eyebrow slightly raised. He stands leaning against a wall with his hands on his hips, elevated slightly above the woman by his place in the frame. Compared to her poise, he is sloppy; because he is caught in the act of looking (putting masculinity as looking itself on the stage to be looked at and found lacking), his position as the one who appraises is dubious. Here Lowenburg does a kind of postmodern cultural work that denaturalizes masculinity and femininity, constructing them as poses we strike and believe in only if we are fools. Bodybuilding and fitness competitions, as his images show, are an exemplary performative of this drama of belief and nonbelief. Some subjects are savvy and even cynical in their enactment of the pose, some are heartrending in their sincere belief. It is here Lowenburg betrays his own complicity in the drama: the position of detached master assumed beyond the frame is itself a pose, but one he must believe in in order to produce his work. The conventions he mocks are also mocked by the very subjects who perform them, just as he mocks photographic convention—but he and his subjects adhere to them anyway, faced on the other side with a void from which there is no turning.

This gives the viewer an understanding of gender and bodies, and why we construct what we construct, and why we see what we see that is more complicated than anything present in Dobbins's work. What is terrifying in Lowenburg's world is his uncanny sensitivity to how much our poses—detached from them though we may be—mean to those who strike them, a sense of how those poses, though ontologically meaningless, are nonetheless all we have and create complicated patterns that join us. The relationship between the woman and the man who looks at her putting herself on display is one such connection, staging the theater of sexual attractiveness and sexual response, starkly rendering the complicated narrative of what people value in themselves and what they sense is valued by others and how this affects their physical embodiment, their display. Lowenburg renders the terror behind the image as well as the image itself.

Lowenburg understandably exposes more thoroughly than any industry insider those aspects of bodybuilding which are absurd: the tearing insecurities, the emotional vagaries that bring this absurdity into play. His choice of subject matter is apt, for bodybuilding may be that absurdity's best witness, the vivid visual documentation of human ambition at its most naked, **119** most pathetic. With that pathos is the dignity of the subject who knows his or her own subjection to the most disquieting aspects of lived experience, but does it anyway. Through much of his bodybuilding narrative, Lowenburg has chronicled those who know their own absurdity but who keep trying to overcome it even though they know it may be a futile task, as well as those who still fervently believe. He may assume that bodybuilders are "people playing out roles they are unaware of, or are only partially aware of," but this assumption is strangely undermined by the pathos of the images in his work. Lowenburg is himself more than "partially aware" of the role he is playing as photographer, someone whose images are informed by his particular views of, among other things, art and photography and the role of the artist. "I try to photograph life as I find it," Lowenburg writes, and it is clear that he finds it indescribably sad, dignified, and absurd simultaneously. If he "regards *all* photography to be a type of fiction, including, and perhaps even especially, documentary photographs," he has also been instrumental in bringing his subjects' most cherished enabling fictions to view.

In the closing paragraph of *Bodyscape: Art, Modernity, and the Ideal Figure*, art historian Nicholas Mirzoeff identifies a shift in twentieth-century conceptions of the artist from what he calls the modern spectator to the postmodern witness. Art, writes Mirzoeff,

> exists in that space between the memory of the witness and those documentary facts that the historian accepts as "objective." It seeks to explore and make visible that indefinable perfect moment, knowable only from instant to instant, in which a person becomes a witness. The choice of Auschwitz as a location for witnessing is not coincidental. The experiences of the late twentieth century make the impartial, rarefied distance of the modern observer or spectator an untenable position. There is no optical neutrality to be had from art, and if there were, it would no longer have anything to offer. The modern spectator must give way to the postmodern witness. Welcome to the stand.[37]

Mirzoeff highlights what is most characteristic in Lowenburg's work—why, finally, despite his "modern spectator" position of detachment from his subjects, he is a postmodern witness to their greatest attempts at making meaning. Mirzoeff uses "witness" in the sense of testimony, of speaking from personal engagement and knowledge. If art exists "in that space between the memory of the witness and . . . documentary facts," Lowenburg has, almost in spite of himself, formed an emotional connection with his subjects that does witness. He explicitly defines his artist practice against such connections, because, in true modernist form, he sees connections themselves as illusions, but his detachment often fails him to positive effect. "Larry Fink, my teacher in photography," he writes, "stressed trying to have what he called a sensual empathy for the people we photograph. Many of his pictures are about the ties that bind people together. I see my work as being more about the barriers that exist between us, and the artificiality of most of the bonds people subscribe to." Yet it is through the revelation of that artificiality that he creates the strongest bond possible: a shared knowledge that we have only ourselves to make meaning, and any joint project performed with another is then even all the more precious.

In this statement Lowenburg articulates the modernist orientation he wants to inform his artistic practice, but which never ultimately does, for this orientation is incommensurate with the complexity of the subjects he studies. According to modernist view, if bonds are artificial illusions and the photographer wants to reveal this truth, then he would necessarily stand aloof from and superior to his subjects, occupying the position of the "subject presumed to know" who sees the higher truths of an alienated world without meaningful connections that his subjects stupidly misinterpret as meaningful. This view finds quintessential expression in Marlow, the narrator in Joseph Conrad's 1899 modernist classic, *Heart of Darkness*, who for a time denies the meaning in human connections and the activities of daily life:

> I found myself back in the sepulchral city resenting the sight of people hurrying through the streets to filch a little money from each other, to devour their infamous cookery, to gulp their unwholesome beer, to dream their insignificant and silly dreams. . . . They trespassed upon my thoughts. They were intruders whose knowledge of life was to me an irritating pretense because I felt so sure they could not possibly know the things I knew. I had no particular desire to enlighten them, but I had

some difficulty in restraining myself from laughing in their faces so full of stupid importance.[38]

Perhaps in what he intends, Lowenburg sees bodybuilders as what the pilgrims are to Marlow: beings in need of enlightenment who dream "insignificant and silly dreams," bearing "faces so full of stupid importance." Many of Lowenburg's photos show just these faces. A typical shot catches a male bodybuilder backstage, flexing before posedown, his eyes on his competition and his expression sure that he is king cream puff. Shot after shot reveals bodybuilding's "insignificant and silly dreams," rows of men lined up, biceps in unison flexing, faces twisted with effort and illusory self-assurance. Looked at quickly, it would seem that Lowenburg "feels sure" that bodybuilders "cannot possibly know the things that [he] knows"—the futility of those dreams, their ultimate meaninglessness, all that flexing and preening, actions staged against the backdrop of the laughing void and stark mortality, tales told by idiots, full of sound and fury, signifying nothing, where everywhere the illusion of progress rings out like a hideous song. Yet the degree of absurdity backfires on modernist intention. Lowenburg's work becomes that of the postmodern witness through the bond it creates with the viewer, who cannot help but feel drawn to the subject's pitiful attempts to make meaning, attempts that resonate all too chillingly with the viewer's own.

Vintage Lowenburg includes an unflattering shot of Mr. Olympia Dorian Yates, shot from behind, head tapering off into shadows, enormous back flatly in the center of the frame like a huge boulder testifying to countless gym hours and eventually deadly steroid abuse—and for what? A hulking gray presence, arms slung from bilateral lats like so many pounds of ham. Two men, deadly serious, tugging a towel between them like middle-aged pups, warming their triceps while another man arches his lats back, pumping himself up in the visual space between them. A woman, also deadly serious, tugging on a towel, her eyes fixed in the distance with a kind of frozen desperation, her mouth drawn in a strange twist of fear, hilarity, and hope; another woman pumping up behind her—beautiful muscular bodies in stark contrast to the peeling paint and decaying wood of their surroundings, betraying transparent longings for immortality stripped from them

Against the backdrop of the laughing void: Vintage Lowenburg. (Photograph by Bill Lowenburg)

even as they stand in gleaming muscular splendor. A mustachioed Cheech, leopard-print headband lifting off from his unfocused eyes, biceps slung up in self-importance against a backdrop of old wires and exit signs he doesn't seem able to see. A blond woman, darkly tanned, her white bikini picking up the whites of the bloated cartoon balloon faces floating on the wall behind her like so many pitiful bodybuilder dreams, those deluded souls trying to take up a stand, make a mark against backdrops that every moment scream their absurdity, their puny selves, their delusions, their heartrending, pointless futility. A black man, pecs distended, hands curled up all around the weight he will heave, mouth twisted into an agonized scream as if he were plagued by himself, his shadow following him so close behind. Three beautifully swollen flexed men looking down at their feet, heads hung in some muscular concentration that wills them into being even as it erases them. A woman bodybuilder, flexed and beautifully striated against a concrete wall scrawled with slurs of paint and random graffiti.

Lowenburg is relentless. Yet a perspective of detachment is itself ideo-logical, a strategy in a game of power plays that works to elevate those who hold it. As Lowenburg's work ultimately makes clear (and as Dobbins's work doesn't even begin to make sense of), detachment is a particular point of view, a ploy that turns Lowenburg and other artists into "subjects pre-sumed to know" rather than giving greater insight into truth. Subjects presumed to know claim to have access to the truth of human absurdity that others willfully ignore or aren't aware of, making themselves into objects of desire for those who want also to know. Just pretend to have answers that your subjects don't have and you will be sought out. Detachment may work as a kind of sadistic manipulative ploy, but it cuts out as much perspective as it fits in. It strips its subjects of a humanity that can be more than absurd, a kind of sublimity in daily abjection. Like bodybuilders pushing absurdity to its furthest extreme, Lowenburg is no longer detached, and reveals that the relentless human drama of haves and have-nots boils down to the des-peration and desire that most give life to the daily scrabble for meaning.

A viewer has to observe Lowenburg's work carefully, spend some time with it. What might initially appear to be contempt for and detachment from his subjects becomes an engagement on repeated viewing, and that

124 seeming detachment should not be mistaken for neutrality and therefore for the truth of bodybuilding. Although it is an old commonplace that it is possible for an artist to act as a neutral recorder, most recent work in cultural theory would show that the way one finds life is heavily inflected by the particularity of one's own daily scrabble. Lowenburg has done important work in the bodybuilding chronicle, but the story is all there only for the patient viewer, the viewer who will return to him again and again. What initially appears is only half the story, for Lowenburg at first seems too distant from his subjects to feel their greatness as well as their absurdity, the achievement of their efforts as well as their futility. Like the anthropologist for whom his subjects remain unspeakably other, initially Lowenburg seems not to have given bodybuilders the dignity that is their due. In all its absurdity, bodybuilding can be a testament to human possibility, to those aspects of the will which refuse to accept the limitations of things as they are and to hold out for, to help create and shape, something else, for no further purpose than the creation of something out of nothing. This is the purpose Bataille's concept of sovereignty explores, the sheer meaning generated through performing an action that has no tangible use outside of doing something that is purely your own, that marks the limits of your being. For many bodybuilders—and this Lowenburg does not fully appreciate because he has refused to form empathetic connections with us—our motivations for building our bodies are much like what he describes as his motivation for taking photographs: "For the foreseeable future [photography] will be an important tool in the job of trying to understand life. On the most fundamental level I believe it is an impossible task, but that it is still important to try."

Two photos in particular do try, and approach the condition of postmodern witness. The first shot (reproduced on the cover) is of a woman, Amelia Altemare, who has been lifting, but at this moment she is sitting, caught in a moment between her sets. Her knees are bent toward her chest, her arms rest on them. She is quiet, still, lost in thought. Her eyes are almost unbearably expressive, her focus away from the camera, staring into some nothingness off to the right, testifying to some sense of pain and futility she has remained strong in the face of, a hint of curiosity mixed with sadness, amusement, resignation. She knows what she is doing, and Lowenburg knows she knows, and his heart is with her. No detached master this time; there is an understanding between photographer and subject that draws the viewer toward her, toward an understanding of her activity, what this bodybuilding thing is about. Her expression of quiet dignity testifies to a strength in perfect conjunction with the muscles in her arms, her composure in the face of the darkness behind and to either side of her an indication of what bodybuilding can do: build a provisional fortress against nothing, forge a shape, define a presence in the world. Lowenburg witnesses to this, inviting the viewer into her life, into the irrefutable fact of her existence. Altemare is self-contained, separate from the viewer's gaze in a way that forces the one to recognize her, to understand her condition, and to make links between that condition and the viewer's own, links that retain the recognition of her discrete being. She's beautiful, sexual, her dark hair and full lips and defined arms could easily signify sexual appeal, but it isn't just sexuality the viewer responds to, for neither the pose, lighting, nor her expression solicit this response.

Even when Altemare is posing in the mirror, as she is in the photo facing page 1, the absurdity marking some of the other photos is not evident here. She looks at herself with the same kind of conscious self-reflection she shows in the cover shot, appraising her body critically, but without the inflated seriousness of some of the others. The space in the photo contributes to her dignity and sense of proportion, for while she is the center of the frame, the gym looms large around her, the steel arms of a bench press framing her on either side. Hemmed in, but fully present, played upon by shadows but standing distinct, she is an ironic anthem to the kind of detachment and self-consciousness that are the requisite conditions of nineties selfhood. Bodybuilding, which in its literality and egoistic preening often seems like a holdover from the eighties, becomes in this shot a kind of negotiation between self and world, body and gaze that leaves the viewer again with a sense of Altemare's irrefutable presence nonetheless inflected by a conscious awareness of its precariousness.

But these photos are not characteristic of most work that has been done. There has yet to emerge a bodybuilding photographer who is fully a postmodern witness, which is why Dobbins and Lowenburg ultimately fail to capture the complexity of bodybuilding in all its pathos and dignity, the full range of its possibilities. Dobbins is too market oriented, playing to the cultural fetish with the visible image, and the female body's privileged place in that fetishization, the place of enticement and promise and heady desire, the place that offers some unspeakable fulfillment always deferred. His relation to his subjects is mostly that of a consumer culture Pygmalion to his Galateas, the shaped bodies he tries to package and bring to life in specifically marketable ways. He makes use of conventions familiar from other contexts for which he sometimes shoots, like *Penthouse* magazine. Lowenburg often plays to the high modernist standards of detachment as truth telling, a place that can make the artist alienated from his subjects. The truth that Lowenburg tells, like all truths, is only partial, and his work is at its best when it gets away from him, when the absurdity of his images crosses the line into empathy and draw the viewer into explicit relationship and metaphysical identification with his subjects. But while Lowenburg is the bodybuilder's most remarkable chronicler yet, he has seen only part of us. In spite of his most strongly worded intentions, the very concept that has formed the basis of his artistic practice—detachment, the denial of an empathetic bond with his subjects—is what brings him the closest to us.

Why does any of this matter? What is at stake? Would more positive photographic representations of female bodybuilders along the lines I have described of Dobbins's more revolutionary work and of Lowenburg's chilling ontologies really effect anything? Is it the case that, as Marcia Ian writes in an Internet posting,

> even if we were to persuade the muscle mags to have more pictures of and for us . . . this will not change anything? Attitudes toward women "in general" will only change, if they ever do, as a result of more actual women having actual power in the world, power to make important DECISIONS affecting the way things happen in government, the media, business, sports, the arts, education, etc. Having a few more pictures of women with powerful bodies won't do diddly.[39]

It is part of my own feeble attempt to make meaning that I have to believe that Ian's view, though true in many ways, is not the final truth about **127**

Bodybuilder Shelley Beattie, deflated a bit for this TwinLab ad, but still doing cultural work for images of female strength. (*All Natural Muscular Development*, May 1997)

these questions of representation and meaning, critical cultural analysis and lived experience. In my narrative, strong women walking around in the world every day, showing themselves, acting out of that physical, emotional, and spiritual strength, *do something*. Pictures of us that show that strength do something, too.

I remember how I felt the first time I saw pictures of Shelley Beattie in *Muscle and Fitness* in the early nineties, the excitement, the curious leaping in my chest. This, I thought, is something I can be. *This* would give expression to what I am. I *expanded*. Haunted by the femininity police, I had previously remained within the boundaries of acceptable femininity, lifting daily but careful never to build too much bulk. Her pictures gave me permission to build myself up, a sense of possibility I didn't have before I saw her. Surprise of surprises and joy of joys: the wider my lats, the more chinups I could do, the stronger I became, the more I spoke up for myself in my life outside the gym. That Beattie's pictures were out in the world made me stronger.

And I remember how I felt when these pictures started to go retro in 1993, when bodybuilders in workout gear lifting weights were replaced by bodybuilders in lingerie spreading themselves over chairs: diminished. My stomach lurched. The world got a little smaller. Choked up. Pictures *do something*. Female bodybuilders do something. We get into the cultural imagination and make it stick, make it grind itself up, choke on its own images, narratives, fears. Literally, figuratively, we are expansive. Photography that witnesses our struggle extends our space in the world, offers a chance to do our time differently, to participate daily in a self-creation that confounds the voices of the femme police who say, *You must stop here, stop here, stop here.* To return to Mirzoeff's categories, I believe that today, in the midst of images of Madonna with child, shards of bombed abortion clinics, skinny, don't-give-a-fuck Calvin Klein models, and bodybuilders decked out for the fitness mags in lingerie and leather gloves, it is all the more crucial for artists who represent bodybuilding to be postmodern witnesses. For our culture ever to understand bodybuilding—what it is, what it can do, the lives it can save and the worlds it can build—we need witnesses who speak to the ways bodybuilding acts out some of our **129** culture's most moving and basic desires. We need engaged images that reveal those desires, rather than the images that proceed from modern spectators who remain detached from their subjects, presenting them as sexual spectacle or sideshow freaks. There are bonds, far too long denied, that must be recognized.

5

Loving
Mr. Hyde

Rethinking Monstrosity

In Praise of Monsters

His face seemed to change and his eyes grew dark with a look in them that was not like Master, but black and full of rage, and his lips, which were parted, seemed to swell and darken. He was so haggard and his eyes, though filled with rage, seemed also to be weary, full of pleading as well.

> VALERIE MINER, *Mary Reilly: The Untold Story of Dr. Jekyll and Mr. Hyde*

"No," I would say—I knew what I would say. "I have made a terrible mistake. Forgive me." I said it, looking at her, seeing the hatred in her eyes—and feeling my own hate spring up to meet it. Again the giddy change, the remembering, the sickening swing back to hate.

> JEAN RHYS, *Wide Sargasso Sea*

A monster is always outside the human community, beyond the pale, what people react to with revulsion and hate, the frenzied crowd pursuing Frankenstein's creation with sticks and flames. Enforcing the limit of what is deemed human, punishing excess. Monster. Something misformed, misshapen. Psychologically, emotionally, physically out of line with the ideal, too far down the continuum:

131

Monster—1 a. an animal or plant of abnormal form or structure b: one who deviates from normal or acceptable behavior or character 2: a threatening force 3 a: an animal of strange or terrifying shape b: one unusually large for its kind 4: something monstrous, esp: a person of unnatural or extreme ugliness, deformity, wickedness, or cruelty

Monstrosity—1 a: a malformation of a plant or animal b: something deviating from the normal: freak 2: the quality or state of being monstrous 3 a: an object of great and often frightening size, force, or complexity b: an excessively bad or shocking example

Monstrous—1: strange, unnatural 2: having extraordinary often overwhelming size 3: having the qualities or appearance of a monster 4 a: extraordinarily ugly or vicious: horrible b: shockingly wrong or ridiculous 5: deviating greatly from the natural form or character: abnormal 6: very great—used as an intensive.[1]

We draw lines to transgress them. No monsters without lines. Definitions of normalcy draw lines like the plastic surgeon's grease pencil cutting away sections on the image of your face, lopping off inches, discarding skin: "The reality of those black grease-pencil lines invokes the use of surgical procedures that literally cut into the face."[2] Who draws the line that says "Abnormal form or structure," or "Ah! the ideal normal form?" After the grease-pencil lines re-create you, were you a monster before?

How is a monster born, what makes it, what makes monsters tick? Frankenstein's monster is made from dead parts (what monsters do we make from our own dead parts?). Dracula is walking dead (how many fully alive?). Maurice Sendak made them friendly. Monsters are our most powerful imaginative creations. We are in love with our monsters, as much as we persecute them in waking life. Conrad's Marlow: "The fascination of the abomination, you know?"[3] Abnormal form, abnormal character: "one unusually large for its kind." Terrifying, threatening, strange. All of us with normal forms can distort ourselves so quickly, disfigured by sadness and rage. It's the hint of what's hidden under the normal surface that is most terrifying. Strange, but in us, of us, one of us. Conrad's Kurtz: "All of Europe contributed to the making of Kurtz."[4] A monster holds sway, "an object of great complexity . . . very great." Beyond the pale, but close enough to recognize yourself. Strange because within.

Monsters are a figure for our time, bringing together things that didn't belong together once, a long time ago, all around us and in us now. A combination of contradictions that can't be contained, that strains the form of logical sense: a deviation that retains traces of the norm. Kat Bjelland, lead singer of Babes in Toyland, diminutive, blond, unearthing a voice that sounds a thousand monsters' lifelong terrors, her good-girl eyes turning back in her head. Different from but the same. Complex, forceful, but too much. Us, but not us. Outside. The limit of human community.[5]

Who and what are monsters, what makes one so called? What behaviors does one exhibit? I used to get called a monster a lot. Once I bit my orthodontist who wanted to make me trade my wolf fangs for the potential of beauty. My mother tried to make sure I would fit in. Ponytails and flowered dresses. Handprints on my face like her, never smashing my fingers through anyone else's face. She held me in front of my father's voice, radios, chair arms, flying fists. She held me in front of her, some force field beyond which he could not hit. In the morning she forced me into dresses. One had ribbons on the front that could be untied. I buried them in my locker, struggling into my friends' discarded pairs of pants. When I yelled and screamed myself they called me monster.

Girls who yell a lot, who argue too much, who don't smile enough are often monsters.

A bodybuilder is a monster. The gargantuan body? Mr. Hyde.

GENDER FEMINISM, POSTMODERN
FEMINISM, AND THE QUESTION
OF SCIENCE: CONTEXTUALIZING
MARY REILLY

In their own rhetoric, bodybuilders are monsters. In the cultural imagination they exist there too, so strangely ballooned, so tangibly swollen into presence. Perhaps they are too literal, too real to be let off the hook, for that same imagination has not granted them the humanity our other monsters have been given. Boris Karloff as Frankenstein's monster, and later the **133** voice of the Grinch, suffering still in his flat-topped head, bolted down by the neck, indescribable pain and some faraway knowledge staring out of his eyes, telling us truths we'll never fathom. And Mr. Hyde. Terrible in his own time but we have come to love him, in John Malkovich's sensual lips and swollen face, his desperate sadness calmed for a moment resting on a comforting hand.

Or so I felt watching Stephen Frears's *Mary Reilly*, which made its brief appearance in the gray and cold of the early months of 1996. It was too relentlessly bleak for many, but I returned to the theater where it ran for a week in my town a total of seven times. It was Mr. Hyde—I was strangely in his grip. Like I was under some spell I kept going back, an automaton haunted by bleak images flickering across the screen, hinting, hinting, some explanation—*what*? Deeply disturbed and compelled, I found my identification was split among Jekyll's despairing listlessness, Hyde's vigor and anger in the face of despair, and Mary's stoicism and compulsive fascination with Hyde. I was all three, somehow, sitting in the darkness trying to take notes, the reel of my feelings split all over the screen. It wasn't until later that I knew why. For the way I resembled all three characters had resulted in that practice, so important to my daily sense of safety, of bodybuilding.

Mary Reilly helped me to make sense of why I bodybuild, and to think of bodybuilding in an entirely new way: as a sword and shield against physical violence and the deformations of personality that violence accomplishes, as a cure for the paralyzing sense of nothingness, the vanishing of meaning violence often accomplishes in its victims' lives.[6] I came to understand the three characters in *Mary Reilly*—Jekyll, Hyde, and Mary herself—as different aspects of the female bodybuilder. Mary, the stoic abuse survivor, the controlled, self-disciplined worker, is one aspect. Jekyll, the scientist who engineers the complete transformation of his own body, is another. And Hyde, the creation, is the body/masculinity some women bodybuilders have created for themselves as a defensive strategy, a way of taking back their bodies from violence and a way of constructing a fortress against future attacks—both treatment and prevention.[7]

For bodybuilding is part of the "extremes and paradoxes, ironies and contradictions inherent to a culture based on self-realization" that David

Peterson del Mar theorizes in his study of domestic violence. The possibility of self-realization for women—a recent historical phenomenon, has, in Peterson de Mar's view, generated "a further rise in violence and in [women's] capacity to resist it."[8] Bodybuilding can be an active part of self-realization that increases women's capacity to resist and heal from domestic violence.

If we begin to think of bodybuilding in this way, we must follow *Mary Reilly* and begin to rethink monstrosity. We must begin to rethink masculinity and femininity, and female masculinity as not-monstrous. We must begin to rethink our experiences, our lives.

Mary Reilly, the movie version, evokes the horrors of its late nineteenth-century setting right along with the similar horrors of our own time—child abuse, incest, urban poverty, as well as the perennial fascination with cultural myths like doubles, good and evil selves, other halves, and the beast within the man. As such, despite its nineteenth-century setting, it reads as much as a meditation on contemporary constructions of gender, technology, and science as it does on nineteenth-century constructions of the same. Reprising the late nineteenth- and early twentieth-century anxiety about human bodies and machines, mortality and aging, and the limits of science and the natural, *Mary Reilly* provides a point of convergence. Here the seemingly disparate threads of childhood abuse, sadomasochistic desire, and the medical technologies that make the body of postmodern plasticity a possibility come together in a way that helped me make sense of the female bodybuilder, helped me make sense of myself.

The movie is informed by issues central to contemporary debates in feminist theory. In *Nomadic Subjects*, Rosi Braidotti identifies two feminist positions on biotechnologies and what she calls the "corpo-r(e)ality of the subject": the "modernist school," represented by Gena Corea, and the postmodern "cyborg feminism" of Donna Haraway. Braidotti herself falls roughly under the (very broad) rubric of "postmodern" or "poststructuralist" feminism that she associates with Haraway, a feminism that rests on three revisions of classic liberal feminism, and of the kind of "biopower" or "disciplined bodies" analyzed in Foucault:

> First, the notion of feminist theory is redefined in terms of nontaxonomical *figurations*; second, feminist subjectivity is reconceptualized as *cyborg*; and third, scientific objectivity is redefined as *situated knowledges*. **135**

. . . Haraway opposes to Foucault's strategy of biopower an approach based on the deconstructive genealogy of the embodied subjectivities of women. . . . [She] takes very seriously the point that contemporary feminism rests on the very signifier "woman," which it must deconstruct. . . . Feminists in the 1990's must replace naive belief in global sisterhood or more strategic alliances based on common interests, with a new kind of politics, based on temporary and mobile coalitions and therefore on *affinity*.

By "figurations," Braidotti and Haraway mean a given culture's foundational myths, a "commonly shared foundation of collective figures of speech." As figurations—stories—these myths are radically changeable and their refiguration should be a point of departure for nineties feminism. Haraway's intervention is the cyborg, a "new figuration for feminist subjectivity . . . a hybrid, or body machine, the cyborg . . . is a figure of interrelationality . . . that deliberately blurs categorical distinctions (human/machine; nature/culture; male/female)." Haraway embraces the figuration of the body-machine while Corea "stress[es] its potential for exploitation and manipulation." Where Haraway goes "beyond" gender binaries and argues for a radical transformation in the rationalist model of science and a new "language of political struggle [that moves] away from the tactic of head-on confrontations in favor of more specific and diffuse strategies based on irony . . . and . . . coalitions on the basis of affinity," Corea argues for a change in the rationalist model that includes a woman-centered perspective and that "highlights the need for a politics of opposition." Where Corea evokes a return to and valuation of the naturalized body of "woman," Haraway sees this return, like oppositional politics, as an impossibility. Corea's is a gender- or cultural-feminist stance, in which biomedical technologies would reduce the specificity of the female body to only a machine, a means to an end, a body replaced by science or used as a means to an end, a reproductive receptacle stripped of its dignity.[9]

A more recent example of the antitechnology stance, which Braidotti does not mention, is Janice Raymond's *Women as Wombs*, which is a critique of the latest reproductive technologies. The book is, Raymond writes, "principally about the consequences of reproductive technologies and contracts for women. Because all these technologies, drugs, and procedures violate the integrity of a woman's body in ways that are dangerous, destructive, debilitating, and demeaning, they are a form of medical violence against women. . . . Technological reproduction is first and foremost about the appropriation of the female body."[10] A more recent example of the "postmodern position" that has come to characterize much thinking post-Haraway is that of Dion Farquhar, who argues the position that "bodies can *both* be in control and shape technologies they desire, utilize, adapt, or resist at the same time they can be controlled and shaped by them."[11]

Both modes of thinking, both responses to "the political struggle of women for control of the reproductive technologies."[12] are still powerful in contemporary culture, and both are central to the dilemmas presented in *Mary Reilly*. On one level the movie operates from a difference-feminist perspective because its view is that science degrades the human body, reducing it to pieces of meat, stripped of human dignity. Once stripped, science releases or unveils the beast within the man (Hyde in Jekyll). Woman (Mary), however, despite her background of childhood abuse and her attraction to beastliness, seems not so beastly, reflecting the "higher" moral judgment some difference feminists argue is essential to women. On another level, however, *Mary Reilly* exhibits an attraction to as well as a repulsion from the question of biomedicine and its transformational effects, just as (maybe) cultural feminism is attracted to cyborgian feminism as well, suggesting the need for a feminism that combines what right now still seem, and are discursively constructed as, contradictory premises. As psychoanalysis has long argued, it is possible to hold two contradictory beliefs at the same time—indeed, that may be an aspect of historical determination for third-wave feminists, raised in a social structure defined by contradiction. Third-wave feminism, as identificatory positions offered by the movie suggest, may be defined by a split commitment to contradictory principles in cultural and postmodern feminism.[13] All of these strains, as I will argue, converge in the female bodybuilder, who, as the literal embodiment of Haraway's "cyborg," but also as the embodiment of some of the limits of Corea's more naturalized female body, invokes both attraction and repulsion in the larger culture, and combines within her single body facets of not just Jekyll and Hyde but Mary as well.

The movie is a postmodern take on high Romanticism, an interpretation of both Stevenson's original and Miner's rewrite that is significantly more sympathetic to Hyde than either. While the Hyde in the original is evil, a decidedly Freudian id, the uncivilized monster lurking just under the surface whom the reader is meant to find physically and morally repulsive, the Hyde of the movie is attractive and sexual in a way to which late twentieth-century audiences have been well trained to respond. There is no doubt that in the movie, despite knowing better and recognizing the resemblances to her abusive father, Mary is attracted to Hyde much more directly than in Miner's novel. The movie is two steps down the road from Stevenson's original, for the character Mary is Miner's addition, while the movie adds the dimension of her attraction to Hyde. His hypermasculinity and proximity to violence has a great deal to do with what makes him sexually attractive — the overwhelming, entirely self-consumed force that sees only itself, that has such a strong presence. *Mary Reilly* critically explores some of the cultural connections between romance and violence that serve to naturalize male violence and make it acceptable, even sexy.

Stevenson's text describes Hyde as "a little man . . . something wrong with his appearance; something displeasing, something down-right detestable. . . . He gives a strong feeling of deformity, although I couldn't specify the point. . . . smaller, slighter than Henry Jekyll."[14] Miner follows suit, and has her Mary write that "the back of his hand is covered with black hair, the fingers blunt, so although, like the rest of him, it is small for a man's, still there is something brutish about it."[15] The movie's Hyde is something else altogether, John Malkovich at his sensual, snarlingly sexual best. Doing himself one better even than his characterization of the Vicomte in *Dangerous Liaisons* (1988), also directed by Stephen Frears, his Hyde is vital and compellingly attractive. While both the Stevenson and Miner versions emphasize Hyde's smallness (said, on page 20 of the original, to mirror "the radiance of a foul soul"), Malkovich's Hyde is physically bigger than Jekyll, and though he walks with the characteristic shuffle mentioned in both novels, in the movie that shuffle seems incidental, meant more to call up similarities between Hyde and Mary's abusive father than anything essential to Hyde's physical presence, which is overwhelming. The speed and decided purposefulness of his walk, his way of occupying as much space as possible as if it were a dominion all his own, the expressive mobility of his face, and the direct sensuality of his long black mane, strands of which he tucks disarmingly behind his ear in the most tense moments, all create a picture of a sexuality for which late twentieth-century audiences have been primed. A dangerous, intellectual Fabio who calls up nothing so much as Heathcliff, Emily Brontë's dangerously sexual, perennially popular, brooding Romantic hero, there is nothing small about this Hyde.

Malkovich's characterization, which creates a figure anything but repulsive, is more in keeping with director Stephen Frears's interpretation of the Jekyll/Hyde story, which differs from both novels. Though it was released in spring of 1996, cameras had been rolling on *Mary Reilly* since the spring of 1994, its release date postponed seven times as a result of conflict between Frears's postmodern take and the studio's more predictable one: "Frears struck out to explore the gray areas between Jekyll and Hyde—and Mary Reilly's strange attraction to both. 'From the beginning he was always a much more complicated character.' . . . Meanwhile TriStar was counting on a more conventional showdown between good and evil."[16] "Showdown between good and evil" *Mary Reilly* ain't. There is no doubt that Mary is more attracted to Hyde than repulsed by him, and her attraction raises questions that make desire a good deal more problematic than simpler equations between evil and avoidance.

Even the movie's most direct confrontation with the question of good and evil, and her relation to it, is highly ambiguous. Mary's question to Hyde "Is evil stronger than good?" is met with "You tell me," at which point he draws her into his bedroom and begins kissing her scars. Her "Please let me go" is not at all convincing, and the camera dwells on her concomitant expressions of pleasure and horror. He withdraws at her request to let her go, and his ironic "I am sorry. I thought you wanted to stay . . . or does my sense of smell deceive me?" is a reference back to an earlier scene. There, Mary dreams that Hyde is in her bed, and in reaction to the protest she makes as he begins to make love to her, he says, "I'm sorry. There must be some misunderstanding. I thought you invited me here." After a long pause, she looks at him directly and says, "I did," no longer resisting. She wakes, waking Annie, who shares her bed. When Mary says "Sorry, bad dream," Annie responds, "Didn't sound so bad," perhaps establishing Mary's **139** attraction to Hyde. The parallel dialogue in the later scene, which is not a dream, makes it clear that Hyde's sense of smell does not in fact deceive him, and a direct cut leaves the question of whether she actually acts on her attraction undecided. It is important that the movie gives her agency: Hyde does not rape her. Repeatedly, if she rebuffs his physical advances, he withdraws, leaving her to sort out her feelings and determine her actions. He taunts her with her attraction to him by forcing her to confront it, recognize it. If Hyde is evil, clearly that evil is not an entirely repulsive thing. In fact it may serve as an aphrodisiac.

If anything in the movie is evil, it is the technology that has produced Hyde and not Hyde himself. The movie's antiscience stance, similar to Corea's, is expressed in more inflected ways through the negative characterization of the transformative possibilities of biomedicine (posited as a cure for the sadness and anger that "comes in like the tide"), but very directly in instances of dialogue spoken by Hyde. Jekyll requests that Mary accompany Hyde on a "scientific errand," which turns out to be a visit to a slaughterhouse for the procurement of various organs. The camera lingers on the buckets of blood that wash down the slaughterhouse steps, a beautiful dull red against the gray cement background and gray light. The camera also dwells mercilessly on hanging carcasses, skinned and in the process of being skinned, from which Hyde requests particular organs, even providing the knife, an exquisitely crafted piece of metal that looks more like an art object than a saw for the ends of intestines. Hyde is undeterred by these sights, gazing avidly into corpse caverns, appraising the pieces, pausing to tuck a wandering strand of his long hair behind his ear. But the camera also dwells on Mary's face, her expressions, which vacillate among horror, fear, disgust, pain, and, sometimes, a hint of perverse interest. Organs in hand, Hyde shepherds Mary to the hospital with the cheerful proclamation, "And now to where they butcher human meat. The hospital and the slaughterhouse share the same gutters—most convenient." The camera cuts immediately to an operating scene, which Hyde eagerly joins, and the blood and sawing operations directly mirror the scene in the slaughterhouse. Mary looks on with the same expressions, the gross material aspects of the human condition literally unveiled before her eyes. That Mrs. Farraday's

bordello is in close proximity to both slaughterhouse and hospital points to a third aspect of the horrors of the flesh, the convergence between the sexual and medical, and, as Raymond puts it in *Women as Wombs* (p. xxxii), the way biotechnology facilitates "sexual access to women."

If medicine is comparable to butchery in *Mary Reilly*, science as a field which produces it is implicated as well. Science seems no more and no less than a complex process for the reduction of humanity into pieces of meat. When Mary asks Hyde what Dr. Jekyll wants the organs for, he replies, "I just supply the organs as required. . . . You've no idea how strange and twisting are the ways of science." He knocks on Jekyll's laboratory door, entering with a loud and cheery "Afternoon, doctor. Visit from the butcher." This scene is quickly followed by a visit from Mrs. Farraday (Glenn Close), the brothel madam who is herself in the business of converting young female bodies into sexual meat. The movie traces a continuum of abuse from Mary's father through the hospital and brothel and back through Hyde.

While the movie seems more equivocal about Hyde himself, science or medicine as the institution that produced him falls under close scrutiny. As Hyde himself says: "I always had an artistic temperament. I know I owe my existence to science but I've never been able to whip up much enthusiasm for it." Stated as this is in a scene where Mary comes upon an clinical anatomy book that has been scrawled over with Hyde's obscene drawings and philosophical pronouncements about pain ("pain is the beginning of understanding"), in this postmodern take on high Romanticism, science comes across as yet another of the normalizing, stultifying social institutions that have led Jekyll to create Hyde in the first place.

Given the (still operational) cultural opposition between science/objectivity/truth and art/subjectivity/fiction and the value given to the first at the expense of the second, *Mary Reilly* makes Hyde and his rebellion against the reductive truth claims of objectivity and science attractive, which raises the same question for claims about the natural body. In the case of the female bodybuilder, as with Hyde, it is science to some extent which makes her possible. It is precisely this call for the return of the natural, less muscular female body in the bodybuilding industry that has led to the expansion of the fitness industry with its evening gown and swimsuit rounds. This call can be linked with some feminist rejections of science and technology, which in this case do much more than prevent the writing of new figura- **141** tional myths. Like Mary's complicated relationship to Jekyll and Hyde, the female bodybuilder's relationship to her own body is often the stage for compulsively reworking primary traumas and creating a palpable presence. Stripped of this right to be visible, stripped of Hyde/science, forced back into nature/diminution, the trauma is reenacted once again, this time in a feminist guise. Rejection of science in this case would result in the recreation of a passive, violable feminine flesh. The growing clamor against the female bodybuilder is perhaps not unrelated to the growing clamor for the return of the traditional nuclear family and the glamorization of pregnancy and childbirth (think Madonna) enacted in contemporary advertising, television, cinema, and other forms of mass media. A rejection of the female bodybuilder, the alternative iconography she represents, and the science that has produced her are part of the recurrent cultural reduction of the female body to its role as mother. If *Mary Reilly* asks us to embrace Hyde but not the science that has created him, I would depart from the movie and take a proscience/technology stance that makes a parallel appeal for the female bodybuilder who is made possible by just that technology, and whose struggle to exist touches on some of our culture's most basic potentials, aspirations, and fears.

VIOLENCE, MONSTROUS VOIDS, AND THE GENDER OF NOTHING

"Violence is violence," writes the women's collective behind *Free to Fight: An Interactive Self-Defense Project*, a spoken word—punk—rap—rock music CD released in 1996 and available from Candy-Ass records with an accompanying workbook. "All abusive behavior," the workbook says,

> is connected: Abusive behavior ranges from acts which make us feel uncomfortable to acts which cause our physical damage or death. This could be our boss telling a racist joke to someone yelling at us on the street or rubbing up against us on the subway to rape and murder. Often, we justify the abuse and consider it "normal." Sometimes we are made to feel stupid or paranoid if we react to the jokes, comments, or stares. These "normal" forms of abuse are offensive because they have an inherent threat of more severe abuse. When we understand the range of abu-

sive behavior, we understand that all women and girls experience some form of sexual abuse during their lifetimes.[17]

What happens, *Free to Fight* asks, when a woman is hit? What is it about a rape or other forms of violence that makes a woman feel she has been erased from this world? Abuse has the function of wiping you out, erasing your singularity, damping the liveliness in your soul with a single stroke. Abuse tells you unquestionably that you are not valued, that your place in the world, your will to live, is a matter of indifference to those around you.

In 1951, the Welsh poet Dylan Thomas was certain he was valued, and wrote his most famous poem, a tribute to his dying father. "Do Not Go Gentle into That Good Night" relies on two repeated lines woven strategically throughout. "Rage, rage against the dying of the light," Thomas pleads. "Do not go gentle into that good night."[18] Articulating that restless urge which first indicates that someone *is*, the poem stands as an unquestionable act of urgency and self-assertion, the declaration of a person's right to live, his or her will to exist, to *be*. But while every person might feel this urge, many are treated as if they have no right to it. "There are always two deaths," novelist Jean Rhys writes in *Wide Sargasso Sea*, "the real one and the one people know about."[19]

"The real death" is often a response to abuse. It is the feeling of being erased, wiped out by forms of violence that are on the continuum the *Free to Fight* collective describes. It can happen to boys as well as girls; according to the Portland, Oregon, Women's Crisis Line, "one in four girls and one in four boys will experience child sexual abuse."[20] Anything that is a direct attack on a person's essential value is abuse. A racist remark can produce a "dying of the light" in the person so devalued, as can a condescending sexist slight from a colleague, intended or not, that tells a woman she is not taken seriously or esteemed. Direct verbal abuse does more killing, and so do the physical attacks that range from black eyes to rape. Every blow a declaration, a blunt cut that is the attacker screaming "You don't matter and I do," every touch an erasure that says "You don't even exist." If an abuse survivor listens, she can feel a form of death that makes her an eviscerated ghost. To survive, she must "rage, rage, against the dying of the light." She must "not go gentle into that good night."

"One in two women will experience domestic violence in her lifetime," reports the Portland Women's Crisis Line. "A man batters a woman every fifteen seconds." I was. I was one of those women from the time I was six, hiding in my room and waiting. It was my father. At first he hit only my mother. Then, when I fought him, he turned from my mother, hit me. But this was nothing compared to what he told us, probably seventeen years and every night. "Ugly bitches. Idiots. Fat whores." "One in four women will be raped by a man," says the Crisis Line, "by the time she is eighteen years old." I was. I was sixteen. "Eighty percent of the time, men rape women who they know on an acquaintance level." He was my coach. It was my first experience of sexual contact more than petting. "Over fifty percent of the time, men rape women in women's own homes." He did. It was in my own bed, that quintessential American-teenager twin with a yellow-and-white checked spread, the same bed I slept in night after night after that.

In the eighties, when this was happening to me, when women all over the country were lobbying tirelessly for a hearing and for funds so that women's crisis hot lines were being established, and women's centers were being built, and women's studies and domestic-violence-prevention programs were put in place and maintained by the energy of these women, when marches like Take Back the Night were first organized and it seemed like many women were speaking the violences that were done to them for the first time, when it seemed like it would be an act of healing to speak, I never thought we would go back to a time when speaking was ridiculed, when injunctions to silence were restored to the norm. When the word *feminist* was something akin to "old maid" or "cancer"—the feminism that has helped me to "rage, rage against the dying of the light." The feminism that has helped me to "not go gentle into that good night."

So here we are in the late nineties, and activism like Take Back the Night marches is represented as dated, old hat, part of a sniveling, weary, dying trend perpetuated by tiresome, dreary whining women motivated solely by their own personal injuries and their inabilities to get men. Issues like sexual harassment, abuse, and rape are once again being silenced, the women speaking about them dismissed with labels like "talk-show confession" or "exhibitionism." According to many who call themselves feminists today, women who discuss these issues are tiresome anachronisms like those annoying "femi-nazis" who burned their bras in 1968 and refused to shave their legs. We are whining, crying victim, crying wolf, and nobody wants to listen. To speak about violence done to you is now unhip. It's too sincere for nineties cynicism; it takes a stand. It's getting stuck on problems we have transcended: "There is no race," an MCI ad for the Internet states, "there are no genders. There are no infirmities—there are only minds." "Now is the time," an ad for Nike women's products line proclaims, "as we strengthen and build our bodies, we build the future of women's sports. The weaker sex? No way. *I am woman; watch me score.*" But pretending that bodies all line up on the same level playing field, that solutions to all problems can be solved at the level of the individual consumer, won't make systematic inequalities go away, not even in cyberspace. Building up your body in response to experiences of abuse, which are always connected to those inequalities, can take you only so far.

In this cultural context, where all forms of disempowerment, including violence against women, are again often seen as the individual's fault, how can we "rage, rage against the dying of the light?" Sometimes, I wake up in the morning and I can't rage against anything at all, I'm too tired. There's some coldness in me, like a blue tinge to the skin, a windup toy run down, what Toni Morrison calls "the sadness at [the] center, the desolated center where the self that was no self made its home."[21] Morrison's words, from *Beloved*, refer specifically to the African American experience within slavery, perhaps the most horrific form of violence done to a people. This experience produced, the novel shows, an entire race of people who have gone through Rhys's "real death," the emotional, psychological, spiritual, and physical annihilation of their being. As a quintessential whitegirl, I have no claim to this devastation. Yet in a lesser form I know the feeling Morrison's words describe as intimately as I know the tastes in my mouth, or the dryness of my skin. While they are not comparable, lesser acts of violence do produce forms of "real death" in persons who have experienced that violence.

From death into life, from nothingness into something, it is perhaps these experiences of "real death" shared by many that can serve as a motivation for the kind of coalition politics writers like bell hooks call for, a shared "yearning to just see this domination end," a political activism that can bring different political coalitions together.[22] In the context of a conservatism insinuating itself everywhere into popular culture from the J. Crew catalog to Cheryl Crowe videos, a context in which the gains of the civil rights and women's movements are systematically being erased and few are protesting, in a context where any kind of sincere commitment or belief is ridiculed as unhip retro whining, where political activism is represented as impossible and impossibly naive, we need these coalitions now more than ever. The choice is ours. For anyone who has suffered the systematic erasure of individual subjectivity or self that Rhys calls the "real death," we can shut up as the culture would like us to and experience that erasure once again.

Or, we can join with others the culture would like to sweep under and speak and write and e-mail and fax so that congresses are lobbied and backlash legislation like anti—affirmative action is changed. In our cultural productions we can work against the tyranny of retro images that enter a conservative plea for a return to a simpler life beyond systematic inequalities based on gender and social class and race. We can produce alternative rhetoric and ways of life to those which have recently domesticated once liberated women, rhetoric like Jane Fonda's declaration that although Ted Turner required her to give up her career for their marriage, she doesn't mind that she doesn't "have a profession . . . anymore," since she is "in a relationship that is a true partnership." We can produce alternative rhetoric to the domestication recently performed on Courtney Love, who is "outgrowing" her feminist "kinder-whore image" according to the January 1997 *Vogue*.[23] We can produce our own rhetoric, craft our own images, practices, write our own books. We can be part of, for instance, the annual NOW Young Feminist conventions, we can join the progressive multicultural activist organization, the Third Wave, founded by Rebecca Walker in New York City. We can refuse to be silent, accepting our responsibilities to act, to do, to speak. And we can build our own bodies. It's because of bodybuilding and feminism that I'm not ready to die yet. Because of bodybuilding and feminism, I can live. It's what helps me "rage, rage, against the dying of the light." It's what helps me "not go gentle into that good night." It helps me rage, and think, and feel, and breathe: because of bodybuilding and feminism, I am a monster.

The story of Dr. Jekyll and Mr. Hyde is the story of monsters, our very own. It is an important part of our cultural mythologies, a figuration, as Donna Haraway would say, that provides a ground for defining the limits of being.[24] There have been many versions since Robert Louis Stevenson's novella in 1886, both written and on film. In Stevenson's version, the monster is a distillation of our "composite natures," invented by a restless, whimsical soul who found his science too dry and his own deviations from its haven of fixed definitions unbearable. In Valerie Miner's version, *Mary Reilly: The Untold Story of Dr. Jekyll and Mr. Hyde*, and Stephen Frears's movie of the same name, both told from the point of view of a maid who is not even really a character in the Stevenson text, Hyde is the *pharmakon*, the remedy that is also a poison. He is the remedy for a sickness that's no deviance from the norm, but rather is shared by many, especially survivors of violence.

Monsters, it seems, come from shared metaphysical ills, the kind you'd never accuse a bodybuilder of having ("What? That lug! They're just not that deep!"). In Mary's words: "There's often this darkness and sadness, unexpected and coming from things that should bring happiness . . . but then it rises up inside like a blackness and I really am in that blackness where my father left me, with no way out and nothing to do but wait until somehow there's some merciful release and I come to myself again."[25] Mary inhabits two worlds, the one of daily, normal perception where things stay in their places and people behave in expected ways. There is an order; things make sense. The other is the land of shadows, what Octavio Paz calls "the country of broken and worn-out things. A gray country, immense and empty, that is not located anywhere."[26]

In "the country of broken and worn-out things," there is no reason to move, just a cold and frozen sadness, paralysis, ashes on the tongue, senses numb. Broken, disjointed, no impetus to move; in this world it's hard to do anything but cry, to see anything, to speak. This world, research has shown, is the world of post-traumatic stress syndrome, a world of anxiety, despair, and a pervasive sense of meaninglessness experienced by battered women and other survivors of violence, such as war veterans. As Ann Jones writes, "After they escape, battered women may be saddled with a load of complicated problems ranging from anxiety, shame, and despair to flashbacks and **147** suicidal ideation. These aftershocks are the symptoms of post-traumatic stress disorder, a psychological syndrome seen also in survivors of rape and incest and in veterans of wartime combat."[27] For these survivors, as for Mary, the gray brokenness is the legacy of violence: "So I feel my father made me thus . . . and [this sadness] will likely never leave me no matter what fortune I have, and it sets me apart from my fellows who seem never to know it. While I can't forgive my father, neither can I regret what I am" (33).[28] And although it is not explained by a similar abuse history, Mary is certain that Jekyll also has a relationship to "darkness and sadness," and both novel and movie reinforce this. They are, according to her, "both souls who knew this sadness and darkness" (33), and sadness and darkness need a cure.

Whatever put sadness and darkness in Jekyll, he suffers from it. He tries to cure it, discard it, drive it out: "For years now," Hyde reports, "the doctor has been suffering from a strange malady. He experimented with many ways to keep it at bay, but it would always return more acute than ever." Mary is right that she and Jekyll shared a heightened relationship to the "sadness and darkness inside," for the "strange malady" from which Jekyll suffers is the same "sadness and darkness" that Mary describes. When she asks him, toward the end of the film, what that malady is, he responds cryptically, amplifying Mary's own description of the same condition: "You might say it is a fracture in my soul . . . that gave me a taste for oblivion." That taste arises from a state of mind where there is, to return to Mary's words, "no way out and nothing to do but wait until somehow there's some merciful release and I come to myself again." Doubled, suffering from a life that flips between presence and absence, ordinary social commerce and the "country of broken and worn-out things," Jekyll tries to consign that brokenness to oblivion: "Finally he distilled two drugs, tested them, and understood that he had found the cure which took an unexpected form . . . me. I was the cure. One formula transformed him into me. The second formula, which he always refers to rather insultingly as the antidote, transforms me back into him. Lately I've found a way to slip his leash to become myself without having to wait for the injection."[29]

For the bodybuilder, her built body can function as a similar cure. The creation of Hyde and the creation of the bodybuilder's body provide an

Mary Reilly's Mr. Hyde and bodybuilder Sue Price: Twin sons of different mothers? (*Top:* Copyright 1996, Tri-Star Pictures, Inc. *Bottom:* Ad for autographed photo in *All Natural Muscular Development*, May 1997)

escape from the country of broken and worn-out things, for they are the antithesis of ashes, of the grayness from which there is no escape. For Jekyll, Hyde is the escape. Unlike Jekyll, who often wants to give up, Hyde loves his life with an enormous hunger, is "ravenous," as Jekyll tries to explain. By contrast to Jekyll's inability to move, every frame with Hyde in it is full of violent action, quick steps and thrusting limbs. He is never still. He is the cure for paralysis, and his sexual attractiveness is directly related to the traditional equation between masculinity and activity and femininity and passivity. For Paz's "broken country" is more specific. It is the place of the feminine, "the cruel incarnation of the feminine condition."

Mary, and Jekyll, cannot move in this place because it is the place of nothingness. "Her passivity is abject: she does not resist violence, but is an inert heap of bones, blood, and dust. Her taint is constitutional and re-sides . . . in her sex. This passivity, open to the outside world, causes her to lose her identity." Contemporary work on domestic violence and battery, however, reveals that abject passivity is not "constitutional" but is rather one characteristic response to violence.[30] And Frears's rendition of Miner's and Stevenson's novels has Jekyll resemble victims of domestic violence, while Hyde, who is a cure for that passivity, is clearly the perpetrator.

Jekyll, unlike Hyde, seems traditionally feminine, and remains supine in his bed, barely able to move, freezing: "Oh Mary, I'm so cold, my hands are frozen though. . . . I'm very tired." Jekyll is cold, gray, shriveled up— almost "an inert heap of bones, blood, and dust"—who needs to be bodily held up by his servants, spoon-fed from bowls. He becomes much more alive in Hyde, "robust" with ruddy skin and bigger body; he moves quickly, decisively, every move an assertion of will. Hyde seems to be a defense against femininity, if the passivity traditionally associated with femininity is the condition of "the country of broken and worn-out things." He is the anger that acts and moves, that covers the sadness that is passive and para-lyzes. The movie indicates a sharp split between sadness and anger—the one associated with femininity, Mary, and Jekyll; the other with masculinity and Hyde. This split is also connected to cultural rules about anger and pat-terns of domestic violence: the cultural commonplace that men direct their anger outward against others and women direct it inward against them-selves. But Jekyll/Hyde is abuser and victim housed within a single skin, which may point to how both masculine and feminine characteristics are necessary and necessarily housed within a single skin, and why—if we are to believe our cultural credos about every individual's right to self-realization and self-determination—femininity in men and masculinity in women can be, instead of monstrous, very positive things.

To the extent that traditional femininity is passive and open, it cannot function as a point of resistance. David Peterson del Mar writes that from the point of view of men who believe in traditional gender roles—a belief which characterized the perpetrators of domestic violence he studied—"modern woman at once demanded too much independence for herself and too much openness from men. The ideal woman, like the pliant image of a *Playboy* centerfold, had no boundaries of her own and presented no demands."[31] To these men, for women to have masculine characteristics (such as independence) and for men to have feminine characteristics (such as openness) was an anathema, a challenge to their position as head of the house. This shows that if traditional femininity—openness, sensitivity to the needs of others—is to function within a human being who has a self, it needs to be inoculated with traditional masculinity—boundaries and one's own demands. Just as Jekyll needs to be inoculated in order to act, do, be, as he is able to do in Hyde, a woman needs masculinity in order to do the same. *Mary Reilly* helps us to find a way of loving Mr. Hyde. Understanding female bodybuilding and female masculinity—seeing them as providing a woman with a sense of self, boundaries, and strength, giving her a sense of her own body as something that is her own, a safe space that functions as a cure for the sense of hopelessness and meaninglessness associated with trauma and abuse—should help us find a way to love female bodybuilders.

Hyde, however, goes too far, and the extent to which he goes too far is the extent to which he is entirely masculine. Hyde is voraciously, constitutionally, active—in the traditional lexicon, masculine. His abusive activities are tied up with that masculinity: as many researchers have indicated, the foundations of violence "rest firmly in [cultural constructions of] masculinity," in the images and definitions of masculinity *as* violence that float indiscriminately everywhere in popular culture from romance novels to journalistic reports, from the movie screen to the legislature.[32] "He was a monster, surely," Jekyll says of Mary's violent father, and asks her why she **151** doesn't hate him. But the movie makes it clear that violence, in some ways, is not seen as monstrous. In the case of Hyde, with whom the viewer is meant to sympathize, it is clear that his violence, his striking out at others instead of himself, fits the cultural parameters for the masculine. In this way, Hyde is no monster but rather a paragon of stereotypical masculinity: self-absorbed, sure of itself, always acting. As Joyce Carol Oates notes in her introduction to the Stevenson text, "There is a sense in which Hyde, for all his monstrosity, is but an addiction like alcohol, nicotine, or drugs."[33] The anger that drives his addiction and actions (or addictive actions) is the unfortunate but more acceptable consequence of a self-generating force, a presence. Anger, always monstrous, is usually seen as monstrous only in women. Contrary to positing a monster who is different from us all, one of the issues the Jekyll/Hyde story addresses is the ordinariness of monstrosity, the ways in which abusive acts are directly tied to cultural norms of masculinity. As Peterson del Mar writes, "The wife beater is not out there somewhere, on the margins of society and history. He is instead our close companion. He is at the center of our culture. He is at the center of our past."[34]

Even though masculinity can lead and has led to violence, however, it can also be used to recover from violence and to recuperate the self destroyed by it. What the Jekyll/Hyde story shows about masculinity and femininity and their relationship to violence and its effects is that one should not attempt to split them into separate categories, personalities, or bodies. An individual contains both masculine and feminine, and it is the splitting them off from each other that is destructive. In the case of the woman who uses bodybuilding as a way of overcoming the sense of passivity that often comes when someone suffers domestic violence, female masculinity may be seen as not monstrous at all but rather as a form of active agency that helps her overcome her victim status. Like Jekyll in his creation of Hyde, to the extent that femininity is traditionally constructed as openness, weakness, and vulnerability, the violence survivor must defend herself against that femininity and take on some of the characteristics of the masculine. Female masculinity is here synonymous with individuality and personhood, with personal freedom and self-realization. While these concepts have always been seen as a fundamental right of the (white) male

American, it has been only within the last thirty years that the women's movement has forced the extension of these concepts to (too often, only to white) women, an extension resisted by many.[35] Persons who ridicule female bodybuilders, who call them monstrous, unfeminine, and want to return the female form to weakness overtly refuse to grant self-realization and personal freedom to women.

BUILDING (ON THE) VOID: POSTMODERN MONSTERS OF THE GYM

Initially, good old Dr. Jekyll and Mr. Hyde—the respectable professional citizen and the beast within—might not seem to have much in common with bodybuilders, particularly female ones. Since bodybuilding has never been as respectable as, say, medicine, it's been seen, until recently, as on the beastly end of things. Not much transformation from civilized to uncivilized here: bodybuilders were weird, strange, narcissistic beasts. Yet a glance at any of the bodybuilding magazines will show at least as much preoccupation with Apollonian features of order and form as with any kind of Dionysian excess. The bodybuilder's work is to create a pure image of order and form, a body that's the perfect package, the right confluence of symmetry and mass. To some extent the bodybuilder's life is a model of regimentation: get up, eat, go to the gym, eat, eat, go back to the gym, eat, sleep. Every gram of carbohydrate, fat, and protein is measured before eaten, every set and rep counted—nothing more or less allowed.

As I have established, in the movie version of *Mary Reilly*, Jekyll, Mary, and Hyde can all be read as aspects of the same self, aspects which also come together in the female bodybuilder. The movie picks up on a moment in Stevenson's original, in which Jekyll confesses that although he has discovered that "man is not truly one but truly two," others will go beyond his dualism: "I say two, because the state of my own knowledge does not pass beyond that point. Others will follow, others will outstrip me on the same lines; and I hazard the guess that man will be ultimately known for a mere polity of multifarious, incongruous and independent denizens."[36] Stevenson's text anticipates postmodern definitions of the subject or self which argue in almost precisely these terms, but unlike most of those theoretical **153** accounts, the movie's use of alcoholism and abuse as a subtext articulate concrete conditions under which a personality's "polity of . . . incongruous and independent denizens" may become most visible. The movie points to ways in which abuse—for the abuser and abused—shatters the illusory totality of the personality, resulting in what the American Psychiatric Association terms "dissociative disorders." In this case, a single personality could metaphorically dissociate or split into at least three seemingly opposed aspects: Hyde, whose rage and sadism represents mostly unmediated aggression; Mary, whose sadness and masochism represents mostly passivity; and Jekyll, who is the mediator between the two, the social actor or mask who carries out normal human relationships in the daily world that do not allow for the aberrations of Hyde, and who has a place for, but devalues, the selflessness of Mary.

While the movie and novel directly posit only Mary's condition as a response to trauma, as my earlier reading suggested, Mary and Jekyll share a similar orientation toward the world, that sense of "sadness and darkness." Although the movie and novel never speculate about the source of Jekyll's malaise, it is clear that there is some form of trauma, some motivating factor that leads him to develop the injection that produces Hyde. Whatever it is for Jekyll (and it may be that his privileged place on the social scale keeps the question from being asked, according to the old mythology that violence isn't part of the lives of the upper classes, it is a lower-class aberration), the battery and sexual violence Mary experiences at the hands of her alcoholic father predisposes her to rigid obedience to social mores, while Jekyll reacts with anger (Hyde). Their different places on the social scale, servant and master, are instrumental in determining the forms their responses take. But the novel and movie are concerned with establishing similarities as well as differences between masters and servants, rich and poor, and draw parallels among Mary's work ethic, Jekyll's obsession with Hyde, and Mary's father's alcoholism, showing a shared root for various forms of addiction.

Mary's most marked response to trauma, and the paralyzing "sadness and darkness" it brings, is hard work. The view she articulates is characteristic of late nineteenth-century life in service, yet the novel also works to show how that characteristic ideology interacts with Mary's experience of trauma. She is "of the opinion that hard work is the best cure for low spirits" (22), and finds that "remembering [her] place, as Mrs. Swit used to say we mu[st] do when we feel uncertain" (9), has a calming effect. She thinks "order in a household is as important to us below stairs as above" (20), and uses that sense of "order" and the work that gives it concrete shape to keep the sadness and darkness at bay. Jekyll jokes with her about this view, telling her she has "a fairly profound view of social order and propriety" (19). This comment shows his privileged position, for Mary's sense of order is one of the few options she has for creating a safe world. For Mary, hard work and the ability to make a garden grow, green spots of life keeping the grayness at bay, are ways of building a world that is a haven from violence and a protection against it. Female bodybuilders, who similarly appreciate hard work, may also find their meaning and sense of safety in it. My point is that for bodybuilders with abuse histories, bodybuilding is one of the few options they have for creating a safe world. Given our contemporary social context, in which advertising constructs the body as a domain over which an individual has complete control and self-determination, the chance to overcome anything (according to a Nike ad, "the path to glory lies in training. It's where we get our strength, speed, endurance, and power. . . . As we strengthen and build our bodies, we build the future of women's sports. The weaker sex? No way. I am woman, watch me score"), we see the building of our bodies as a concrete, tangible way to create a safe space we can inhabit.

Our options for creating such spaces differ across the spectra of gender, race, and class. That Jekyll can be engaged in work that ultimately questions forms of order, senses of place and identity, is a function of his place. When he tells Mary, "My work doesn't have such pleasing results as yours. It may finally be of benefit to no one. It may only make the world more strange than it is already, and more frightening to those who haven't the courage to know the worst . . . yet I must do it" (105), Jekyll gets to pose as a fearless crusader for truth as a way to deal with his metaphysical malaise while Mary must subscribe to an illusory sense of order that exploits her. As we have seen, this is how many feminists interpret exercise compulsions **155** like bodybuilding—as an illusory sense of order, a self-imposed enslavement to work on their bodies that exploits the women who anxiously haunt the gyms, churning the Stair Masters day after day.

Mary's work is the work of keeping the house in order, everything in its place and clean, which involves the subsumption of self to a larger order and the denial of self-expression, while Jekyll's work is the work that produces Hyde, who is, although socially unacceptable, precisely a form of self-expression. Gender as well as class enter into the dynamic here for the obvious reasons that self-expression is encouraged for one sex and discouraged in the other—in the nineteenth century and today. Peggy Orenstein's research on contemporary American secondary schools showed that teachers still reward behavior in girls that shows obedience and compliance, whereas boys received attention and distinction for rebellious behavior.[37] Mary's philosophy of hard work is in perfect accordance with the intersecting expectations of gender and class that require women and those not in the upper classes to subsume their individual interests to a social structure not in their interests at all. As I will argue in chapter 6, however, despite appearances to the contrary, bodybuilding can function very differently— as a declaration of independence, as a carving out of a space for the self even as that self becomes enslaved to the need to keep carving.

Although not so marked in terms of a rigid demarcation of class, contemporary body ideals for women function similarly to Mary's work. The hard work of building the perfect body is performed in addition to the hard work of service, or the work of a professional job. Working out the body has become a cross-class phenomena, recently expanding from its predominance in blue-collar (male) culture and prisons to encompass a wide cross-section of the population. Women in positions of greater economic privilege, of course, may have more time to work out, and the money to afford the posh gym, but there are gyms that market themselves to every economic strata. To the extent that many women spend a significant proportion of their leisure time working on their bodies, they subsume individual interests to a collective ideal in the name of developing their most precious individual asset, the sexual desirability of their bodies. In dominant cultural body ideology, you're good, commendable, admirable if you go to the gym and work out; bad, lazy, slothful if you do not. "Supporting a habit," a Nike ad reads (astutely picking up on the way exercise can become a form of addiction). "Step junkie, gym freak, high-impact mama, she has many names. One thing is for certain, she's a regular. Five to six times a week she's in the gym, burning it up. She thrives on the frequency and intensity of her workouts." That very addiction is culturally venerated as discipline and dedication.

But dedication to what? From one point of view, a dedication to herself, to her own development, her own sense of self, of safety, space. From another point of view, dedication to an impossible ideal that diverts her attention from more productive activist causes. According to the body ideals that have been prevalent at least since the early eighties, the most sexually desirable bodies are the ones that have done the most working out (or had the most plastic surgery). A woman who sees herself as part of mainstream culture struggles with this body paradox every day: Jekyll in her claim to individual expression and Mary in the subsumption of that expression to the larger order of achieving the individual success of the standardized image. Working out is a legacy of equity feminism, which did achieve significant goals in giving women access to previously all-male spheres, including athletics. In the last fifteen years women have largely been allowed the kind of individualistic ideology and scope that Jekyll expresses. Yet the old ideology that dictates that women subsume their individuality to the higher good of their families remains present simultaneously, along with the ideology that subsumes the individual to the higher good of the standardized body: thin but firm, lightly muscled, no cellulite or other fat anywhere. It should be noted that while body image is becoming increasingly important to men, their bodies commodified and subjectivities consumerized in the creation of new markets so that their individual interests and leisure time are subsumed to the ideal of the "buff" male body as well, this marks the cultural drift of a paradoxical process that can serve as a potent form of containment masquerading as individual achievement and value.

This argument applies even more to bodybuilders than to the average fitness enthusiast. The ideological schizophrenia that posits individual achievement through the attainment of a standardized ideal manifests itself even more vehemently in bodybuilding, where, contradictorily, the quest for individual distinction (Jekyll) exists hand in hand with a quest to embody the most dominant bodily ideals within the sport (Mary). If you add **157** the question of histories of abuse for some bodybuilders to the equation (Mary/Hyde), this is another permutation on how you get Jekyll, Mary, and Hyde all housed within the same figure. The female bodybuilder's body is the simultaneous attempt to express her anger at both her devalued social position and the abuse history that proceeds from that devaluation, and to keep that anger in by directing it toward an acceptable social aim. She wants to protest and comply simultaneously.

If bodybuilding is approached on this fundamental level of identity, it begins to mark one way out of the impasse found in analyses that interpret from a purely gender-feminist or from a purely postmodern-feminist position, an impasse reflected in interpretations of the female bodybuilder as either liberating or completely controlled. It is a reading of the built body as both liberated and controlled. The built body can be seen to function as an abused woman's double, her Mr. Hyde, her transformation brought about by chemical injection. The built, engineered body that science makes possible is the stage for compulsively reworking the original trauma and creating a body that is experienced as visible and present, unlike the feelings of erasure experienced by the abused body. The figures of Jekyll, Hyde, and Mary converge in the female bodybuilder around the issues of violence, science, and identity. The female bodybuilder's need to perform her embodiment is one highly visible manifestation of a turn in the construction of contemporary American identities that might be summed up by "I have an audience, therefore I am."

In an article on MTV's *Real World* in *Rolling Stone*, David Wild writes, "One senses *The Real World* speaks to an entire generation of viewers that can hardly wait to get a camera crew on its ass. An application in *The Real World* book led to 10,000 new young bodies anxious to sign on for house duty. One imagines packs of twentysomethings lying in wait for a quick way out of the ghetto of obscurity."[38] While Wild's description can be read as just another jab at the foibles and superficiality of Generation X, it points to a sense that many in contemporary culture experience as real: a sense that they are invisible, meaningless, confined to a "ghetto of obscurity" unless they have an audience to rescue them and confer, through the attention of that audience, a momentary sense of identity upon the one who performs.

158 Feelings of invisibility are perhaps even more endemic to women who have been abused. For these women in particular, the performative dimension can be healing, a reclamation and recognition that cancels their previous erasure out. One subculture that has made explicit connections between performance and healing is Riot Grrrl, the young punk feminist movement that first gained attention in 1991. According to Gottlieb and Wald,

> Since . . . abuses of girls' and women's bodies . . . are generally associated with women's alienation from their bodies, the ability to *be* embodied—the deployment of the body in performance—provides an antidote to its previous violations. Girls wield their bodies in performance . . . in such a way as to make their bodies highly visible: this visibility counteracts the (feelings of) erasure and invisibility produced by persistent degradation in a sexist society. Such performance recuperates to-be-looked-at-ness as something that constitutes, rather than erodes or impedes, female subjectivity.[39]

It is my contention that bodybuilding for women performs a similarly positive function: recuperating to-be-looked-at-ness as something that helps consolidate a sense of subjectivity formerly experienced as under erasure. The subculture of female bodybuilding rises more generally out of the historical context of subjectivity-as-performance and more particularly out of the context of violence against women.

Bodybuilding for women solves this vulnerability/invisibility problem on two levels. It makes the body the focus of attention, involving it in daily performance, complete with audience (the workout, the gym crowd), and it makes the body strong: hard, tight, experienced as inviolable, plugging into the iconography of invulnerability (think *Xena: Warrior Princess*). A form of violence against the self, bodybuilding functions as a repetition of trauma that, through the transformation of weak, vulnerable flesh into flesh that seems like steel, is also trauma's cure. While I am not saying that all bodybuilders have abuse histories, I am saying that bodybuilding can function this way for those who do, and that this is an important way in which bodybuilding is more than an activity that diverts women's attention from more important political causes. It is also one way of dealing with experiences of rape, harassment, and sexual abuse that second-wave feminism raised as important social issues. It is one way of overcoming victim status, as **159** conservative third-wave feminism has been urging us to do. While it is crucial that women fight together politically to try to change the social conditions that tend to produce the abuse in the first place, it is also crucial for individual women to have a way of healing themselves from abusive experiences, a healing that can be shared with other women and occupy an important position on the activist continuum. The contradictions a female bodybuilder embodies and negotiates surely deserve a place in the canon of other third-wave feminist practices, such as women who strip their way through college or twentysomething bodies reconstructed by plastic surgery. Unlike these other practices, however, the female bodybuilder's body is the simultaneous attempt to express her anger at both her devalued social position and the history that proceeds from it, and to keep that anger in. She tries to make herself monstrous within acceptable social norms.

In February 1996 the question of why women lift weights or bodybuild came up on the "Women's Bodybuilding Forum" (Femuscle), an Internet discussion group devoted to the subject of women's bodybuilding. One contributor, who is an editor of and writes for the women's bodybuilding magazine *Women's Physique World*, and who has interviewed a number of the top competitors over the years and asked them that same question, provided a Top Ten list:

10. "I just always liked the look of muscles. On a guy, a girl, or on an animal. I just always thought that it looked cool."
9. As an aid to overcoming something emotional, like stress or depression.
8. As an aid to overcoming an eating disorder.
7. As part of an athletic injury rehabilitation.
6. Because they'd been sedentary after playing high school or college sports and didn't like the shape they were in.
5. To share in an interest that already existed in a husband or boyfriend.
4. As a means of improving performance in another sport.
3. To get back into shape after childbirth.
2. To gain shape on a thin body.
1. To lose weight.[40]

This list shows that feminist criticisms of activities like bodybuilding (that it just imposes an even more restrictive and impossible ideal on women) have a basis. The ubiquitous "to lose weight" marks an allegiance to cultural ideals about the slender body that began in the sixties and was grafted onto the hard-body image of the eighties, a grafting revealed in "to gain shape on a thin body." This shift in body ideals is documented by music videos. VH-1's "Eight Track Flashback," for instance, provides a look at seventies bodies that is a strong reminder of how different ideals—and the bodies produced by those ideals—are now. One segment aired in January 1996 included clips from Maria Muldaur, Ike and Tina Turner, and Linda Ronstadt playing in 1975. Tina Turner had the hardest body, but a few shots which focused on her back (she was wearing a backless dress) revealed the soft rolls characteristic of the unworked-out body, thin but not sculpted. By today's standards, Maria Muldaur in her hip huggers and flaring peasant blouse that tied up under her breasts looked positively fat, her small waist flowing into that soft thick paunch of flesh over her pelvis that might have been celebrated as part of the feminine form in the mid-seventies, but which by the eighties was flattened out by hours and hours of aerobics and abs of steel. Ronstadt, in a flowing dress, revealed only chubby bare arms, but they were enough to show a very unsculpted, unworked-out body as well. What most surprised me but perhaps shouldn't have was how much I fell into the lose-weight mentality and how ugly I found their bodies (despite knowing I'm not supposed to feel that way—I'm more conscious than that), and how I couldn't refrain, more than twenty years too late, from yelling at the screen, "Get yourself into the gym!"

The list of reasons women bodybuild, while not exhaustive, hits a number of key points in the construction of a sense of self for women in the late twentieth century that come together in bodybuilding. All of the reasons, in one way or another, touch upon achieving, constructing yourself according to popular ideas about the female body in dominant American culture, the attainment of which marks personal success. Yet bodybuilding (as numbers eight and nine might begin to indicate), contains elements of subversiveness of those ideals as well. It creates bodies that are both in line and out of line, severely disciplined and powerfully rebellious. Current bodybuilding media darling Ericca Kern, for instance, used the occasion of her   **161** mostly nonexploitative and absolutely gorgeous nude *Flex* pictorial to write, "Through serious weight training, I changed my body and my attitude completely: I've gone through a process from anorexia and self-hatred to emotional strength and much less inhibition. Now I look in the mirror and I love what I see."[41] As most of the images of Kern and as her own language suggest, if bodybuilding can be used to overcome depression and eating disorders, a sense of valuelessness and self-censorship, it can begin to create a female embodiment, a way of living in a female body, that is something other than purely made up to please other people.

Although this is what the built body can *do*, it is often depicted in ways that suggest the opposite. Another success story, fitness competitor Jennifer Goodwin's account of her healing from anorexia, "How Bodybuilding Saved My Life!" is written and framed within conventions that trivialize it. It is written in the language of the clichéd pandering familiar from bad-cable-social-problem movies (the title, "How Bodybuilding Saved My Life!" even comes with the requisite exclamation point), and is full of hyperbole like "miraculous transformation" and "danc[ing] amber/green eyes."[42] But even worse are the images, the picture of anorexic Jennifer in biking shorts, shades, and tee shirt, looking like a ordinary person except too thin, and Jennifer the sex goddess, miraculously transformed from stick to chick with a single blink of the photographer's shutter. The images of the "after" are insulting: Jennifer looking pleadingly at you with doe eyes, lips slightly open; Jennifer looking defiant as she unzips her latex short-shorts just that little bit; Jennifer shot from the rear in a bathing suit at a gas pump, her hands provocatively working the hoses, her mouth open just so . . . it's enough to make at least this viewer find a greater comfort in the anorexic images if the alternative is this kind of clichéd prurience. But in 1997, catering to prurience is apparently what stands for successful healing. Her body, which could be framed in such a way that it would communicate the kind of strength and positive growth that the article claims, is represented instead as a stock fantasy object, explicitly framed by conventions that construct her body in a way that has nothing to do with its health, integrity, or strength.

The diminution performed by Jennifer's photos and others like hers is similar to that performed by the current movement toward smaller women in bodybuilding combined with the ascendance of fitness competitions. Both diminutions jeopardize the healing potential of bodybuilding. As cultural critic Doug Aoki puts it,

> Mainstream response to the bodybuilding body reveals the widespread prejudices and bigotries that found supposedly "individual" decisions about what is feminine or masculine or attractive or unattractive. . . . The challenge that female bodybuilding presents to existing and limiting notions of sex and gender . . . [makes it] a truly revolutionary enterprise, whatever the varied convictions of those who pursue it. In that light, one of the problems with fitness competition is that it is not simply an alternative to bodybuilding; it does not represent merely a different but equal kind of beauty. Situated as it is in a mainstream that already rejects the bodybuilder, the rise of the fitness woman is one more tactic that aids and abets that rejection.[43]

In rejecting the female bodybuilder, dominant culture rejects Mr. Hyde and women's right to anger and self-determination (again). Bodybuilders as distinguished from fitness women use their bodies to depart from as well as incarnate the norm, and are a sword as well as a shield in the fight against an outside world that may have devalued them. In the movie version of *Mary Reilly*, Jekyll explains on his deathbed that Hyde was his means of achieving "what [he] had always wanted—to be the knife, as well as the wound." The female bodybuilder's body as sword and shield, weapon and defense, points to the ways in which a woman's bodybuilding cannot simply be seen as enslavement to cultural ideals of beauty or as blindly buying into the just-do-it rhetoric of empowerment provided by the sports equipment and apparel industry.

Read metaphorically, Hyde is the body/masculinity women have created for themselves as a defensive strategy, a way of taking back their bodies from violence and a way of constructing a fortress against future attacks. Since the experience of domestic violence is the antithesis of self-realization for women, and research shows that its perpetrators violently reinforce traditional gender roles that associate masculinity with power and control, bodybuilding can most effectively work as a response to abuse if it is done in the context of a broader understanding of feminist activism and **163** changed gender roles, and if it is seen not just as individual development but as the strengthening of women's position in a general way.[44] For, as Ann Jones writes, "The widespread practice of wife beating intimidates all women and reinforces our society's habitual pattern of male violence. . . . It helps keep a man's world a man's world."[45] Do we really want to label as monstrous the bodybuilding which fights this violence, which provides a possibility for healing from the negation of self that the violence performs, which holds out a possibility for self-realization to women? If the female bodybuilder, who can incarnate this self-realization, is monstrous, we need to rethink the idea of monstrosity. Exclamation points aside, as an anchoring point, a space of (or at least the temporary illusion of) metaphysical safety, bodybuilding has literally saved some women's lives. It has saved mine. It takes no injection to turn me into Hyde. Like Jekyll in the end, I might wake up as him; I might not. There's just no telling.

6

American Girls, Raised on Promises

Why Women Build; or, Why I Prefer Henry Rollins to Beck

SOVEREIGNTY

Whenever you enter the space of a serious lifter's gym, there is sure to be some form of rock music loudly thrashing through the speakers. There has long been a connection between hard rock or metal and hefty bodies slinging serious poundage in the gym. The classic rock anthem is one of the best aids (excepting supplements and drugs) to get a great pump, the condition in which your muscles are full of blood and you are literally pumped up, because the anger and energy that drives the music helps to psyche you up enough to lift heavier, longer, heaving iron to the beat, unleashing your own energy and anger. Bodybuilders often joke about how personal tragedy or crisis is good for training in that you tend to lift much harder when angry or distressed, and hard rock can help you connect with that anger. A hard-core bodybuilding gym is often distinguished from the mainstream fitness gym by characteristics like huge free-weight sections and various supplements for sale in the front case, but perhaps the most definitive characteristic of the hard-core gym is that it plays classic rock like Skynyrd and Roses and Zeppelin, damn it, not feminized mainstream fluff like Hootie and the Blowfish or Mariah Carey.

But what does it mean for the female builder that the hard rock anthem, like the free-weight space in the gym, is explicitly constructed and defined against the domesticity and regulation that views the female body with derision and as a trap? Simon Reynolds and Joy Press argue that rock is one of the major vehicles of expression of the American fascination with the frontiersman rebel: "Women represent everything the rebel is not (passivity, inhibition) and everything that threatens to shackle him (domesticity, social norms). This ambivalence toward the feminine domain is the defining mark of all the classic instances of rock rebellion, from the Stones through the Doors, Led Zeppelin, the Stooges, to the Sex Pistols, Guns N' Roses and Nirvana."[1] Touchstones like Zeppelin's "Stairway to Heaven" or Skynyrd's "Free Bird" are good examples of this. Lyrically, "Stairway to Heaven" combines a critique of feminine consumer culture with the mythological imagery of truth and permanence, a pseudo-philosophical indictment of her belief that "all that glitters is gold," that one can buy the stairway to heaven. A ubiquitous late seventies anthem to the shallowness of both femininity and the culture of consumption associated with it, the song represents (for those of us coming into adolescence at that time) some of our first encounters with the opposite sex in that "Stairway" was inevitably the grand slow-dance finale to that formative institution of the negotiation of male/female relations—the junior high school dance. Similarly, Lynyrd Skynyrd's hallowed "Free Bird" is an explicit anthem of the male flight from the feminine: the free bird the woman can't change, domesticate, tie down, no matter how hard she tries. Free to fly and fly away, "Free

Bird" demonstrates the idea of male rebellion against and detachment from the feminine, where the male self is made possible by this very action of detachment.

But this rebellion is clearly not limited to rock; rather, in rock the characteristic "fear and loathing of the feminine" is given visceral embodiment. Bodybuilding is the enactment of this loathing when it functions in such a way as to purge signs of femininity from the body. As Marcia Ian writes, "Female bodybuilders . . . want to eradicate from themselves their sentimentalized 'femininity,' and its historical equivalent, immanent passivity."[2] Bodybuilders, like rockers, are expressing rebellion, as well as movement and physical strength, in this case through shaped flesh. As Sam Fussell writes in *Muscle*, bodybuilders form a subculture that views building as an activity which visibly transgresses social norms, that sets the builder apart from mere mortals: "We builders were nothing if not isolated, sequestered in willful disobedience against the rest of the world, and steroids were our agents of divorce. It was us against them, bodybuilders against mankind."[3] Fussell's language, although not marked explicitly, spells out the gender dynamics Ian documents. Bodybuilders "divorce" themselves from the rest of the world, that is, from the "tamed," domestic spaces, and are "willfully disobedient," evoking images of transgressions against some familial norm. "Them" is more accurately described as the feminized, ordinary populace, a "mankind" too domesticated, not virile enough.

The frontiersman analogy is apt because of the way in which bodybuilding, like so much of American culture, relies on the most cherished tenets of individualism, only to a more extreme degree. Veteran bodybuilder David Dearth voices this succinctly:

I train alone. I psych alone. I am alone. And that's how it must be, because the success or failure of my bodybuilding efforts depends entirely on the strength of my will to succeed. I empathize with the lone warriors of the past: the cowboy, the samurai, the medieval knight. After all, it is strength that makes all things possible—nothing survives without it. Who knows what delicate wonders have passed out of existence for want of the strength to survive?[4]

Since warriors, cowboys, samurai, and knights were historically all men, and since physical strength, traditionally considered a masculine attribute, is opposed to the feminized "delicate wonders" that have "passed out of existence" for "want of [that] strength," it is clear that in Dearth's thinking the feminine is a set of characteristics that needs to be overcome at all costs. His insistence that he is alone is a code for what he sees as transcendence of limitation: the ability to escape entanglements and relations of any kind, softer "delicate" attachments which would keep him, not just from success but from survival. His success is dependent on the relentless reduction of the world to his weights: "I go to sleep thinking of my workout. . . . I awaken to these same thoughts."[5] Poor guy. While this kind of single-minded dedication may have been admired in the eighties, in the hip and cynical nineties, which has a ready-made set of refutations for any argument, a rhetorical appropriation for any direct expression or firmly held set of beliefs, Dearth's thinking seems a bit naive and passé, far too sincere to be hip.

To some extent Dearth, whose thinking finds its musical corollary in classic rock, seems like a dinosaur today. Maybe that's why classic rock is now seen by music industry hipsters as similarly passé despite its massive listener base and huge number of radio stations devoted to the classic rock format. We can't all be hip, after all, for hipsters need those sorry retrogrades to define themselves against. While *some* retro is currently "all that," "the bomb," it tends at the moment to be disco that is more appropriable to today's feel-good ethos. Classic rock's a clunky dinosaur that still coughs up sales on those pitiful Journey and Kansas reunion tours, but anyone with a bit of nineties savvy knows to avoid it. Still, Dearth's assumptions, like those restless antidomestic strivings Reynolds and Press document in classic rebel rock point to a concept crucial to the bodybuilding mentality (similarly retro?): that of sovereignty.

"Rock," write Reynolds and Press, "is riddled with the idea of Phallus Power. The subtext is that in a world of men castrated by the system, here is a REAL MAN."[6] The reality of one's manliness is proven by the divorce from and transcendence of the artist (bodybuilder, academic—the list could go on) over the common, everyday world—gendered feminine (which is not to say that women can't or don't participate in schemes of transcendence)—of mere mortals. This system of thought neatly combines ideologies of individualism and masculinity into their logical apotheosis, that of sovereignty, a concept which is clearly expressed in the thinking of, among others, French philosopher Georges Bataille, who argues that "a world in which nothing is sovereign is the most unfavorable one. . . . Life *beyond utility* is the domain of sovereignty."[7] Consumption without production, life without specific use, being for itself—these are the domains of sovereignty, of modern-day kings. As Reynolds and Press point out,

> Rock is full of kings . . . [who] in a wider sense . . . represent *total possibility*, the zenith of the imaginable. . . . The rock star is the incarnation of his fans' forbidden desires and impossible dreams. . . . Rock stars . . . always cultivated an aesthetic of excess. Their values are aristocratic, a rejection of the bourgeois creed of deferred gratification, accumulation, investment. . . . A sovereign existence is one that isn't subordinated to utility, that doesn't involve the employment of the present for the sake of the future."[8]

At first glance, with its emphasis on sacrifice and goals, bodybuilding would seem to have nothing to do with the cultural logic of sovereignty. Yet if placed in a larger frame, that of an individual's life and the place of bodybuilding in it, bodybuilding can have no further use than that of self-assertion, the extension of the self into the world through the medium of muscle. Even most of the champions in the sport don't make a living from bodybuilding itself; from a use-value perspective it is hard to justify the endless hours of training, cardiovascular exercise, and diet that go into the creation of the bodybuilder physique when so little that is tangibly productive is gained in return. Bodybuilding brings none but a very few individuals lucrative endorsements, and the prize money offered in contests never even covers the costs of training and supplements. "Why would anyone want to waste their time just to look like that?" is a question commonly voiced by nonbuilders, but the emphasis on looks diverts from the deeper motivations. Bodybuilding would be, then, in a use-value mode of thinking, a bad investment, an endless expenditure of energy that has no purpose.

"What distinguishes sovereignty," Bataille writes, is the consumption of **169** wealth, as against labor and servitude, which produce wealth without consuming it. The sovereign individual consumes and doesn't labor."[9] Bodybuilding is sovereign because it is the consumption of an individual's free time and resources, which could be diverted to much more productive ends. It is a form of "labor and servitude" for the self rather than for someone else, a labor performed in the service of nothing. It's about feeling like you have some kind of control over your own life, some space you can claim and say "Forget everything else, everything I need to get done, THIS is mine!" On the deepest levels, bodybuilding has no further purpose than (the illusion of) self-ownership, of the ability to squander one's own time if one so desires, to put one's own energy into production for the self, not for others. Such is the province of the sovereign.

While a sovereign logic is inherent in bodybuilding iconography—replete as it is with superheroes and gods, figures of fantasy that rise above the realm of ordinary mortals—it has been repressed and ignored in the written expression of bodybuilding ideology, which voices the logic of self-sacrifice, dedication, and health benefits. Bodybuilding has a use, in this way of thinking. It is done in service of health; it is done in service of the good American goals of achievement like "being the best you can be," and being the best requires personal sacrifices like time spent at the gym that could be spent at the pub eating chicken wings, and eating a pleasureless, fat-free diet of tuna fish supplements. But this is the official rhetoric, which protests too much to be fully believable. Iconography that shows bodybuilder superheroes in comic books or that propelled Arnold Schwarzenegger's phenomenal success is much closer to psychological truth. It is the repressed logic of sovereignty inherent in bodybuilding that makes middle-class America so uncomfortable, that makes bodybuilding an object of public fascination and repulsion, awe and ridicule, particularly for women, who are still expected to have a for-others orientation and are seen as appalling, selfish, and unnatural if they do not.

Bodybuilding to some extent has become as popular as it has because culturally there is a longing for sovereignty, a space where one can just do and say as one pleases, for no purpose, without consequences, without having to slave away for some corporation or at some even more menial job: just look at the slacker phenomenon and at the popularity of Howard Stern, as well as the public outcry against political correctness, which accurately or inaccurately is seen as imposing limitations on what people are permitted to think and say. Why otherwise would so many people—from the baby boomers on down—want to be in bands, which in the popular imagination are linked to excesses of all kinds, to the right to behave outrageously? Our culture is starved for individual sovereignty, for a way out of the daily grind that reduces us to our productivity and use value. And of course, because social injunctions against sovereign desires are so vitriolic, and public censure so great for most people (hence the idolatry practiced with accepted stars), a state of sovereignty is desired all the more fervently. True hedonists we, the sovereign is what many people want to be, the place many people want to get. It is the position most culturally valued at the deepest, unspoken levels, despite official rhetoric of sacrifice for others and responsibility that would dictate otherwise. For better *and* worse, we are a nation of individuals who, at the most fundamental levels, don't want to be told what to do.[10] Women's bodybuilding is about the ability of women to partake of some sense of sovereignty, too—and in a way that expresses it physically, visually. Bodybuilding is an in-your-face confrontation with traditional roles, an unavoidable assertion of: "I don't care if this is a waste of time or diverts me from more important political causes or if you think it makes me unfeminine, it's what I want to do." Women's bodybuilding is an unequivocal self-expression, an indication of women's right to *be*, for themselves, not for children, partners, fellow activists, not for anyone else. In a culture that still mostly defines women's purpose as service for others, no wonder female bodybuilding is so controversial.

In their discussion of sovereignty Reynolds and Press trace a parallel trajectory in rock that makes clear some otherwise confusing tensions between the American celebrity system and the professed political philosophy of democracy, tensions based on the paradox that everyone wants to be king ("It's good to be king / just for a while" is Tom Petty's wistfully cynical 1994 version—we *know already* that we can't all be king, but it's nice to desire it anyway—of this paradox). *I know but all the same . . .* the ideological fetish that keeps desire in play—in this case, the desire to stand out, be above the masses, different, a star. As mid-nineties antistar Beck puts it, "*Rock star* conjures up something like a mystic: someone who sees himself as above other people, someone who has the key to the secret that people want to know. . . . I've never related to that. . . . [For me] it's not a self-glorification thing."[11] Rock stars by definition embody the illusion of standing above, in the place of the subject presumed to know, as does a bodybuilding star even more literally since their difference, superiority, sovereignty, is inscribed in their own flesh. And stars are a pre-nineties thing, at least in terms of what they profess.

For things have gotten much more complicated than they were in the excess of the eighties, whose ideologies—for both good and ill—were more tolerant of unmitigated self-assertion and desire. Ideology in the nineties doesn't tolerate such a straightforward, all-out expression of will, or narcissistic desire, or self-interestedness. To do so is to take too much of a definite position, and any definite position can be attacked. Beck explains this in generational terms, saying "I think my whole generation's mission is to kill the cliché. . . . It's one of the reasons a lot of my generation are always on the fence about things. They're afraid to commit to anything for fear of seeming like a cliché. They're afraid to commit to their *lives* because they see so much of the world as a cliché."[12] Since any definite stand or stab at sovereignty can be mocked as a cliché, one must be self-deprecating and ironic, seemingly will-less, and, contrary to the will-to-power, must decry success, dub oneself "zero," like Billy Corgan of the Smashing Pumpkins, even though the star system is perhaps even more vehemently in place.[13]

This is why someone like the muscle-bound Henry Rollins, rocking out and preaching his metal-fueled will-to-self-determination, seems passé in the music world today, where faceless, starless amalgams like techno and anything that exhibits a hybrid of genres currently rule the roost. Beck is "where it's at" because his low-key, antistar persona and the mixture of styles in his music do to a certain extent sit "on the fence." The ideology of sovereignty that Reynolds and Press detect as central to rock's pantheon marks the passing of an era, a dedication to single groups or figures, stars, that the constant craving for novelty will not tolerate. Music industry analysts have documented a shift in consumer buying patterns from allegiance to a single figure or group, buying everything their beloved band puts out, to a decentered drift from group to group, look to look, sound to sound.

Dedication to *anything* is uncool—which poses definite problems for any kind of political activism. Classic rock's now dated, seemingly unsophisticated, outright expression of antifeminine, ego-centered, delusional will-to-power had serious problems. But at least it was honest; at least it took a stand; at least it was a form of self-assertion. This is why, even if intellectually I am in sympathy with Beck and his antistar, world-as-cliché stance, emotionally I recognize a compatriot in Rollins. Ironically, he ends up a political ally because he is willing to take a stand, to risk cliché, to admit a desire for sovereignty—that same sovereignty which was previously denied to women, but once we got a chance at it, our own critiques had rendered it cliché. This is one of the most ironic contradictions third-wave feminism faces, but I'm not going to sit on the fence. Give me red-painted Rollins over silver-tongued Beck any day. Now that was a REAL MAN.

The psychology of rebellion against the feminine documented by Reynolds and Press and exemplified in figures like Rollins sets up a contradiction for the female builder. Trespassing in a space defined against her gender (hard against soft, isolation against connection, detachment against emotion), participating vicariously in an anger directed against her, motivated by a music that gains its energy from canceling her out, she must prove her ability to be one of the guys at the same time she provides reassurance of her femininity. What does it mean for a woman to identify with the king psychology endemic to classic rock? What is the relationship among rock stars, female bodybuilding, female athletes, and male identification? Why is it that, at the moment when some women were gaining access to at least the provisional possibility of participating in the cultural logic of sovereignty, with all its pleasures and problems, to do so is suddenly dated, passé, an ethos departed into the technological ether? My most convincing answers come from my own fascination with sovereignty in classic rock, and my love affair with the music of one of its main satellites, Tom Petty.

IT'S GOOD TO BE KING

Tom Petty's "It's Good to Be King," from 1994's *Wildflowers*, ironically but fondly expresses the American fascination with sovereignty: the king who gets his own way is a lost dream that he can't help having even though it is **173** lost. So while Petty's song may express the wistful angst of a diminished cultural power in mid-nineties masculinity, it also expresses the wistful angst of a male-identified third-wave feminist bodybuilder. I was born in 1964, which places me right on the edge of Generation X. For some of us straddling the divide between Generation X and whatever it was that came before us, perhaps the more appropriate name would be the classic-rock generation, because for us, and in a very specific manner for a specific group of women that makes up one part of that "us," the master narrative that stepped in to take the place of more traditional models was not Hemingway or Dos Passos or Sartre or Nietzsche, but rather Tom Petty and the Heartbreakers. Understanding what it means for a thirtysomething, male-identified, straight, white chick to have Tom Petty's music, attitude, and persona provide a horizon of meaning is, in Ann Powers's words, a way of understanding "a legacy that's at turns unspeakably degrading and impossibly, joyfully liberating."[14] It's understanding the strange confusions at the heart of third-wave feminism.

Tom Petty is rock and roll in the old silhouettes-of-women-on-the-mudflaps-of-big-trucks tradition, a singer who, in "Don't Do Me Like That," and "Free Falling," urges women not to take personal initiative and leave him while he gets to "free fall" away from a relationship and be a bad boy whenever it suits him. Although a milder version of the Rolling Stones' under-my-thumb tradition, Petty is not the kind of figure who would immediately spring to mind along with the word "feminist." Yet he has provided a form of identification for at least this particular blood-red, table-thumping feminist even after she had the tools with which to relegate to the realm of the laughable Petty-isms like "Here Comes My Girl," in which he expresses the anachronistic cultural mythology of the man going out and working hard all day to support his girl, who returns this favor by inspiring him to go on through her sexiness and devotion to him. Her selflessness makes it all worthwhile. Any self-respecting feminist would hear lyrics such as these and scream, "Nineteenth-century separation-of-the-spheres, angel-in-the-house, woman-as-muse tradition!" and lambaste the song's expression of the old ideology of the woman who stands by and behind her man, who provides him with a purpose for going out into the world and working while she provides a stable emotional ground to which he can return.

Feminists would object to the notion that it's a woman who "looks so right" who provides him with "all he needs tonight," as well as his discussion of his woman's "walk" with its hints of sexual possession, and that possession providing him with a sense of meaning and purpose and reason to be a breadwinner. Come on, Tom, this is fifties schmaltz, appearing on *Damn the Torpedoes*, your breakthrough album, in 1979, a time when women are earning their own bread and finding modes of existence other than "looking right" for their men. So how could a singer whose focus is the old-master narrative of rigid gender roles provide a horizon of meaning for a feminist who has the deepest emotional investments in undermining, helping to facilitate the exhaustion of, and replacing that very narrative the song glorifies? An answer, I think, is historically located in the women's movement itself, and in its absorption by popular culture in the seventies and eighties.

To turn to "American Girl," and the American girl I definitely was at the time that this song made its appearance in 1976, the lyrics of the song hold a personal significance informed by its historical context. What might have been both "so close" and "still so far out of reach" for a twelve-year-old American girl in 1976? What promises had been made to her and why? What was lacking in her own life so that "she couldn't help thinking that there was a little more life somewhere else"? What is it that is "so painful"? And what does the mysterious He, who "creeps back in her memory" for "one desperate moment" have to do with that sense of lack and pain?

In 1976, the second-wave women's movement had been under way for roughly eight years. Following on the heels of the civil rights movement, collective supporters of women's rights gained some reproductive control in 1973 with the *Roe v. Wade* decision legalizing abortion, and the seventies in general saw the mass movement of women into the workplace, marking what seemed to be a widespread cultural agreement with the feminist notion that women are people. In 1976, a twelve-year-old girl was raised on the promise that she could do anything a man could do, that opportunity was available to her wherever she looked, that—to use another Petty lyric from "Into the Great Wide Open" (1991)—"the sky was the limit." White, middle-class, twelve-year-old girls were promised that they, too, could finally cruise, like the boys, into an open horizon. **175**

For the first time, we were offered the white male subject position of fully autonomous, individuated, rugged rebel—offered, even, a glimpse of the sovereignty and transcendence of the ordinary that the rebel rocker lives out. Anger and rebellion could be expressed through male identification, and that identification was in turn seen as liberation. We didn't have to be like our mothers, we were told—sometimes by our mothers themselves, who were busy going back to school and getting MBAs (although when my own mother was doing this in 1981, I didn't even know what she was up to, I just knew I was glad she was gone some nights). Clearly, even as some of our mothers were cruising into the great wide open themselves (mothers in other racial and class groups had always had to work, but since white, middle-class women were taken as the standard for all women, this had been largely ignored), there was silence or looking away surrounding our recognition of our mothers' achievements.

Our identities, like those of many sons before us, were formed by not being like our mothers, which meant, then, being like our fathers. The father and his position were offered up as available to us, too—opportunities everywhere. Let's face it: when we hung posters of Tom Petty and Mick Jagger and Jim Morrison on our bedroom walls, it wasn't just that they were hot enough to make us sweat. It wasn't the fit of their butts in the right cut of jean. It wasn't just that we wanted them—their assertiveness, freedom, their mischievous, self-delighted I-can-do-or-say-anything-and-you'll-still-love-me. We wanted to *be* them. And all the cultural truisms of the time told us that we could. This is America. You can be whatever you want.

Petty knew that the American girl of the post-sixties generation was raised on the promise that she could do anything—that every opportunity was open to her, and he knew that this promise sometimes rang hollow. "American Girl" was one of the first hits from the 1976 album *Tom Petty and the Heartbreakers,* and perfectly expresses the mingling of high hopes, sadness, and quiet confusion about why those hopes haven't solidified that can characterize the life of women raised on the equal-opportunity promises of second-wave feminism. The way the song captures the hopes and disappointments of much of a female generation was not lost on Jonathan

Demme, the director of the film *The Silence of the Lambs* (1991), who, in a scene meant to convey the characteristic illusion of self-possession, safety, and empowerment shared by women born in the sixties and later, has one of his serial killer's female victims rocking out to "American Girl" just before she runs into her attacker. Both Petty's song and Demme's clever use of it provide a cultural context for the problem of why I love Tom Petty, that self-proclaimed associate of heartbreakers.

For it is clear that the brokenhearted subject of "American Girl" is involved with more than clichéd romantic feminine dreams. For the unnamed She who is the subject of the song, the song lyrics spell out the terrible irony and desire of a goal just missed, a dream a hairbreadth away from fulfillment, gone. Something was "so painful," something "still so far out of reach." Given what we were promised, some American girls certainly thought that "there was a little more life somewhere else," and that this life was available to us if we acted like boys, if we disowned those aspects of ourselves even remotely resembling our mothers. Male identification offered us "a little more life," and was attainable if we gave up anything considered traditionally feminine, including our bodies, which meant that having a body as close to a boy's as possible signified power—and people still wonder why eating disorders proliferated right around this time. The eating disorders were one indication that something was wrong, one of the first whispers that indicated pain.[15] "American Girl" probably refers to a failed romantic relationship, but in this particular historical context it can also for many of us be taken to refer to that first failed relationship with our fathers who, perhaps desiring sons and getting daughters instead, took advantage of the historical moment and encouraged those daughters, in order to gain their fathers' love, to be sons—to become, fundamentally, something they could never be, so close but still so far. We could never become (and as Nike ads reassure us, shouldn't have needed to become) boys, but we gave it a hell of a try anyway, turning from most of our feminine characteristics as from the plague. The life of the white son that white daughters struggled to gain access to and found themselves inexplicably failing in was extraordinarily "painful," and was, by definition out of reach because it required the impossible.

It required persons who had female bodies and who were therefore branded unalterably according to one set of cultural characteristics (such as beauty, sexual attractiveness to men, and emphasis on personal relation-ships) both to enact and to renounce those characteristics simultaneously. You are a girl, the code read, and that means you have to create a certain image and attract men if you want to live a meaningful life, but you also shouldn't be like a girl. Only weak people are like girls. Be beautiful, and attract a man, but also *be* a man, which means you shouldn't worry about relationships, only achievements. It was a contradictory code that offered male identification as the promise of a way out of the restrictiveness of traditional roles, but undermined that possibility through the simultaneous requirement of impeccable femininity as well as the cultural power of being taken seriously only to the extent that one did not act like a girl.

Many of us, myself included, wanting the love of the father/culture, torn by the contradictions of desire for, wanting to be, and hating the "father"— that is, the male image of strength and omnipotence that is a child's image of her father—ended up in competitive athletics. Here the highest honor was to perform like a guy, to be considered in the same category or level of competitiveness, again achieved by distinguishing oneself from other women. The milestones of my high school life were being given the privi-lege of working out with the men's cross-country team since I was so good, so far ahead of the rest of the women's team, and the documentation of this elite position in the local paper when a perceptive interviewer titled his lead article "Amphi's Heywood—One of the Guys." Publicly designated as "one of the guys," I thought my life was nearly complete. To reinforce this difference from other women and therefore my superior position, I re-fused even to talk to anyone on the women's team, and reveled in the fact that I was the only one to make it to the state meet. When in my senior year my points alone added up to second place in the state as a team, I saw this as the ultimate triumph since I had achieved such a high team distinction individually. My position as "one of the guys" was the basis for my whole identity in one sense—a sense that collided rather dramatically with that other basis, still functioning, still as thick in the air as that promise offered by male identification—the identity offered by looking "so right" and all the cultural significance that seemed to accompany it.

I knew that the way I looked had a lot to do with the amount of press I received, so frequently that local athletes wrote into the paper to complain.

There were black women, and white women who didn't look as traditionally feminine as I did, who often won just as many events, yet they were never featured. I was only dimly aware of this then, and just felt happy to get the coverage, but I only "looked so right" from a very traditional point of view. My whiteness contributed to the ability of newspapers to market me as traditionally feminine. Given a long racist history and continuing racism and class discrimination in the U.S., my personification of acceptable femininity was facilitated by that history. As Cahn writes, "African American women's work history as slaves, tenant farmers, domestics, and wageworkers disqualified them from standards of femininity defined around the frail or inactive female body. . . . Black women are often represented in dominant culture as masculine females lacking in feminine grace, delicacy, and refinement. . . . [There has been a] long exclusion of both African American women and female athletes from categories of acceptable femininity." [16] Given that changes in gender roles in the seventies and eighties affected primarily white women, that I was given cultural value as one of the guys but still represented as acceptably feminine had more to do with historical connections among femininity, whiteness, and middle-class-ness than it had to do with me and some essential personal value (though at the time I sure took it that way).

The demand that an eighties girl should be one of the guys but still look like a girl brought the cultural confusion about changing gender roles for women to the fore. The newspaper article that designated me "one of the guys" demonstrates the clash in ideologies, and people trying to bridge it:

> Leslie Heywood is just "one of the guys," as far as the Amphi High School cross country team is concerned. The pretty blonde, blue-eyed junior is the best runner on the girls team, but she regularly works out with the boys team. . . . "I want her to stop thinking like a girl runner," [the Panther coach] said. "Not that I want her to stop being a girl, but because I want her to work and think like an athlete. Right now she's just one of the guys." [17]

My coach's comments provide only a brief, attenuated glimpse of "the pressures," that Bruce Kidd describes "on female athletes to be what is   **179** considered feminine." From my coach's remarks, it is clear that he considers someone who "works and thinks like an athlete" male, and that I could only, in spite of his insistence that he doesn't "want me to stop being a girl," be an "athlete" if I were in fact "just one of the guys." The contradiction between acceptable femininity and individual achievement was constant, as was the requirement that I act out both.

The immediate qualification of the statement that I was "one of the guys" with a description of me as a "pretty blonde, blue-eyed junior," so often seen in bodybuilding magazines and other journalism that involves female athletes, works to soften the effect, to reassure readers of my femininity since femininity clashed with the dominant view that athleticism is a male province in which one establishes one's agency and personal value. As Kidd writes, "I realize that I would have been devastated if a girl—no matter how gifted—had played for any of the teams I was so proud to make. Such a situation would have proclaimed to the world that I was 'like a girl' and therefore inadequate."[18] The newspaper demonstrates the very view Kidd articulates when it reports, "'She pushes the guys, too,' says [the girls coach]. 'There's a lot of mutual benefit. If she beats one of the JV runners, then we can rib them and they'll work a little harder.'" The guys were publicly shamed when I beat them in a practice. The picture that accompanied the article showed me leading a pack of guys on a run up a steep hill, and the actual guys in the photo behind me were upset as well as teased and denigrated for weeks about getting caught and displayed in the local newspaper running *behind* a girl. Further, since as David Whitson writes, sports is "an institution that encourages men to identify with other men and provides the regular rehearsal of such identifications," my status as "one of the guys" disrupted this system of identification and the valuation of men and masculinity it performs to a certain extent.[19] What would it mean for one of the guys on the team to identify with me, a girl? To the extent that this identification did happen, my position was potentially subversive. Yet that subversion was contained by two things: that I was in a marginalized sport to begin with, a sport seen as less masculine than major sports like football, and the fact that I was myself male identified. The newspaper article goes on to say,

The only place either of the coaches sees a problem is in what [the girls coach] calls the team concept. He says that without Heywood working with the girls team, the other girls don't think they can compete with her. "I would like all of the girls to believe that they can compete with Leslie for at least the first mile or so. . . . I think the girls feel it would hurt her. It would hold her back, keep her from reaching her potential. That in turn would hurt the team."

Even the girls I was devaluing in my acceptance of the creed that to be a real athlete I had to distance myself from them felt it would "keep me from reaching my potential" to be part of their group. My identification with males, my acceptance of the view that maleness is what is valuable, ensured that the "team concept" was something that made me physically nauseated, for I was emotionally invested in demonstrating my distance and difference from the girls in as graphic and literal terms as possible since an alliance with them would have signified weakness, lack of potential, and that I need not be taken seriously. For I knew that, as Susan Cahn writes, "many Americans simply [do] not separate the concept of athletic superiority from its cultural affiliation with masculine sport and the male body."[20] In order to uphold that affiliation (because I thought that to do so would bring me the valuation usually denied women) my only strategy in meets was to take off as fast as I could at the sound of the gun, get as far away from the other female bodies as I could, and never look back.

Again, trying to have it both ways, like the rhetoric accompanying every pictorial of a female bodybuilder in a magazine, this article attempted to demonstrate that despite my guyness and difference from girls I wasn't a freak or a monster—hence the emphasis on my more acceptable "other interests" like "varsity cheerleading," which proved that I wasn't "one-dimensional," that I still enacted the characteristics of lack and male support, that I hadn't broken entirely away. As Silverman writes,

Female subjectivity represents the site at which the male subject deposits his lack. . . . The castration which is synonymous with sexual difference is not endemic to the female body but is emblazoned across it by the male subject through projection. . . . Conventional masculinity can

1 8 1

best be understood as the denial of castration, and hence as a refusal to acknowledge the defining limits of subjectivity. The category of "femininity" is to a very large degree the result. . . . Defense against what is in the final analysis male lack . . . The "ideal" female subject refuses to recognize male lack.[21]

My situation came perilously close to disrupting these categories, and both the media and my self-representation worked to contain that disruption. It became difficult for the guys on the team to project lack on a body that was beating them up the hills, disrupting the dynamic that would allow them to deny their lack by placing it on girls, those representatives of "femininity" who by definition weren't supposed to keep up with them, thereby proving male sufficiency and female lack. I reminded them in the most graphic terms that their lack of lack was a fiction, but that fictionality was contained by my willingness to take the category of lack onto myself *even as* I denied it, by presenting myself also as "varsity cheerleader," as the "pretty blonde, blue-eyed junior."

This other position showed that I wasn't "just one of the guys," that I did contain the necessary lack to designate me as "other" and thereby remained within the limits of the acceptable. I acted out and supported the very set of characteristics—femininity and the mindless support of dominant cultural traditions of gender—that in the context of athleticism I denigrated, radically dissociated myself from to the extent of refusing to speak to women. Talk about a "divided self." But why? If I was so interested in being "one of the guys," in denying my own lack, why did I also take up the other position? The identity offered by "looking so right," as the Petty song put it, and the cultural rewards that went with it made the acceptance of lack seem like a tangible form of power. Because I looked "so right"— that is, because I constructed myself according to a feminine ideal that signified lack, that I existed to attract male attention—I did get attention. My position as varsity cheerleader made it socially empowering for the guys on the cross-country team who were low on the social totem pole to be seen in my company, and would fight among themselves every day to see who would get to sit next to me on the way to practice or at the movies, and who would get to pay for my ticket. To a fifteen-year-old, this looks like power.

What others unconsciously read as lack I read as power, and I did everything I could to fortify my position as someone who looks "so right" (wearing full makeup to every practice, ribbons in my hair) thereby fortifying a lack I interpreted as strength while always feeling that some inexplicable thing was not quite right.

Tom Petty probably never figured out why the "American girls" he sang about would express their lives by "God, it's so painful," but he did, through male identification, seem to offer for the duration of his songs at least, full access to that male space we "couldn't quite reach" due to our attempts to "look so right" and to the fact that while we could almost do it, we were never quite the real thing. I was an honorary guy on that cross-country team, loved much more for my difference than for my similarities to them. In a Tom Petty song I could be just one of the guys, faced with his dilemmas and possibilities, his bravado in the face of uncertainty or pain. The "I" in the Tom Petty songs was the "I" that I wanted to be, that I had been promised access to but painfully denied in reality. It took me years to realize that this "I" had its own problems. And while I now know that consciously, the promise of fulfillment that it seemed to offer still has a powerful unconscious pull.

On a recent trip, cruising up the Pacific Coast Highway in a Saab with its sunroof open and Petty's *Let Me Up, I've Had Enough* (1987) blasting on the CD player, I came fully to terms with what it is that I (still) like about Tom Petty, and therefore where my emotional investments still are. Caught in a state of longing for the masculine subject position, the chance to fight for sovereignty I was promised but never fully gained, paralyzed by the sense of lack my failure to gain it engendered, my still close connection to Petty, despite knowing better, was living proof of both Zizek's and Silverman's formulations. Even though I can take apart a song like "Here Comes My Girl" and berate it for its nineteenth-century story line, this does not explain the great pleasure and sense of power I got out of driving fast up the coast singing along with "Jamming Me." As Zizek writes, "Cynical distance is just one way—one of many ways—to blind ourselves to the structuring power of ideological fantasy: even if we do not take things seriously, even if we keep an ironical distance, *we are still doing them.*" [22] Here I was, intact in my cynical difference from Petty and the ideas his music and **183** lyrics express, while loving them anyway. Not the ideas about angels in houses, but the idea of the power and sovereignty that could be mine, wholly, intact, for the duration of those moments I could sing along with that voice that was asserting it. The appeal Petty holds is the appeal of an extended promise, a power that he has that I can have, too. I know better, know that this power is an empty lure and that the traditional masculine subject-position is not much empowered than the feminine one. Nonetheless I will do it again, and feel reassured—if divided from myself—at those moments. As Silverman writes, "Ideological belief operates at a level exterior to consciousness, and the subject can continue to 'recognize' itself and its desires within certain kinds of sounds, images, and narrative paradigms long after consciously refuting them. . . . There is no subject whose identity and desires has not been shaped to some degree by it."[23] Loving Petty, I confront, in Ann Powers's words, "the conundrum of loving a double dose of what's supposed to be bad for you: on the one hand, a pop fantasy that can dehumanize; on the other, a feminist ideology that declares dangerous what most attracts you."[24]

Even as someone who spends a great deal of her life speaking about problems with and emotional costs of the ideology of individualism that Petty's music expresses, I recognize myself and my desires in his assertive rejections of femininity and women, which his music allows me to participate in vicariously. I know it is an ambivalent identification because the feeling of empowerment is the product of and made possible by self-rejection, but I am doing it anyway. I'm still like Faulkner's Thomas Sutpen, trying to pass, embracing the very values of autonomy, privatization, and separation that cancel me out, that make me into "lack."[25] To love Tom Petty is to love the masculine and reject the feminine, culturally coded as the popular, as seen in the denigration of pop music, usually populated by female singers. Petty is another example of a popular singer who rejects the popular and romanticizes heroic individualism instead. His songs provided me with an anthem of empowerment as I drove up the coast, feeling better than I had in the months since I last heard him. His songs momentarily fill a yearning for power—a yearning that can lead to other things.

In "Liberation Scenes" bell hooks writes about a kind of cultural work that "emerg[es] from an oppositional, progressive, cultural politic that seeks to link theory and practice, that has as its central agenda sharing knowledge and information in ways that transform how we think about our social reality." She describes the kind of work I hope to do precisely because I feel the yearning that leads me to still love Petty's music. Many thinkers argue with hooks that we need to form coalitions and act, and that we can do so for starters by analyzing our own emotional connections to popular culture as well as the social context for those connections. Hooks looks for "common passions, sentiments shared by folks across race, class, gender, and sexual practice . . . a depth of longing in many of us . . . The shared space and feeling of yearning opens up the possibility of common ground where all these differences might meet and engage one another."[26] Analysis of cultural texts like Tom Petty's music, and the personal and historical reasons for my engagement with it, points to a drive in pop culture to work against the kind of collective movement hooks speaks of here, and thus works against the yearning so many of us feel for empowerment and change. But, through expressing a desire for liberation and sovereignty that awakens and validates our own expression, pop culture also enables us to see ways our yearning is shared, and give us a reason to work collectively to bring about precisely such empowerment and change.

Fifty-Foot Queenie: Why Women Build

Through the contradictory longing expressed by "American Girl," it is possible to guess one of the reasons at least some women bodybuild: to attain the promise of sovereignty or self-ownership that, in the aftermath of second-wave feminism, was offered to some American girls. Many of those girls, who routinely experience violence, are desperately attempting to gain that promise. But can such an individualist activity, such an individualist desire, ever lead to coalition, to a group effort to change anything, especially if bodybuilding does fulfill the promise of "something that was so close and still so far out of reach"? If the very yearning for change is brought about by a sense that the promise of gender equality has not been fulfilled, and bodybuilding seems to fulfill the promise, then how can it ever be more than a compensation, an ideological suture which marks a dream of gender equality deferred?[27]

In the academic criticism, as well as the larger culture in which women strain and sweat, proudly exhibiting their chiseled bodies, there are two contradictory views of female bodybuilding, both of which are true: bodybuilding conforms to dominant norms, discouraging group activism and the need for further change, and bodybuilding offers a way out of the kind of cultural ideas—women are small and weak, for instance—that can kill you. If you don't feel small and weak, you are also more likely to feel you can do something, effect some kind of change. Your personal change, your personal feelings of strength, become an inspiration for other women, who, through believing in themselves and acting strong, force others to treat them differently. A form of third-wave activism, certainly, an alternative to the picket lines, but is it enough if it just stops there?

So here's where I conform: 24 percent of my waking hours, almost one-fourth of my life since adolescence, has been spent working out—that many hours lost to any activist cause. A quarter of my hours and sometimes more (although I didn't run or go to the gym today so I could finish writing this). But those hours are my sanity, my identity, my life. The weight plates, stacking up the hours to nowhere, the runs down the sidewalk for mile upon mile, my eyes never wavering, focused on nothing, on everything: hopes, fears, dreams. Building out of that nothingness, I am a feminist bodybuilder. My Frankenstein boots mark my presence on the ground. There is no way that you will ever knock me down. To touch me is to touch a flesh that is inhumanly forged, thickened, marked, shaped into a wall you'll never fit through. Grams of protein, grams of fat. Teaspoons of creatine, capsules of time, the test tubes of chemicals I ingest. You have to see me, can't look away. I intrude on your screen, inevitability itself, the final curtain. I have these delusions sometimes. I'm a monster. And I hope, knowing this, you will still listen.

To build, or not to build? Retrograde or hip? Admirable or laughable? Legitimately self-expressive or shamelessly self-centered? All of these? More?

Bodybuilding is about individual change, and as my own history has shown, can sometimes function to divert energy away from activist causes and keep change from happening. But it is also a way to claim a forbidden **186** space, to assert oneself into the public sphere in unprecedented ways. For

a woman to walk into the free-weight space of a gym is always to trespass—
disparaging looks shot at her lifting her wimpy weights communicate this
immediately; or if she can lift a lot of weight, remarks like "Are you sure
you want to lift that much? You'll get big" reaffirm traditional gender roles
that decree a woman should not get big (except maybe her breasts)—ostensibly the purpose of lifting.

Yet despite all this, the gym remains a place where the female body,
unlike other places, can, by getting strong, earn a little respect. Respect
for her body's integrity, boundaries, for her self-ownership, a respect often
denied women in their daily lives. The practice of lifting and developing
strength can make a woman who has been physically or emotionally abused
and diminished feel stronger, more invincible, more whole. Lifting can
make a woman who has been culturally devalued in any of the usual ways—
"You throw (or talk or act) like a girl"—feel stronger, more certain of herself and her place in the world, the right she has to take up space. Even if
the fitness babes are taking over the magazines, in the daily subculture
things are a little different. As you get stronger, you gain the admiration
and respect of regular gym members who ask your advice on how to hit legs
harder or what a particular exercise does. You may also, as I did just last
week, become the butt of admiring jokes: "She could bench press you,
man." "She could bench press you, too." "Hell, she could bench press all
of us put together."

Feeling I have the right to take up space works magic. And with that
magic inside me, a holdover from the afternoon's workout, I'm watching
some video compilations the other night. I've got on the Rolling Stones,
Voodoo Lounge, and then Tom Petty and the Heartbreakers, *Playback*. En-
dorphins still in my blood, my chest still pumped from my bench, it hits
me. On the television screen, unlike when I've got them screaming out of
every speaker in my Pathfinder, helping me take the corners and the traf-
fic lights by storm, Tom and Mick have bodies. Limits. Those voices from
my childhood, insinuating themselves into all my adolescent desires, the
voices that had filled the room, so *big*, so *there* that I just had to listen . . .
this time, when I'm watching them on TV, what I see is those voices coming out of skinny guys' chests. And my chest is twice their size and I'm not
talking about my breasts. **187**

As this dawns on me, slowly—hey, you know, I could take him down with my left arm—I can feel their voices' spacious magic, power, start to drift off with their words, disappearing out over the thousands of worshipfully bobbing heads, over my TV screen, out of my thickly muscled chest where I had kept them. Their aura fades. Suddenly, things feel different: the Heartbreakers, Stones are skinny. They wield guitars and voices and drums,but they've got no pecs. Just guys, a little geeky, the jerky movements of their thin arms and hips more than a little like chickens. Just guys.

So it's now, this moment, not skinny, grown into myself, that I know. Because of weights, after eighteen years I have arrived at a place where I've got my own fantasies of power, self-ownership, strength. I don't need Mick's or Tom's deflected glory, aura, their sovereignty so boldly writing itself over the world and my heart and my mind: I have my own. The fact simply is, I could bench press Mick. I could bench press Tom. Hell, I could bench press them all. Their voices will never have the same hold over me again.

ENTER THE DRAGON

In a piece of cultural criticism that makes me cry each and every time I read it, Susan Bordo uses the movie *Babe* (1995) to demonstrate how the power feminist just-do-it rhetoric of nineties empowerment encourages the workout ethos of consumer culture, an ethos which suggests that every aspect of our lives—including mortality, aging, and social and economic success—is under our control if only we try hard enough. "Freedom. Choice. Autonomy. Self. Agency," Bordo writes. "These are powerful words in our culture, fighting words. But they are also words which are increasingly empty in many people's experience. Are we invoking the rhetoric with such desperation precisely because the felt reality is slipping away, running through our fingers?" As Bordo asserts, freedom, choice, autonomy, self, and agency are precisely what many claim about their bodies in late twentieth-century culture; working on them and working them out is figured as the ability to be whatever they choose. Yet if the workout is the medium in which one exercises that autonomy and choice (as much of consumer culture suggests we should), lived experience is that "many of us exercise in *order* to be able to eat. . . . [Exercise becomes] a compulsive daily ritual around which people organize and subordinate all other activities." The issue, Bordo argues, is not that exercise is bad, or that we follow cultural images to these kinds of extremes, but rather *why* we follow them, for permeating consumer culture and many people's lives is the "sense that [we] are of no use, no value, ugly, unacceptable, without a future, unless [we] can get [our] bodies into prescribed shape" and continue to work out and diet to keep them that way.[28] The feeling that we will never make the grade and finally be good enough and be able to stop creates the sense that any achievement is tenuous and temporary. Such feelings about our bodies can be linked to uncertainties in other areas—the kind of economic uncertainty that comes with corporate downsizing and other forms of diminishing job security, for instance, uncertainties that characterize most contemporary American lives.

Babe was the breakaway movie of 1995. In it a pig, through sticking to his nondominating world view, becomes a better sheepherding dog than the dogs themselves. It is in the context of existential uncertainty that Bordo draws what at first seems an unlikely parallel between the animals in *Babe*, whose sense of existence and value is made precarious by the fact that most of them will get eaten, and contemporary consumers, pumping their bodies in the guise of mastery and self-determination in a world of commercials that "capture a moment of 'empowerment' and make it stand for the reality of things." But the reality of our consumer lives, she argues, is not unlike the reality of Babe's world, where "existence is precarious for the animals on the farm, as it is materially for many people, and as it is 'existentially' for all of us—whether we recognize it or not. We can try to avoid this recognition with illusions of 'agency,' fantasies of staying young forever, and the distractions of 'self-improvement,' but it only lies in wait for us."[29] The gym is a place of just such distraction, illusion, and fantasy. These are the fantasies that bring us through the doors, day after day. They give our lives meaning, a sense of purpose and accomplishment—a sense of keeping impending disaster at bay.

The only problem is that that sense requires constant reinforcement, constant work. "My students know," Bordo writes, "that as long as they keep up their daily hours at the gym, they can feel pumped-up. . . . But how, they wonder, can they possibly keep it up their entire lives? They **189** know there is no equilibrium there, that the conditions of their feeling all right about themselves are *precarious*." The precariousness Bordo refers to has to do with a basic sense of well-being, basic human desires for acceptance and love, desires simply to exist without having continually to prove one's worth, desires which the rhetorical just-do-it masks. Raised in 'just do it' culture, empowered by second-wave feminism and Title IX, which were wonderful, crucial, enabling things, I have been just doing it, daily proving my worth physically and otherwise from the age of thirteen. Which is exhausting. So for me, the most touching part of Bordo's analysis, the part that makes me cry every time I even think about it (and I, as a good *macha*, am not particularly given to crying), is the last section of the chapter, where she interprets the farmer's closing words to Babe: "That will do, Pig. That will do." These words, Bordo writes, "represent an acknowledgment that so many of us fervently long for in our lives, and are so rarely given. So many of us feel like Babe, trying our hardest to become something valued and loved, uncertain about whether or not we will ever be granted the right to simply exist. 'That will do. That will do.' These are words to break the heart. Enough. You've worked hard enough. I accept you. You can rest."[30]

The terrible implication of Bordo's analysis is that in contemporary consumer culture, of course, we will never be granted that right, for it would bring to a halt the business that depends on our continual self-work. And the further implication, although she does not go into this, is that much of the meaning in our lives, much of our daily pleasure, comes from the struggle for that right. The meaning is in the struggle, and if that struggle were resolved, if we were granted the right simply to exist, as much as we desire it now we wouldn't desire it then. In the contemporary context, what other sources of meaning and pleasure do we have?

Bordo's analysis raises several crucial questions, and has caused, for me, a kind of crisis of faith. In so clearly articulating the treadmill-workout ethos that characterizes my sense of being, identity, existence, and place, and linking that ethos to consumer culture and its need to produce subjects willing to work on themselves continually, to see themselves as lacking and able to empower themselves only through more self-work, she begins to make sense of the exhaustion that has characterized my life. In the world of contemporary consumer culture, no one will ever tell me, as the farmer tells Babe, "That will do." No one will ever tell me, "Enough. You've worked hard enough. I accept you. You can rest." Everything around me says, "Do more." Indeed, in contemporary rhetoric, even to have a desire to rest, to be accepted, is to construct myself as a victim, to give myself over to someone else's control. Just do it, and keep doing it. The empowerment is the image and my sense of proximity to it—the image of the athlete struggling to overcome barriers, and triumphing, so daily life is constructed as struggle and triumph. And even though I like to be heroic, this wears me out, though I normally don't show it: exhaustion masquerading as empowerment.

In *Twilight Zones*, as in her other books, Bordo's work is a generative mode of cultural criticism that opens the door to a more complicated understanding of totally confusing issues. It is work that, while pointing to very real sites of cultural containment (like advertising), also points to ways—like women's bodybuilding—that living bodies negotiate containment. In the face of Bordo's analysis, I am forced to question my most cherished motivations, beliefs, and ideals. One more struggle, with a great deal at stake. Have I been able to triumph this time, come up with an argument that can restore to my beliefs their driving sense of reality and shape, their passion, their body, their blood? For some of the questions Bordo raises for those of us living, breathing beings out there on the treadmill sweating our life's blood away are these: Will images of strong women help women in general be strong? Does physical strength have any relation—other than imagined—to our power and strength in the social world? Does my own existence as a strong woman who is seen as such daily in two different gyms and at local powerlifting contests do anything to affect other women in a positive way? Does it have any impact? Does anyone care?

Precarious though my faith may be, I have to believe that it does. I have to believe that consciously or unconsciously, intentionally or no, any babe who sports a muscle symbolically strikes a blow against traditional ideas about male supremacy and such practices of male domination as domestic violence. I have to believe that any woman with muscles makes a statement in support of women's equality, self-realization, women's rights. A woman with muscles shouts out about female sovereignty, about women's right to be for themselves, not others, about their right to exist, take up space. And **191** while I believe that David Peterson del Mar is right that as a culture "it is time for us to qualify our commitment to personal freedom" since too much focus on self and individual rights can make it very difficult to "recognize . . . that our individual health and our collective health cannot be separated from each other," I also believe that he is more right than anyone I have read in a long time when he says that "women, who are still far from realizing the full benefits of individualism . . . in many respects . . . require a larger dose of self-realization. A movement toward mutuality is the responsibility of the most privileged, not the least."[31]

So *let's do it.* Let's take the promise of equal opportunity at its word. Let's get self-realized. Let's leave those aerobics and high repetitions designed only for toning back in the dustbins of history, throw them in that same trash heap which contains the old laws that let husbands beat wives with rods no more than an inch thick. Let's get more than an inch thick. Let's get big, feel our muscles, our power, our terrible, wonderful, monstrous strengths. Let's hit the gym, hit the weights, claim our space. Fifty-foot queenies, *let's pump.*

Notes

1. INTRODUCTION

1. Bill Dobbins, "Introduction," *The Women: Photographs of the Top Female Bodybuilders* (New York: Artisan, 1994), p. 8.

2. Kenneth R. Dutton, *The Perfectible Body: The Western Ideal of Male Physical Development* (New York: Continuum, 1995), p. 13.

3. As Leslee A. Fisher has documented, some competitive bodybuilders reserve the term *bodybuilder* for those who compete: "Dieting and all the other restrictions in preparing for a bodybuilding contest separate bodybuilders from everyone else. These deprivations earn them the right to be called 'bodybuilder'" ("'Building One's Self Up': Bodybuilding and the Construction of Identity among Professional Female Bodybuilders," in *Building Bodies*, ed. Pamela L. Moore [New Brunswick, N.J.: Rutgers University Press, 1997], p. 153). To many competitive bodybuilders, the fact that they have gone the extra mile, so to speak, means that the term *bodybuilder* applies only to them—all others work out or lift weights. This is like a distinction with which I am personally more familiar, in track and cross-country, where we who competed and ran sub–six-minute miles were *runners*, and everyone else was a *jogger*. I respect and am in sympathy with the position that competitive bodybuilders should be granted a distinction from those who don't compete; it is not a distinction, however, that is tenable for my purposes in this book. Because I am emphasizing connections between the dominant culture and the bodybuilding subculture, I use the term more broadly to include the large numbers of women who lift weights regularly and see this practice as an important part of their lives but who don't compete.

4. Arnold Schwarzenegger, "Foreword" to *The Women*, by Dobbins, p. 7.

5. Alan M. Klein, "Sally's Corner: The Women of Olympic," in *Little Big Men: Bodybuilding Subculture and Gender Construction* (Albany: SUNY Press, 1993), pp. 159–193; Anne Bolin, "Vandalized Vanity: Feminine Physiques Betrayed and

Portrayed," in *Tattoo, Torture, Mutilation, and Adornment*, ed. Frances E. Mascia-Lees and Patricia Sharpe (Albany: SUNY Press, 1992), pp. 79–99 and "Flex Appeal, Food, and Fat: Competitive Bodybuilding, Gender, and Diet" in *Building Bodies*, ed. Pamela L. Moore (New Brunswick, N.J.: Rutgers University Press, 1997), pp. 184–208; Yvonne Tasker, "Action Heroines in the 1980s: The Limits of 'Musculinity,'" *Spectacular Bodies: Gender, Genre, and the Action Cinema* (New York: Routledge, 1993), pp. 141–146. See also Laurie Schulze, "On the Muscle," in *Fabrications: Costume and the Female Body*, ed. Jane Gaines and Charlotte Herzog (London: Routledge, 1990), pp. 59–78; Annette Kuhn, "The Body and Cinema: Some Problems for Feminism," in *Grafts: Essays in Feminist Cultural Theory*, ed. Susan Sheridan (London: Verso, 1988), pp. 11–23; Marcia Ian, "How Do You Wear Your Body?: Bodybuilding and the Sublimity of Drag," in *Negotiating Lesbian and Gay Subjects*, ed. Monica Dorenkamp and Richard Henke (New York: Routledge, 1995), pp. 71–88; Gloria Steinem, "The Strongest Woman in the World," *Moving Beyond Words* (New York: Simon and Schuster, 1994), pp. 93–122; Anne Balsamo, "Feminist Bodybuilding," *Technologies of the Gendered Body: Reading Cyborg Women* (Durham, N.C.: Duke University Press, 1996), pp. 41–55.

6. Some of the most nuanced writing on female bodybuilders is that of Marcia Ian, Laurie Schulze, and Anne Bolin, who are bodybuilders themselves as well as academics. Bolin, in a discussion about competitive bodybuilding and diet, argues that the bodybuilder's soma "challenges and transforms conventional notions of femininity, yet it embeds and endorses conventional notions as well" ("Flex Appeal," p. 184). Ian points to the complexity of the contradictions within bodybuilding: "Bodybuilding . . . both depends on and tries to minimize or camouflage the Cartesian dualism which has historically structured our relations to our 'own' owned bodies, the sense that we are subjectivities surreally wearing our bodies, that our bodies conform to and play variations on types and styles just as our clothes, our hairdos, our gestures do. . . . The champion female bodybuilder . . . is both transforming the female body she used to wear into a manly one, and altering the fit of the female body" ("How Do You Wear Your Body?" pp. 77, 79).

In "On the Muscle," Schulze invokes the work of John Fiske and the resistance-theory axis of cultural studies in order to explore connections between "professional female bodybuilding and its pleasures" and "the terrain of resistance and refusal that Fiske describes" (p. 17). Theorizing resistance, Fiske himself argues the popular culture flourishes in the "space between social norms and their application in particular circumstances, a space where compliance or contestation is negotiated, and a space between determining social relations and people's attempt to control their own identities and relationships." He defines popular culture as "the art of making do with what is available," arguing that "in industrialized societies people make their culture out of resources that are not of their own making and are not under their control" ("Popular Culture," in *Critical Terms for Literary Study*, ed. Frank Lentricchia and Thomas McLaughlin, 2d ed. [Chicago: University of Chicago Press, 1995], pp. 322, 326). Female bodybuilding can be seen as a site of this kind of negotiation, where women take the existing structure of gender roles and, through constructing their bodies, push its limits.

Like other third-wave feminist practices, women's bodybuilding is always a negotiation between resistance and containment, defiance of dominant cultural ideas about gender and compliance with them. While it is crucial to point out ways women's bodybuilding functions as a "commercial mode of incorporation of subcultural resistance into the dominant consumer culture," it is just as crucial to point out ways that the bodybuilder is not entirely contained. To give precedence to one or the other disguises how, on the one hand, media culture powerfully works to shape our flesh in regressive ways, and how, on the other, we try to direct that shaping to more affirmative ends. The disruptive potential of the female bodybuilder and the cultural conditions and controversies that surround her is understandable only by being able to think contradictions simultaneously.

At the time this book went to press, one other full-length study of women's bodybuilding, Maria R. Lowe, *Women of Steel: Female Bodybuilders and the Struggle for Self-Definition*, was announced as forthcoming by NYU Press.

7. Marcia Ian, "Female Bodybuilding and Fitness," Femuscle@lightning.com, March 19, 1996.

8. Ian, "How Do You Wear Your Body?" p. 88.

9. I discuss Lowenburg's work at length in chapter 4.

10. Femuscle: The Women's Bodybuilding Forum, Femuscle@lightning.com.

11. When I say "our culture" I am by no means positing the United States as a country with a unitary culture. As countless cultural theorists have argued, hybridity and contradiction, combinations of cultures, along with many distinct cultures, mark the landscape. The only culture "we" share is that of consumer capitalism, which some of us have much greater access to than others. Nonetheless, the culture of commodity, image, and spectacle, greatly enhanced by mass media, is something everyone in America must confront and negotiate to varying degrees. Douglas Kellner, among others, names this shared culture "media culture," and argues for the development of what he terms a "critical media literacy" if we are to succeed at understanding and negotiating it. It is precisely this media culture I take up here, and I hope to contribute to a critical literacy, particularly around contemporary issues of female embodiment in that culture. See Kellner, *Media Culture: Cultural* **197**

Studies, Identity, and Politics Between the Modern and the Postmodern (New York: Routledge, 1995).

12. Although ideal cultural images for women and men have required the kind of sculpted physique that could only be crafted in the gym, recently some women's magazines have been advocating otherwise. In January 1997, for instance, New Year's resolution number one in *Vogue* magazine urged readers to "Get Out of the Gym!" See Vicki Woods, "A Fresh Take," *Vogue* (January 1997): 95.

13. Christine Hoff Sommers, *Who Stole Feminism?* (New York: Simon and Schuster, 1994), p. 21.

14. Courtney Love, *Pretty on the Inside*, Caroline Records, 1991.

15. Ann Jones, *Next Time She'll Be Dead: Battering and How to Stop It* (Boston: Beacon Press, 1994), p. 7.

16. Sam Fussell, *Muscle: Confessions of an Unlikely Bodybuilder* (New York: Avon Books, 1991), p. 137.

17. The relationship between contradiction and third-wave feminism, as well as its antecedents in the second wave, is developed more fully in Leslie Heywood and Jennifer Drake, "Introduction," *Third Wave Agenda: Being Feminist, Doing Feminism* (Minneapolis: University of Minnesota Press, 1997).

18. Jean Baudrillard, *America*, trans. Chris Turner (London: Verso, 1988), pp. 84, 35, 58.

19. Crystal Kile, "Hello Kitty Explains Kinderwhore to You: Third-Wave Feminism and Riot Grrrl Style (Paper presented at the Feminist Generations Conference, Bowling Green State University, Bowling Green, Ohio, February 2–4, 1996).

20. On Riot Grrrl, see Joan Gottlieb and Gayle Wald, "Smells Like Teen Spirit: Riot Grrrls, Revolution, and Women in Independent Rock," in *Microphone Fiends: Youth Music and Youth Culture*, ed. Andrew Ross and Tricia Rose (New York: Routledge, 1994).

21. Representative quotations from letters from readers in from *Flex*'s "Talkback" column, 1995–1996; Steve Wennerstrom, "The Gray Matter Gang," *Flex* 14 (July 1996): 194.

22. See, for instance, David Peterson del Mar, *What Trouble I Have Seen: A History of Violence Against Wives* (Cambridge, Mass.: Harvard University Press, 1996), who argues that "quantitative evidence also indicates that violence against wives rose late in the twentieth century. Studies from across the United States showed that violent husbands used physical force frequently by the 1970s, with most such husbands hitting their wives at least once every few months or weeks" (p. 146). Ann Jones argues that "no one claims these days that battering is part of man's essential nature, for there are lots of men—probably more than half the male

population—who have never done it and who never will. But no one claims that battering is 'abnormal' behavior for men either. . . . Great numbers of men, in every segment of the population, still swagger through 'relationships' with all the finesse of Rambo. And many young men—the MTV fans who are fast making date rape and fraternity gang rape campus traditions—seem to regard the use of violence against women as, if not part of man's nature, certainly man's *right*" (*Next Time*, p. 99). The added twist to Jones's argument here is that in contemporary rhetoric, her analysis would immediately be dismissed as "male bashing" and thus overlooked, a cultural practice that further authorizes violence.

23. Jones, *Next Time*, p. 15.

24. On the facetiousness of the contemporary rhetoric of choice, see Susan Bordo, *Twilight Zones: The Hidden Life of Cultural Images from Plato to O.J.* (Berkeley and Los Angeles: University of California Press, 1997), especially chap. 1.

25. Jones, *Next Time*, p. 4.

2. BUILDING BACKLASH

1. Susan Faludi, *Backlash: The Undeclared War Against American Women* (New York: Crown Publishers, 1991).

2. Naomi Wolf, *The Beauty Myth: How Images of Beauty Are Used Against Women* (New York: William Morrow, 1991); Katie Roiphe, *Fire with Fire: The New Female Power and How It Will Change the Twenty-first Century* (New York: Random House, 1993), p. xvii.

3. See Camille Paglia, *Sex, Art, and American Culture* (New York: Vintage, 1992); Katie Roiphe, *The Morning After: Fear, Sex, and Feminism on College Campuses* (New York: Little, Brown, 1993); Christina Hoff Sommers, *Who Stole Feminism?: How Women Have Betrayed Women* (New York: Simon and Schuster, 1994), pp. 33, 21; Rene Denfeld, *The New Victorians: A Young Woman's Challenge to the Old Feminist Order* (New York: Warner Books, 1995).

4. Sommers, *Who Stole Feminism?*, pp. 33, 21.

5. Webster's *Ninth New Collegiate Dictionary* (Springfield, Mass.: Merriam-Webster, 1986), p. 1295.

6. Sommers, *Who Stole Feminism?*, p. 26.

7. Ibid., p. 27.

8. Ibid., p. 40.

9. Ibid., pp. 17, 15, 22, 24, 45.

10. Ibid., p. 74.

11. Ibid., p. 45

12. Joan Wallach Scott, "The Campaign Against Political Correctness," in *PC Wars: Politics and Theory in the Academy*, ed. Jeffrey Williams (New York: Routledge, 1995), p. 22.

13. Sommers, *Who Stole Feminism?*, p. 55.

14. Linda J. Nicholson, *Feminism/Postmodernism* (New York: Routledge, 1990); Marianne Hirsh and Evelyn Fox Keller, *Conflicts in Feminism* (New York: Routledge, 1990); Seyla Benhabib, Judith Butler, Drucilla Cornell, and Nancy Fraser, *Feminist Contentions* (New York: Routledge, 1995).

15. The Third Wave's mission statement was in the Spring 1996 issue of *HUES* (Hear Us Emerging Sisters) magazine, a multicultural alternative to young women's magazines like *Glamour* and *Seventeen*, which is run by Tali and Ophira Edut and Dyann Logwood, three graduates of the University of Michigan.

16. Sommers, *Who Stole Feminism?*, p. 229.

17. Katha Pollitt, "Born Again vs. Porn, Again," *Nation* 264, no 4 (February 3, 1997): 9.

18. Bordo, *Twilight Zones*, p. 18.

19. The phrase is Douglas Kellner's; see *Media Culture: Cultural Studies, Identity, and Politics Between the Modern and the Postmodern* (New York: Routledge, 1995).

20. Dutton, *Perfectible Body*, p. 105.

21. See Dobbins's introduction to *The Women*, p. 26.

22. Schulze, "On the Muscle," p. 60.

23. There is no corresponding fitness competition for men, although there is a separate master's competition for bodybuilding for men and not women.

24. Quoted in Dobbins, *The Women*, p. 20.

25. Chris Aceto, "Sex or Flex," *Flex* 14, no. 1 (March 1996): 275. I consistently rely on *Flex* rather than any of the other bodybuilding or fitness publications as a primary source throughout the book because it is known as the "hard-core" bodybuilding publication not necessarily intended for a more popular audience, as are other Weider magazines, like *Muscle and Fitness* and *Shape*.

26. See Douglas, *Where the Girls Are*, chap. 10, on how the "catfight" between two women or groups of women functions politically to derail activism and positive cultural change.

27. Octavio Paz, "The Sons of La Malinche," *The Labyrinth of Solitude*, trans. Lysander Kemp, Vara Milos, and Rachel Phillips Belash (New York: Grove Press, 1985), pp. 85–86.

28. Chris Holmlund, "Visible Difference and Flex Appeal: The Body, Sex, Sexuality, and Race in the *Pumping Iron* Films," in *Building Bodies*, ed. Pamela L. Moore (New Brunswick, N.J.: Rutgers University Press, 1997), pp. 87, 93.

29. Lenda Murray, "Breathless: Ms. Olympia Lenda Murray in Words and Images," *Sensuous Muscle: The Women of Bodybuilding*, special edition of *Flex* (Summer 1995): 14. All previous quotations in this paragraph are from the same special issue, pp. 23, 61, 90, 129, and 165–166.

30. *Flex* 13, no. 4 (June 1995): 125.

31. Fussell, *Muscle*, p. 73.

32. Cory Everson, *Superflex: Ms. Olympia's Guide to Building a Strong and Sexy Body* (Chicago: Contemporary Books, 1987), pp. 73–75. The reference is to Donna Haraway, "A Cyborg Manifesto," chap. 8 in *Simians, Cyborgs, Women: The Reinvention of Nature* (New York: Routledge, 1991).

33. Bill Dobbins, "Bimbo Layouts," Femuscle@lightning.com, January 25, 1996.

34. Steve Holman, quoted in Brie Sansotta, "Muscle Mags and Female Bodybuilding," Femuscle@lightning.com, March 12, 1996.

35. John Romano, "Playboy Hardbodies vs. Ironman," *All Natural Muscular Development* 34, no. 5 (May 1997): 194.

36. See Kellner, *Media Culture*, chaps. 1–3.

37. Susan Bordo, *Unbearable Weight* (Berkeley and Los Angeles: University of California Press, 1993), p. 166.

38. See Sara Evans, *Personal Politics* (New York: Vintage, 1979), especially chap. 5.

39. "A Regular Joe," *Flex* 12, no. 7 (September 1994): 21–22.

40. Kiana Tom, *Kiana's Bodysculpting* (New York: St. Martin's, 1994), pp. 2, 3.

41. Steinem, *Moving Beyond Words*, p. 95.

42. Paglia, *Sex, Art*, p. 15.

43. Arnold Schwarzenegger, with Douglas Kent Hall, *Arnold: The Education of a Bodybuilder* (New York: Simon and Schuster, 1977), p. 34.

44. Quoted in Francesca Stanfill, "Woman Warrior," *New York* (March 4, 1991): 28, 27.

45. Schwarzenegger and Hall, *Arnold*, p. 28.

46. Tom, *Kiana's Bodysculpting*, p. 3.

47. Fussell, *Muscle*, p. 24.

48. Bordo, *Unbearable Weight*, p. 297.

49. Fussell, *Muscle*, p. 30.

50. Susan Jeffords, "Can Masculinity Be Terminated?" in *Screening the Male*, ed. Steven Cohan and Ina Rae Hark (New York: Routledge, 1993), p. 245.

51. Susan Jeffords, *Hard Bodies: Hollywood Masculinity in the Reagan Era* (New Brunswick, N.J.: Rutgers University Press, 1994), pp. 167, 173.

52. Ibid., p. 176.

53. Evans, *Personal Politics*, p. 148.

54. Merri Lisa Johnson, "Under the Covers: Cumming to Consciousness in the Music of Tori Amos," unpublished manuscript, p. 2.

55. For a more detailed exploration of the redefinitions and disputes relevant to third-wave feminist activism, see Rebecca Walker, "Introduction," *To Be Real* (New York: Anchor Books, 1995), and Heywood and Drake, eds., *Third Wave Agenda*, introduction.

56. Kellner, *Media Culture*, p. 66.

57. Mariah Burton Nelson, *The Stronger Women Get, the More Men Love Football* (New York: Harcourt, 1994), p. 31.

58. Recent work in men's studies does show, however, that the seeming "for self" guise of masculinity actually covers alligiance to a role every bit as restrictive as that of traditional femininity. Participation in sports culture is one place that has traditionally offered men an escape, a set of activities done for oneself. See Michael A. Messner and Donald F. Sabo, eds., *Sport, Men, and the Gender Order: Critical Feminist Perspectives* (Champaign, Ill.: Human Kinetics Books, 1990), esp. the introduction and chaps. 1, 2, 8, and 9.

59. On a more positive note, at least since the popularity of women's sports in the 1996 Summer Olympics, television advertisements featuring athletic women have surfaced. Especially notable are a Mountain Dew spot that features women engaged in various Extreme Sports, with a punked-up version of "Thank Heaven for Little Girls"; and the Lady Footlocker spot, which features many different women athletes playing their sports to a punk-rock version of Helen Reddy's second-wave feminist anthem "I Am Woman." I read the ads, with their focus on athletic women and decidedly harder-edged remakes of popular songs of older eras, as good examples of a third-wave feminist sensibility.

60. See, among thousands of other references, *People* 46, no. 18 (October 28, 1996): 48–51.

61. Nelson, *The Stronger Women Get*, p. 30.

3. ZERO

1. Kaja Silverman, *Male Subjectivity at the Margins* (New York: Routledge, 1992), p. 4.

2. Ibid.

3. Achim Albrecht, "Magnificent Muscle," *Flex* 12, no. 7 (September 1994): 54.

4. Bordo, *Unbearable Weight*, p. 30.

5. Holmlund, "Masculinity as Multiple Masquerade," in *Screening the Male*, ed. Cohan and Hark, p. 217.

6. Ibid., p. 218.

7. Klein, *Little Big Men*, p. 153.

8. Ibid., pp. 246, 140.

9. Zoe Heller, "Sly's Body Electric," *Vanity Fair* (November 1993): 144, 145.

10. Creed quoted in Yvonne Tasker, "Dumb Movies for Dumb People: Masculinity, the Body, and the Voice in Contemporary Action Cinema," in *Screening the Male*, ed. Cohan and Hark, p. 232.

11. On anorexia as a form of "passing," see Leslie Heywood, *Dedication to Hunger: The Anorexic Aesthetic in Modern Culture* (Berkeley and Los Angeles: University of California Press, 1996).

12. In Lacan's work *aphanisis* describes the paradox of the split subject, which "fades" in the moment of its constitution since being is sacrificed for meaning: "The subject appears on one side as meaning and on the other as fading—disappearance" (quoted in Juliet Mitchell, "Introduction I," in Jacques Lacan, *Feminine Sexuality* [New York: Norton, 1982], p. 16).

13. Tasker, "Dumb Movies," p. 242.

14. Klein, *Little Big Men*, p. 246.

15. Frank Zane, *Fabulously Fit Forever* (Palm Springs, Calif.: Zananda, 1993), p. 15.

16. Klein, *Little Big Men*, pp. 237, 246.

17. Zane, *Fabulously Fit Forever*, pp. 17–18, 257.

18. Quoted in George Butler, *Arnold Schwarzenegger: A Portrait* (New York: Simon and Schuster, 1990), pp. 96, 92.

19. Fussell, *Muscle*, pp. 137, 138.

20. bell hooks, "Reflections on Race and Sex," *Yearning: Race, Gender, and Cultural Politics* (Boston: South End Press, 1990), p. 63.

21. Richard Majors, "Cool Pose: Black Masculinity and Sports," in *Sport, Men, and the Gender Order*, ed. Sabo and Messner, pp. 109, 114.

22. Kenneth L. Shropshire, *In Black and White: Race and Sports in America* (New York: NYU Press, 1996), pp. xxii, xxi.

23. hooks, *Yearning*, p. 71.

24. "Magnificent Muscle," *Flex* 12, no. 7 (September 1994): 52–57.

25. Sue Dobos, letter in "Talkback," *Flex* 12, no. 3 (May 1994): 179.

26. Elaine Bell Kaplan, "'I Don't Do No Windows': Competition Between the Domestic Worker and the Housewife," in *Competition: A Feminist Taboo*, ed. Valerie Miner and Helen E. Longino (New York: The Feminist Press, 1987), p. 93.

27. Susan K. Cahn, *Coming On Strong: Gender and Sexuality in Twentieth-Century Women's Sport* (New York: Macmillan, 1994), especially "'Cinderellas' of Sport: Black Women in Track and Field," pp. 110–139.

28. Ibid., p. 114.

29. John Romano, "Women on Steroids," *Muscular Development* 33, no. 3 (March 1996): 132. Romano's article is specifically about female bodybuilders on steroids rather than female bodybuilders in general, but it is the case that every time a woman develops significant muscularity she is accused of taking steroids (see Dobbins, *The Women*, p. 27). This still works to support my point that muscular female bodybuilders—steroid or nonsteroid—are described in similar language to the language used to describe female track and field athletes earlier in the century.

30. Cahn, *Coming On Strong*, p. 128.

31. hooks, *Yearning*, p. 62.

32. "Trained Beauty," *Flex* 13, no. 0 (Summer 1995): 34–38; "Mastery," *Flex* 14, no. 1 (March 1996): 124–129.

33. bell hooks, "Selling Hot Pussy," *Black Looks: Race and Representation* (Boston: South End Press, 1992), p. 62. See also Sander Gilman, "Black Bodies, White Bodies: Toward an Iconography of Female Sexuality in Late Nineteenth-Century Art, Medicine, and Literature," *Critical Inquiry* 12 (Autumn 1985): 204–242, and hooks's reading of Gilman in this chapter. My reading of the racialization of women bodybuilders is indebted to hooks's analysis of similar operations in contemporary cinema.

34. Evans, *Personal Politics*, p. 88.

35. Dobbins, *The Women*, p. 127.

36. *Flex* 12, no. 5 (July 1994): 127.

37. See especially Wolf, *Fire With Fire*.

38. See especially Roiphe, *The Morning After*.

39. T. S. Eliot, "Tradition and Individual Talent," *Selected Essays* (New York: Harcourt Brace Jovanovitch, 1978), p. 4.

40. Toni Morrison, *Playing in the Dark: Whiteness and the Literary Imagination* (New York: Vintage, 1992).

4. Hard Times

1. Bruce Chatwin, "An Eye and Some Body," in Robert Mapplethorpe, *Lady: Lisa Lyon* (New York: St. Martin's, 1983), p. 11.

2. Leslee A. Fisher's fieldwork, as well the research of others she cites, documents an impoverished sense of being in the women bodybuilders (all competitive at high levels) who were the subjects of her study. "Although the female bodybuilders interviewed," writes Fisher, "found motivation and achievement through manipulation of their bodies, that achievement was sought as a result of an impov-

erished sense of self, a feeling of personal inadequacy. The women described a kind of 'spirituality of imperfection' that involved attempts to fill the void inside through manipulation of the external. Coparticipants described how their sense of self-esteem was not very good at all, either currently or prior to beginning competitive bodybuilding" ("'Building One's Self Up,'" p. 151). Fisher's findings parallel Alan M. Klein's on male bodybuilders (*Little Big Men*), as well as Sam Fussell's narrative account in *Muscle* (see my discussion in chapter 3). Harry Crews's novel *Body* (New York: Poseidon Press, 1990) explores a similar psychology.

What Fisher and Klein do not ask, however, and what Fussell and Crews begin to imagine, is why bodybuilders in particular suffer from this insubstantiality of being. Historically, and even today stereotypically, bodybuilders are accused of narcissism or excessive self-preoccupation. But the sense of a "void inside" that Fisher found characteristic of her subjects is also characteristic of trauma survivors (see my discussion in chapter 5). I would argue that there is a connection between bodybuilding practice and some form of abuse history, that often bodybuilding is an attempt to overcome a sense of diminishment or to heal psychological wounds of various kinds, whether that diminishment has come from more directly abusive situations such as domestic violence or sexual assault, or more covert abuses such as the experience of racism, sexism, classism, or other forms of discrimination. Bodybuilding may be a response to such treatment, an attempt, as Fisher puts it, "to build one's self up" in the face of a world that has diminished or devalued that self. As such, bodybuilding can be seen as an affirmative strategy of self-healing.

Competitive bodybuilding, however, with its emphasis on isolated individual achievement and winning at all costs may, ironically, contribute to an individual's sense of valuelessness. One's body becomes, as it did for Fisher's subjects, a constant reminder of one's "flaws" (p. 154). Bodybuilding as a practice may be a way to address a sense of personal valuelessness within the context of a knowledge about and a concern for the larger social and cultural issues that contributed to the sense of valuelessness in the first place.

3. Chatwin, "An Eye and Some Body," p. 14.

4. "Foreword," Dobbins, *The Women*, p. 7.

5. Heather Tristany, "The Ideal Female," *Flex* 11, no. 1 (March 1993): 166–170.

6. K. C. Compton sees the ability of girls to spit during their workouts, just as boys do, as a measure of progress, connected to the rise in sports participation by girls: "My daughter and her generation of young women . . . play soccer with a take-no-prisoners attitude that my friends and I, we of the sit-on-the-sidelines, watch-the-boys-play generation, could not have imagined. . . . I love to see them **205**

out there . . . walking away from the track or the court with such casual ease. They belong there, belong in their bodies, belong in this world naturally in a way the women of my generation had to work hard to claim" ("Learning to Spit," *Women's Sports and Fitness* [August 1997]: 90). Compton points to the ways in which the bodily freedoms Tristany would like to limit reflect perogative or lack of it.

7. Dobbins, *The Women*, p. 10.

8. See Bordo, *Unbearable Weight*, pp. 245–246.

9. Dobbins, *The Women*, p. 11.

10. In taking this particular line of argument I am not saying that female body-builders are uniformly rejected or found unappealing. Alan Guttmann asks, "Is it not time to acknowledge that today's female athletes are more likely to be admired than to encounter hostility and denigration?" He offers public response to female bodybuilders as the litmus test of this. *Women's Sports: A History* (New York: Columbia University Press, 1991), p. 217.

Often female bodybuilders are admired and accepted. But if acceptance for women's bodybuilding has grown on a subcultural level, the bodybuilding industry has made a deliberate ploy to make that acceptance take a sexual form, perhaps undermining what would otherwise indicate positive change. Accepting muscular women as sexual is a change of sorts but serves to shift the focus from athleticism.

11. See Holmlund, "Visible Difference," p. 94.

12. Nelson, *The Stronger Women Get*, p. 197; emphasis in original.

13. Ibid.

14. Ibid., p. 198.

15. Ibid., p. 214.

16. Quoted in M. G. Lord, "Pornutopia: How Feminist Scholars Learned to Love Dirty Pictures," *Lingua Franca* 7, no. 4 (April/May 1997): 3.

17. Ann Jones, for instance, argues in *Next Time*, "I call particular attention to the many ways in which pornography impinges on women's lives because it is all the more difficult for women to secure freedom from bodily harm when our free speech is silenced by the subjects we must shout about. . . . We can't escape the peculiar amalgam of sex and violence that is now widely regarded as normal love" (pp. 117, 119). To the extent that some pornography promotes the idea of natural masculine sexual violence and that the "free" expression of sexuality may include violence against women, I agree with the critique that says this provides a model for behavior in actual experience, and that there are many women who don't see violence against them as a form of pleasurable sex, although there may be some that do. Critique, however, is different from censorship, and I am not advocating the censorship of pornography any more than I am advocating the censorship of

the bodybuilding magazine pictorials (which I am not). What I am advocating is a critical reading of those images, an understanding of their assumptions and the kind of cultural work the images do in the world by making particular assumptions seem normal, "the way things are."

18. Graf did appear in the April 1990 issue of *Vogue* in a black Norma Kamali maillot dress, bent so as to adjust her high heels and make her cleavage the focus of the shot.

19. Bill Dobbins, "Iron Man," Femuscle@lightning.com, January 27, 1996.

20. Quoted in Nelson, *The Stronger Women Get*, p. 214.

21. See Holmlund, "Visible Difference," pp. 94–95.

22. *Flex* 12, no. 11 (January 1995): 232.

23. Tina Brzozowski, letter in "Talkback," *Flex* 12, no. 8 (October 1994): 19.

24. Bordo, *Twilight Zones*, pp. 124–125.

25. Bill Dobbins, "The Female Bodybuilding Revolution," Femuscle@lightning.com, January 23, 1996.

26. Guttmann, *Women's Sports*, pp. 263–265 and passim.

27. Photographs by Joe McNally, *Life* (July 1996): 50–64.

28. Occasionally pictorials of the black male bodybuilders use a more explicitly sexualized style. The feature on Aaron Baker, for instance, in the October 1994 *Flex*, poses Baker in leopard-skin trunks and heavy sterling silver cross in two of the shots using props—a chair in one, some kind of sword in the other—which are not often used in pictorials of the men. Usually they are photographed in competition briefs and without props. More on the representation of black bodybuilders in chapter 3.

29. These quotations are from the jacket flap of Dobbins, *The Women*.

30. Dobbins, "Iron Man."

31. On this trend see Rosemary Hennessy, "New Woman, New History," *Materialist Feminism and the Politics of Discourse* (New York: Routledge, 1993), pp. 100–151.

32. Dobbins, "Bimbo Layouts."

33. Dobbins, "Iron Man."

34. Elizabeth Grosz, *Jacques Lacan: A Feminist Introduction* (New York: Routledge, 1990), p. 137.

35. William Faulkner, *Absalom, Absalom!* (1936; rpt. New York: Vintage International, 1990), p. 102.

36. My quotations from Lowenburg in this section are taken from an untitled document, written in April 1996, that he wrote specifically to give me background on his work.

37. Nicholas Mirzoeff, *Bodyscape: Art, Modernity, and the Ideal Figure* (New York: Routledge, 1995), p. 204.

38. Joseph Conrad, *Heart of Darkness*, ed. Robert Kimbrough (1899; rpt. New York: Norton, 1988), p. 70.

39. Ian, "Female Bodybuilding and Fitness."

5. LOVING MR. HYDE

1. *Webster's Ninth New Collegiate Dictionary*.

2. Balsamo, *Technologies*, p. 74.

3. Conrad, *Heart of Darkness*, p. 10.

4. Ibid.

5. Some fascinating recent analyses of monstrosity from a literary critical perspective include Judith Halberstam, *Skin Shows: Gothic Horror and the Technology of Monsters* (Durham: Duke University Press, 1995); and Jerrold E. Hogle, "The Struggle for a Dichotomy: Abjection in Jekyll and His Interpreters," in *Dr. Jekyll and Mr. Hyde after One Hundred Years* (Chicago: University of Chicago Press, 1988), pp. 161–207.

6. Elaine Hilberman's pioneering examination of battered women shows that they "were a study in paralyzing terror that was reminiscent of the rape trauma syndrome, except the stress was unending and the threat of assault ever present. Agitation and anxiety bordering on panic were almost always present. . . . The waking lives of these women were characterized by overwhelming passivity and inability to act. They were drained, fatigued, and numb, without the energy to do more than minimal household chores and child care. They had a pervasive sense of hopelessness and despair about themselves and their lives. They saw themselves as incompetent, unworthy, and unlovable and were ridden with guilt and shame. They thought they deserved the abuse, saw no options, and felt powerless to make changes" (quoted in Jones, *Next Time*, p. 179).

7. I offer this reading of female bodybuilding and *Mary Reilly* as a hypothesis. I know of no clinical studies that prove a correlation between female bodybuilding and the experience of physical abuse, no empirical data that prove my hypothesis. Ideally, my hypothesis could generate such study in the future.

8. Peterson del Mar, *What Trouble I Have Seen*, p. 135.

9. Rosi Braidotti, *Nomadic Subjects* (New York: Columbia University Press, 1994), pp. 42, 107, 102, 104–105, 106.

10. Janice E. Raymond, *Women as Wombs: Reproductive Technologies and the Battle over Women's Freedom* (San Francisco: HarperCollins, 1993), pp. viii, xxxi. Raymond, herself a doctor and a feminist activist, has written a book graphic

enough to give even the most rigorously "postmodern," protechnology feminist pause. Raymond envisions her work in part as an antidote to postmodern feminism, which she sees as complicit with male domination in medical technologies: "Increasingly, in feminist and biomedical circles, reproductive technologies and contracts are debated not only as if they have nothing to do with sexual access to women but as if they have nothing to do with women at all—as if they are mere ideas or academic exercises. . . . Frequently, feminsts 'debate' about whether these technologies are not *simply* abusive to women but can be used by women as well, as if we all need lessons in the complexity and nuances of violation. In the postmodernist world of social criticism in which essays, books, and conference papers have taken on the role of distanced commentary, it is my hope that this book will be a dose of reality. Feminism is only real if it is continuously involved in women's lives" (p. xxxii). My split commitment to difference *and* postmodernist feminism— to some of the basic and often contradictory assumptions of each—leads me to have a divided reaction to Raymond's position here. While I would be reluctant to oppose postmodern feminist thinking to "reality" since it is, in part, a critical investigation of traditional conceptions of reality that points to their construction within historically determined relations of power, I would agree with Raymond that feminism must be "continually involved in women's lives," and that the kind of academic writing she objects to often privileges the theoretical over the anecdotal in such a way as to obscure real, concrete relations of power. Her book, at any rate, is a sobering account of how reproductive technology is currently used to further substantiate traditional patterns of male dominance and control of women's bodies and thereby their lives.

11. Dion Farquhar, *The Other Machine: Discourse and Reproductive Technologies* (New York: Routledge, 1996), p. 4.

12. Braidotti, *Nomadic Subjects*, p. 108.

13. On contradiction as a fundamental principle of third-wave feminism, see Walker, ed., *To Be Real*, pp. xviii–xl; and Heywood and Drake, eds., *Third Wave Agenda*, pp. 1–20.

14. Robert Louis Stevenson, *The Strange Case of Dr. Jekyll and Mr. Hyde* (1886; rpt. New York: Vintage Classics, 1991), pp. 6, 10, 80.

15. Valerie Miner, *Mary Reilly: The Untold Story of Dr. Jekyll and Mr. Hyde* (New York: Pocket Books, 1990), p. 145.

16. Jeff Gordinier, "Living the Life of Reilly," *Entertainment*, no. 315/316 (February 23/March 1, 1996): 24.

17. *Free to Fight: An Interactive Self-Defense Project*, Candy-Ass Records, 1996 (sound recording with workbook).

The first part of this section is taken from my keynote speech to a "Take Back the Night" rally at SUNY–Binghamton, March 5, 1997.

18. Dylan Thomas, "Do Not Go Gentle into That Good Night," in *The Norton Anthology of English Literature* 4th ed., vol. 2 (New York: Norton, 1979), p. 2416.

19. Jean Rhys, *Wide Sargasso Sea* (New York: Norton, 1982), p. 128.

20. Statistics are from the *Free to Fight* workbook.

21. Toni Morrison, *Beloved* (New York: Plume, 1987), p. 140.

22. bell hooks, *Outlaw Culture: Resisting Representations* (New York: Routledge, 1994), p. 217.

23. The cover of the October 28, 1996 *People* magazine shouts "MAMA MADONNA! Exclusive: Madonna and her friends talk about the happy arrival of little Lourdes Maria, 6 lbs. 9 ozs. Says the singer: 'This is the greatest miracle of my life.'" The quote from Jane Fonda is in Joanna Powell, "*Good Housekeeping* Interview with Jane Fonda," *Good Housekeeping* 222, no. 2, (February 1996): 26; the quotes from Courtney Love are in Vicki Woods, "A Labor of Love," *Vogue* (January 1997): 133.

24. See Haraway, *Simians*.

25. Miner, *Mary Reilly*, pp. 32–33.

26. Paz, "Sons of La Malinche," p. 79.

27. Jones, *Next Time*, p. 87.

28. Page numbers in parentheses refer to Miner's novel *Mary Reilly*. Quotations in this section with no page number are transcriptions from the movie soundtrack of *Mary Reilly*.

29. This passage is from the movie soundtrack is a distillation of several passages in the Miner novel.

30. Jones, *Next Time*, p. 179.

31. Peterson del Mar, *What Trouble I Have Seen*, p. 168.

32. Ibid., p. 173.

33. Joyce Carol Oates, "Introduction," to Robert Louis Stevenson, *The Strange Case of Dr. Jekyll and Mr. Hyde* (New York: Vintage Classics, 1990).

34. Peterson del Mar, *What Trouble I Have Seen*, p. 174.

35. Ann Jones writes, "Despite the idealism of our assumptions, the right to be free from bodily harm has never been absolute. Like all our other rights, it was for a long time the privilege of only some of the 'people'—mainly well-to-do white men who drafted the laws and administered their enforcement. English men enjoyed privileges that were enshrined in the common law as their legal *rights*, and among them was the right to rule the family. Building on the foundation of English
common law, American legislation and jurisprudence imported those male 'rights'

wholesale. And just as English women had complained for centuries about the undue power men held over women and children, American women also began to campaign for equal rights, especially for equal rights *within the family*" (*Next Time*, p. 19).

36. Stevenson, *Dr. Jekyll and Mr. Hyde*, p. 76.

37. Peggy Orenstein, *School Girls: Young Women, Self-Esteem, and the Confidence Gap* (New York: Doubleday, 1994).

38. David Wild, "Television Reality Bites Back," *Rolling Stone* 742 (September 5, 1996): 71.

39. Gottlieb and Wald, "Smells Like Teen Spirit," p. 268.

40. Michael Bogen, "Why Women Build—The Top Ten," Femuscle@lightning.com, February 2, 1996.

41. Ericca Kern, "Timid No More," *Flex* 13, no. 10 (November 1995): 126 (photography by Bill Dobbins).

42. Carol Ann Weber, "Jennifer Goodwin: Bodybuilding Saved My Life!" *All Natural Muscular Development* 34, no. 5 (May 1997): 110.

43. Doug Aoki, "Fitness Women vs. Female Bodybuilders," Femuscle@lightning.com, March 13, 1996.

44. On the association between male perpetrators of domestic violence and their belief in and adherence to traditional gender roles, see Peterson del Mar, *What Trouble*, pp. 150–158.

45. Jones, *Next Time*, p. 96.

6. AMERICAN GIRLS, RAISED ON PROMISES

1. Simon Reynolds and Joy Press, *The Sex Revolts: Gender, Rebellion, and Rock 'n' Roll* (Cambridge: Harvard University Press, 1995), p. 3.

2. Ian, "How Do You Wear Your Body?" p. 78.

3. Fussell, *Muscle*, p. 131.

4. "David Dearth," *Flex* 12, no. 9 (November 1994): 47.

5. Ibid., p. 51.

6. Reynolds and Press, *Sex Revolts*, p. 117.

7. Georges Bataille, *The Accursed Share*, vols. 2 and 3, trans. Robert Hurley (New York: Zone Books, 1992), pp. 16, 198.

8. Reynolds and Press, *Sex Revolts*, p. 123.

9. Bataille, *Accursed Share*, p. 198.

10. Susan Bordo's analysis of postmodernism, cultural images of self-determination, and "power feminism" astutely discusses how this desire for agency, for self-determination, is used against us in consumer capitalism, as evidenced by the

rhetoric of personal choice that is employed in the context of following what can only be culturally influenced norms. "The worst thing," Bordo writes, "in the Braveheart/Nike universe of values, is to be bossed around, told what to do. This creates a dilemma for advertisers, who somehow must convince hundreds of thousands of people to purchase the same product while assuring them they are bold and innovative individualists for doing so" (*Twilight Zones*, p. 27). While one can see and feel the facetiousness of Nike's rhetoric of self-determination, one which, by this logic, women's bodybuilding would support, the question of *why* a particular woman bodybuilds becomes crucial here. If it is just to match an idealized cultural image, it would hardly count as self-expression. But if it is about feeling physically and emotionally stronger, about cultivating a willingness to be assertive and impose limits on time reserved for the self and time spent in service of others, this is a different question. "Culture criticism," writes Bordo, "isn't about lacking sympathy for other people's personal choices. . . . It's about preserving consciousness of the larger context in which our personal choices occur, so that we will be better informed about their potential consequences—for ourselves as well as others" (*Twilight Zones*, p. 16). I would argue that one can be hyperconscious of the context in which the personal choice to bodybuild occurs, including the context of changed beauty ideals more sympathetic to the muscular woman, and say that while *some* of bodybuilding may be about attaining a body ideal, that attainment is the fortunate by-product of the deeper motivation, which is to feel physically and emotionally strong, less vulnerable to domestic and other forms of violence. And on a less legitimate level, the logic of sovereignty would be precisely about the ability not to have to worry about the potential consequences of our actions for others, the ability to say—in just this *one* place in our lives, unlike all the other places where we worry incessantly about the consequences of our actions for others—"I just don't give a damn."

11. Beck is quoted in Mark Kemp, "Beck: The *Rolling Stone* Interview," *Rolling Stone* 758 (April 17, 1997): 62.

12. Ibid.

13. It's too early to tell, but the "return of the rock star" heralded by Marilyn Manson may mark a turn against self-deprecation and a return to more "classic" blatant expressions of sovereignty. See Neil Straus, "Marilyn Manson," *Rolling Stone* 752 (January 23, 1997): 48–52.

14. Ann Powers, "Who's That Girl?" in *Rock She Wrote*, ed. Evelyn MacDonald and Ann Powers (New York: Delta, 1995), p. 466.

15. Twelve years after its first appearance, Susan Bordo's "Anorexia Nervosa: Psychopathology as the Crystallization of Culture" is still the definitive text on this.

See *Unbearable Weight*, pp. 139–164. See also Heywood, *Dedication to Hunger*, especially chap. 1.

16. Cahn, *Coming On Strong*, p. 127.

17. John Truitt, "Amphi's Heywood "One of the Guys,'" *Arizona Daily Star* (October 15, 1980).

18. Bruce Kidd, "The Men's Cultural Centre: Sports and the Dynamic of Women's Oppression/Men's Repression," in *Sport, Men*, ed. Messner and Sabo, p. 39.

19. David Whitson, "Sport in the Social Construction of Masculinity," in *Sport, Men, and the Gender Order*, p. 21.

20. Cahn, *Coming on Strong*, p. 2. A paperback version of this book was published by Harvard University Press in 1996.

21. Silverman, *Male Subjectivity*, pp. 46–47.

22. Slavoj Zizek, *The Sublime Object of Ideology* (New York: Verso, 1989), p. 33.

23. Silverman, *Male Subjectivity*, p. 48.

24. Powers, "Who's That Girl?" p. 465.

25. Faulkner, *Absalom, Absalom!*

26. bell hooks, "Liberation Scenes: Speak This Yearning," in *Yearning*, pp. 6, 13.

27. Langston Hughes's *Montage of a Dream Deferred* shows how the dream for racial equality is deflected, and is the reference for my formulation. See *Selected Poems of Langston Hughes* (New York: Vintage, 1974), pp. 221—227.

28. Bordo, *Twilight Zones*, pp. 57, 59, 58.

29. Ibid., pp. 60, 61.

30. Ibid., pp. 64, 65.

31. Peterson del Mar, *What Trouble*, p. 173.

Index

About the Author

LESLIE HEYWOOD is an assistant professor of English at the State University of New York, Binghamton. She is author of *Dedication to Hunger: The Anorexic Athlete in Modern Culture* and coeditor, with Jennifer Drake, of *Third Wave Agenda: Being Feminist, Doing Feminism*. Her next book will be an autobiographical account of her life as a female athlete, to be published in 1998.

DATE DUE